WATCHING
WILDLIFE
CENTRAL AMERICA

Luke Hunter
David Andrew

Lonely Planet Publications
Melbourne Oakland London Paris

CENTRAL AMERICA

MEXICO

Chetumal
Corozal
Orange Walk

Blue Creek
Village

Ambergris Caye
San Pedro
Caye Caulker

San Ignacio
Belize City

MEXICO

Lago de Petén Itzá

BELMOPAN

BELIZE

Turneffe
Islands

Dangriga

Cordillera de los Cuchumatanes

GUATEMALA

Río Chixoy

Placencia

Maya Mtns

Golfo de Honduras

Punta Gorda

Modesto
Méndez

Lago de Izabal

Sierra de las Minas

Río Motagua

Lago de Yojoa

Río Ulúa

Montañas de Comayagua

Río Aguán

Río Patuca

Río Coco

HONDURAS

GUATEMALA CITY

SAN SALVADOR

EL SALVADOR

TEGUCIGALPA

Cordillera Entre Ríos

Cordillera Isabella

Río Wawa

NICARAGUA

Río Grande de

Lago de Managua

MANAGUA

Lago de Nicaragua

La Cruz

Río Escondido

Golfo de Papagayo

Liberia

COSTA RICA

Puerto Viejo
de Sarapiquí

Tamarindo

Laguna de Arenal

Santa
Elena

Cordillera Central

Península de Nicoya

Puntarenas

SAN JOSÉ

Carta

Golfo de Nicoya

San Isidro de
El General

Bahía Drake

*Península
de Osa*

PACIFIC OCEAN

BELIZE
Cruise Belize's coral cayes to visit frenetic seabird colonies, search for the endangered manatee, and enjoy snorkeling and diving with tame sharks and rays

BELIZE
Wander the world's first and only jaguar sanctuary at Cockscomb Basin: You'll see colourful toucans, Yucatán black howler and, if you're lucky, el tigre itself

COSTA RICA
Monteverde's epiphyte-laden cloud forest – dripping with mist and atmosphere, and home to some of Costa Rica's most-wanted including the legendary quetzal

0   50   100km
0   25   50mi
1:7,000,000

JAMAICA

☆ KINGSTON

ELEVATION

	6500ft
	5000ft
	3300ft
	1600ft
	650ft
	0

C A R I B B E A N   S E A

PANAMA
Superb lowland rainforest on
Pipeline Road boasts some of
the world's best and most
accessible birdwatching –
hundreds of species recorded in a day

PANAMA
Remote rainforests of PN Darién –
stronghold of the mighty harpy eagle,
where sensational birding features
numerous endemics and
squadrons of multicolored macaws

COSTA RICA
Scarlet macaws wing across
PN Corcovado, one of
the country's finest reserves,
as you search for tapirs,
peccaries and monkeys galore

Puerto Limón

Bribri
Changuinola

Cordillera

Laguna de
Chiriquí

Golfo de los
Mosquitos

Colón

Cartí

Corazón de Jesús

Cordillera de San Blas

Chepo

La Chorrera

Lago
Bayano

Serranía de Majé

Caledonia

Serranía del Darién

almar
orte

San Vito

Chiriquí
Grande

Neily

PANAMA

Cordillera

Central

PANAMA
CITY

Santa Fé

Golfito

David

Las Lajas

Santa Fé

San Miguel

Isla
del Rey

La Palma

Yaviza

Río Mataro

Golfo
Dulce

Bahía de
Charco Azul

Las
Palmas

Santiago

Soná

Bahía de
Parita

Golfo de
Panama

Serranía del Sapo

Río Salaquí

Caño León

Golfo de Chiriquí

Isla de
Coiba

Isla
Cébaco

Chitré

Península
de Azuero

Tonosí

Río Salaquí

COLOMBIA

Isla Jicarón

Watching Wildlife Central America
1st edition – September 2002

Published by
Lonely Planet Publications Pty Ltd ABN 36 005 607 983
90 Maribyrnong St, Footscray, Victoria 3011, Australia

Lonely Planet offices
Australia Locked Bag 1, Footscray, Victoria 3011
USA 150 Linden St, Oakland, CA 94607
UK 10a Spring Place, London NW5 3BH
France 1 rue du Dahomey, 75011 Paris

Photographs
Many of the images in this guide are available for licensing from
Lonely Planet Images.
email: lpi@lonelyplanet.com.au
Web site: www.lonelyplanetimages.com

Front cover photograph
Rainbow-billed (or keel-billed) toucan (Alfredo Maiquez)

Back cover photographs (from left to right)
Jaguar (Tom Boyden)
Red-eyed tree frog (Greg Basco)
King vulture (Michael & Patricia Fogden)

ISBN 1 86450 034 4

text & maps © Lonely Planet Publications Pty Ltd 2002
photos © as indicated (pages 228-9) 2002

Printed by The Bookmaker International Ltd
Printed in China

CONTENTS

6 Contents

INTRODUCTION

A trip into a Central American rainforest is to be enveloped by life. Indeed, with hundreds of species still awaiting classification, there are few places on the planet where there is *so* much life. But of course, far more so than tiny or cryptic undiscovered species, it's the wealth of more obvious wildlife which makes Central America one of the world's great wildlife-watching hotspots. With over 900 bird species, boa constrictors and basilisks, a unique mix of mammals which includes monkeys and marsupials, and flamboyantly beautiful small fry like poison-dart frogs and blue morpho butterflies, a Central American safari promises some exceptional viewing.

This book aims to assist and enhance the process. For the first-timer, we cover the basic 'how-to' information for planning a visit, specifying the best times, the various tour options, suitable equipment and clothing, the best places to see particular species and so on. Then, for everyone from the complete novice to the wildlife specialist, we detail how to extract the most once you're here. The best wildlife-watching reserves of Belize, Costa Rica and Panama are reviewed in detail, providing information on the specific wildlife attractions of each destination and the finer points of finding them. We've covered a range of different parks and reserves, from the largest national parks to lesser-known attractions noted for particular species that are difficult to find elsewhere. Additionally, we've gone for diversity over duplication so that dry forest reserves, cayes, wetlands and volcano parks appear alongside the rainforest and cloudforest sites for which Central America is so well-known. The book does not aim to cover every reserve – there are more than 300 of them in Central America – but you will find the very best of them here.

To help with identification, a comprehensive Wildlife Gallery illustrates more than 200 species most likely to be seen, all of them in color photographs. But more than that, the Gallery also provides a little interpretation of animal behavior and ecology. Beyond simply ticking species off a list, enjoying wildlife is about understanding it. Whether you wonder what it means when howler monkeys begin their booming dawn chorus, why jaguars are so hard to find or simply where to go to see a particular species, we hope you'll find this book provides the clues.

Above all, we hope it inspires you to keep on watching wildlife. Whether it encourages and aids your first trip, a return visit or even just an armchair safari, we want the book to increase your enjoyment of wildlife. Money from wildlife-watching tourism is increasingly one of the crucial factors for conservation in developing countries. ∎

AUTHORS

Luke Hunter

Melbourne-born Luke completed his PhD at the University of Pretoria's Mammal Research Institute, working out methods for reintroducing cheetahs and lions into areas where people had wiped them out. Seven years in Southern Africa convinced him that wildlife-oriented tourism will be one of the most significant factors protecting the world's great wildlife regions in the 21st century. This interest led him to take on his first Lonely Planet title, *Watching Wildlife Southern Africa*. He has also written and taken the photos for a book on cheetahs and worked as a senior researcher for the Australian Broadcasting Corporation's Natural History Unit. The Carnivore Section Chair of the IUCN Reintroduction Specialist Group and a member of the IUCN Cat Specialist Group, Luke is now based at Monash University, from where he continues his research on wild cats.

David Andrew

After his father was mauled by a gorilla at Howletts Zoo, David's family fled the wilds of England to live somewhere safer – Australia! There David created *Wingspan* and *Australian Birding* magazines; edited *Wildlife Australia* magazine; and among other jobs has been a research assistant in Kakadu NP, a birding guide for English comedian Bill Oddie and an editor of Lonely Planet guides. He was coordinating author for LP's *Watching Wildlife East Africa*, contributed to *Watching Wildlife Australia* and *Watching Wildlife Southern Africa*, and is now the Publishing Manager for the Watching Wildlife series.

FROM THE AUTHORS

Luke Hunter

I owe thanks to a great many people whose hospitality and advice in Costa Rica and Belize made this project so enjoyable. Topping the list, Carlos Alberto Lopez, whose magnificent help and friendship made all the difference; and to Costa Rica Expeditions, especially Rebeca Zuñiga, who extended superb support. Costa Rica Trekking Expeditions provided outstanding assistance for PN Chirripó; thanks to Noel Ureña, Walter Odio, Jilberth Valverde, Julian Odio, Rodolfo Elizondo and to Rosita Lopez for arranging everything. Many thanks also to George Soriano of Horizontes and Marco Thomas of Costa Rica Suntours. At Tortuga Lodge, thanks to Guido Montero, Luis Gonzales and Fernando Estrada, to Diego Quesada at Poco-a-Poco and to Dr Roy Young at Nature Resort. Belize Audubon Society was were helpful, especially Ian Courtenay, Sergio Hoare and Nellie Catzim. Thanks also to Programme for Belize's Anita Gladden, Ava Davis and Wilbur Sabido. Many specialists assisted me with my endless queries; thanks to Greg Basco, Esteban Biamonte, Dorothy Beveridge, Eckarth Flowers, Tony Garel, Aaron Hidalgo, Susan Lala, Jim Lewis, Sharon Matola, Monrique Montes Obando, Linde Ostro, Thomas Rainwater, Sebastian Troëng and to Jim Wolfe for beers, butterflies and bocas. Thanks also to Santa Rosa's welcoming biologists: Maria Marta Chauarria, Roger Blanco, Alejandro Macis and Tihisia Boshart. Special thanks to everyone at Lamanai: Mark and

Monique Howels, Blanca Manzanilla, Carlos Godoy, Reuben Arevajo and to Steve Reichling for the tarantula info. To Judy Blake, Carol Bult and Anna Henly, thanks for the great company on the road.

David Andrew
Thanks are owed to everyone who smoothed my tour of the great country of Panama: The staff and management of Ancón Expeditions, especially Marco Gandásegui, Hernan Auruz and John Shyne; Raúl Arias de Para and staff of Canopy Tower; and Ken Klotz and Allen Hale of EcoVentures. Rebeca Zuñiga of Costa Rica Expeditions was of inestimable help in organizing my visit to Costa Rica (and was especially helpful when things went wrong). Thanks also to Scott Doggett for sharing his wealth of experience of all things Panamanian; to Greg Basco for snapping away on request with his camera right up till the last minute; and to all the nature guides, drivers and fellow wildlife enthusiasts I met on the road.

THIS BOOK

LUKE Hunter researched and wrote the Nature in Central America, and Wildlife-Watching chapters; the Costa Rica and Belize sections of the Parks and Places chapter; the Mammals and More Creatures Great and Small sections of the Wildlife Gallery chapter; and part of the Habitats chapter and the Introduction. David Andrew researched and wrote the Birds section of the Wildlife Gallery chapter, the Panama section of the Parks and Places chapter, part of the Habitats chapter and the Birdwatching section in the Wildlife-Watching chapter. Miranda Wills contributed text to several sections of the Wildlife-Watching chapter and to the Ecotourism section.

FROM THE PUBLISHER

THE idea for this series came from David Andrew and was supported by Chris Klep, Nick Tapp and Sue Galley. The concept was developed further by Sean Pywell and Jane Bennett; Sean became the first series editor and Mathew Burfoot designed the layout for the series. Maps for *Watching Wildlife Central America* were drawn by Karen Fry, Eoin Dunlevy and Chris Klep. Editing and proofing were done by Miranda Wills, Thalia Kalkipsakis, Peter Cruttenden and David Andrew. Layout was done by Wendy Wright and Indra Kilfoyle, with assistance from Vicki Beale. Most of the photos were sourced and supplied by LPI – special thanks to all at LPI who put in much extra effort for this title. Simon Bracken designed the cover. Mapping was checked by Glenn van der Knijff; layout was checked by David Andrew, Lindsay Brown, Glenn van der Knijff and Andrew Smith.

HOW TO USE THIS BOOK

YOU'RE here to see the animals and we're here to help you: *Watching Wildlife Central America* shows you how to recognise the major players and advises you on where to find them. This book is also packed with background information on wildlife habitats, advice on getting started, when to go and how to prepare. There are also detailed watching tips (eg, which trail to hike), and clues on the best time to look. Read on to help plan your wildlife-watching adventure and get the best out of this treasure-trove.

Nature

Wildlife-Watching

Habitats

Parks and Places

Wildlife Gallery

Each chapter is color coded to help you navigate through the book – look for the thumb tabs.

Getting Started There are two main ways to go about watching wildlife: pick your animals and then find out where to go; or choose where you want to go and then find out what's there. In Central America you'll see some wildlife in a lot of places (eg, Central American agoutis, white-faced capuchins); but for other animals you'll need to go to certain places (eg, resplendent quetzals in cloud forest reserves). The key chapters cover both approaches: Parks and Places describes where to go and what's there; and the Wildlife Gallery tells you about the animals. Flipping between these chapters will tell you almost everything you need to know.

Index The quickest way to find out about an animal or reserve is to look it up in the Index. Animals are arranged into groups according to their common names (scarlet macaw comes under macaw) – page numbers in bold indicate a photo of that animal. Reserves are listed alphabetically by name.

Table of Contents This gives you a quick overview of the book. We've color-coded each chapter to help you find your way around until you're more familiar with the layout.

Group page *Highlight page*

Wildlife Gallery This is a rundown of all the key species and groups: What they look like (and how to tell them apart) and the kinds of things you can see them doing. This chapter is divided by thumbtabs: Mammals, Birds, and More Creatures Great and Small (eg, reptiles).

Key animals are presented as feature pages, which describe unusual and interesting aspects of their ecology. A sidebar next to the main text summarizes some of their main characteristics (eg, behavior, breeding and habitat); and a Hotspots box lists some

Hotspots: where to find animals *Summary information*

11

places where they might be found (use this as a link to the Parks and Places chapter). Other animals appear in family groups or are grouped according to the habitat in which they are most likely to be found – these pages are packed with photos to help you work out what's what.

Parks and Places Organised country by country and starting with an introduction to the overall region, this chapter describes the best national parks, reserves and other places in which to see wildlife. Each country section begins with an overview (including itineraries). Specific destinations, eg, national parks and other reserves, are ordered alphabetically according to their importance for wildlife-watching. Thus major attractions, such as PN Corcovado, are given more-detailed treatment and less-frequented reserves may be covered in only one page. Facts for travellers (like location, contacts, accommodations and wildlife rhythms), watching tips and wildlife highlights are summarised for each; and a color map points out major features and good wildlife-viewing areas.

Wildlife-Watching Essential as background reading, this chapter tells you when to go and how to look, and explains the ins and outs of guides, equipment and field guides. Special features cover birdwatching, photography, sea-turtle and whale-watching, spotlighting, and diving and snorkeling.

Nature in Central America We explain the reasons behind Central America's great biodiversity and introduce some of the conservation issues.

Habitats Describes Central American ecosystems in simple terms.

Resource Guide This lists recommended field guides and other books, reliable tour operators and wildlife-related Web sites.

Glossary Explains any confusing or unfamiliar words that appear in the text.

Wildlife highlights Parks and Places *Park map*

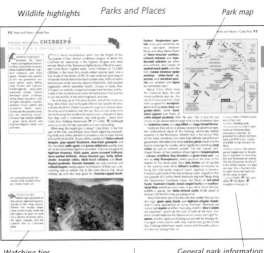

Watching tips | *General park information*

Wildlife-Watching

ECOTOURISM

BE it exploring the rainforests of Brazil or diving Australia's Great Barrier Reef, the urge to experience the globe's pristine places is strong for many travellers. But while verdant jungles and stunning seascapes delight, for the majority they are just a glorious backdrop – what they have really come to see is wildlife. From tracking chimpanzees in Uganda to spotting whales in the Bahamas, seeing the world's most famous wildlife has become a popular international pastime. Since their East African beginnings in the 1970's, nature tours have gone global and they are now a significant source of revenue for many developing and developed countries. Today's nature tour hotspots include East and Southern Africa, Australia, Nepal, Thailand, Alaska, the Amazon Basin, the Galápagos Islands and of course, Central America.

'Ecotourism' takes the concept of a nature tour and pushes it one step further. The essence of ecotourism is not only about seeing and interacting with nature, it's also about doing so in a way that preserves and sustains it. At its simplest, merely paying park entrance fees helps channel your dollars back into conservation when those fees are ensuring the ongoing protection of the park. But more than that, genuine ecotourism ensures that the people living in and around those parks also benefit, and so have a vested interest in conserving nature and wildlife. For example, by going on a wildlife tour run by a local indigenous community in Belize, you are supporting that community and giving them the incentive to preserve their environment and wildlife instead of making a living by logging or hunting. That connection is lost when you opt for a foreign-owned company which does not employ local people or somehow contribute to their subsistence. It may even be diminished with

---

Ecotourism or egotourism?

To ensure that you help rather than hinder the wildlife and places you visit, do a little research. A starting point is the recommended list of tour operators in the Resource Guide at the back of this book (or other similar publications) and ask the following questions:

Does the company:
- Employ local people and use local products and services?
- Make contributions to the parks and places they visit?
- Sponsor local environmental projects?
- Keep tour groups small to reduce impact on the environment and local cultures?
- Aid environmental and wildlife researchers?
- Educate travellers about wildlife, the environment and local cultures?

Ecotour operators offer an incredible variety of tours and contribute to the principles of ecotourism in a number of different ways. Don't expect a 'yes' to each of the above questions, but if you get a 'no' to every one, ask the company to explain in detail how it contributes to ecotourism; if the answer doesn't satisfy you, consider looking further afield.

Ecotourism in Central America

With everything from taxi services to cyber cafes bearing the eco-tag in Central America, it can be a minefield establishing a company's credentials. Arming yourself with the right questions is a good start (see the 'Ecotourism or egotourism' boxed text) but even then, it's easy for operators to pay lip-service to the ecotourism ideal. So, how then to decide what is a reasonable contribution? Firstly just because it's large doesn't mean it isn't green. Two of the region's largest operators, Costa Rica Expeditions and Horizontes Nature Tours have together donated more than $25,000 to the national parks authority for equipment and resources needed by park guards, only one of the many ways they contribute. The very professional Ancon Expeditions is operated by Ancon, Panama's foremost private conservation organisation. At the other end of the corporate scale, Costa Rica Trekking Expeditions makes park signs and interpretive displays for PN Chirripó and hires local guides to accompany their trips into the park. For some sites, it's even simpler to cut through the confusion: Hire independent local guides at the park itself. Numerous parks and reserves have a system for drawing on the surrounding communities to guide tourists; see the Getting Around section in the Wildlife-Watching chapter for more details.

locally-based companies if all their staff are city-living and all the revenue from their tours ends up there.

Today, ecotourism is probably tourism's fastest growth sector and while not everyone who travels to nature hotspots wishes to see *only* wildlife, it is almost certain they will visit a national park or reserve and try to view some. Unfortunately, the rising popularity of ecotours with travellers (fueled by increasing international publicity about the environment and concern for its demise) has led to flamboyant misuse of the term among tour operators seeking profit. Brochures and Web sites abound with the label, but many organizations are eco-sensitive in name only; at worst they exhibit the greatest failings of the tourist industry, ultimately destroying the places they tout through overdevelopment and exploitation of local people and wildlife. Fortunately there are many tour operators that offer the real thing. There are also a variety of organizations (including the United Nations and international conservation and human rights groups) working to promote guidelines and standards for ecotour operators and monitor their activities. For tips on choosing an ecotour company, see the boxed texts.

Don't forget wherever you are to make your own eco-contributions: Respect local cultures, avoid disturbing wildlife and don't buy wildlife products (unless they are legal and encourage conservation of the resource; for more tips see Close Encounters in the Wildlife-Watching chapter). More so than at any other time in history, travellers today have the incredible wealth of life on earth at their fingertips; there is almost nowhere on the planet that is truly inaccessible and, theoretically at least, no species that cannot be viewed and enjoyed. Equally though, many of the charismatic animals that tourists wish to see are facing extinction within the next century. By undertaking travel which adheres to the principles of ecotourism, you the traveler are helping prevent that. ∎

NATURE IN
CENTRAL AMERICA

*An introduction to Central America's
natural history*

ENVIRONMENT

From above the rainforest canopy looks like a sea of giant broccoli. Unbroken tracts of forest are now rare outside Central America's major conservation reserves.

CENTRAL America is a narrow filament of land stretched between the great continents of North and South America and, compared with them, it is tiny. Its seven countries – Belize, Guatemala, El Salvador, Honduras, Nicaragua, Costa Rica and Panama – are collectively smaller than Texas, all crammed into a ribbon of earth spanning 175mi (282km) at its widest point and only 30mi (48km) at its most narrow. But size gives little indication of its spectacular diversity; for that, the critical factor is location. Geologically and biologically, Central America is the locus for an astonishing convergence of forces. For most of its 40-million-year history, it existed as an archipelago of individual volcanic islands, thrown up by the rupture of the earth's crust below. The violent meeting point of four tectonic plates, Central America's foundations have been colliding with one another for millions of years and even today, the floor of the Pacific Ocean is dragged beneath the earth's surface at the geologically lightning rate of about four inches (10cm) a year. Around three million years ago, the upwelling of regurgitated rock culminated in a union of the scattered islands and created the land bridge we know today. In that event, the previously separate American continents were joined and the once continuous Atlantic and Pacific Oceans were divided.

The same forces have given rise to Central America's convoluted terrain. Created by the volcanism which continues today, the dominant feature of the land bridge is its steep mountainous spine. Beginning in the Maya Mountains of Belize and running to Panama's remote Serreniá de Darién, an almost continuous chain of cordilleras (mountain ranges) rises to over 2.5mi (4km) above sea level at its highest point. Throughout, from Guatemala's Volcán Tajumulco to Panama's Volcán Barú, the slopes are peppered with more than 250 volcanoes and craters. Most are extinct, or at least dormant, but this is still the most volcanically active area of the Americas and volcanoes should be treated with caution (see the boxed text 'Natural Disasters'). Many continue to both manufacture and destroy the Central American landscape today.

Flanking the foothills of the mountains in a slender band that ends at the ocean, a fertile plain runs the length of each coast:

Natural disasters

Geographically, Central America is ideally placed for an onslaught from the most violent of the earth's forces. It sits poised above the junction of four tectonic plates and is battered by the storms and tides of two oceans, which once ran together unimpeded. For all that, truly dangerous natural disasters are rare and, indeed, many people come here for a safe taste of them

Topping the list are volcanoes. There are none in Belize and all of Panama's volcanoes are extinct, but Costa Rica has seven that are still erupting. All can be visited safely, but if the signs tell you not to climb them, then don't; climbers ignoring the warnings at Arenal have been killed or injured. Hurricanes are relatively frequent along the Caribbean coast, but again, rarely fatal. If you're worried about them, avoid the hurricane season (June to November). Finally, earthquakes are possible, but the chances of being caught in one are about the same as seeing a jaguar – *extremely* low!

1478mi (2378km) on the Caribbean side and 2043mi (3287km) on the Pacific. Cloaked with volcanic ash from above, the lowlands are heavily populated with people and considerably altered by human activities, but they are also home to some of the most wildlife-rich habitats of the region. The Habitats chapter describes major Central American ecosystems.

The New Tropics

Central America sits entirely within the tropics – the hot, humid strip encircling the globe between the tropics of Cancer and Capricorn with the equator as its midline. To distinguish the American tropics from the world's other tropical regions, biologists refer to them as the Neotropics (because they're in the New World), a region which, from the north, begins in a band that runs though central Mexico and southern Florida and ends in far northern Chile, central Paraguay and southern Brazil.

All of Central America is in the Northern Hemisphere, but the climate here bears little resemblance to that of Eurasia and North America. High temperatures and high rainfall dominate, although Central America's extraordinary topography brings about far more variation than is often assumed. The hottest areas are the lowlands, usually taken as sea level to 3280ft (1000m); daytime temperatures average around 84 to 90°F (29 to 32°C) and nights are a humid 70 to 75°F (21 to 24°C). Between 3280 to 6560ft (1000 to 2000m) is known as the temperate zone where daytime temperatures are a few degrees lower and nights drop to around 59°F (15°C), but rarely lower. The cold zone (above 6560ft/2000m) has mild daytime temperatures, but nights can hover around freezing point (32°F/0°C); Costa Rica's Cerro Chirripó and Panama's Volcán Barú are both higher than 9840ft (3000m) and, along with occasionally freezing days, regularly experience nights below freezing.

Temperatures vary remarkably little throughout the year in Central America and the usual seasonal labels of the Northern Hemisphere don't apply here. Instead, seasons are gauged by rainfall and, like Africa, fall broadly into a rainy period and a dry one. For most of the region, the rainy season runs from around April to November, and although it's only slightly cooler, is called invierno (winter); the latter half of invierno is also the hurricane season. The dry season from November to April is called verano (summer), but for much of Central America it's only a little less rainy. On the Caribbean side of the continental divide, rain falls heavily year-round and, indeed, the Caribbean slope receives twice as much rainfall as the Pacific side. It also rains during verano on the Pacific coast, but a few regions like Costa Rica's Guanacaste province experience a prolonged, parched, dry season. With the exception of these pockets, even if you spend only a week in Central America, rain on at least a couple of days is normal regardless of the season. Because of that, most visitors come to Central America in the dry season, but invierno can be equally rewarding: mornings are often clear and sunny with rain later in the day. More importantly for the wildlifewatcher, each season has its distinct attractions – see the Parks and Places and Wildlife Gallery chapters. Plan according to your want-list rather than the chance of rain. ∎

WILDLIFE

The poison-dart frogs are unique to the Neotropics. This lovely poison-dart frog is carrying tadpoles on its back.

As we know it, Central America is only a few million years old and most of its wildlife can be viewed as recent arrivals (in paleontological terms) or their descendants. But of course, their origins lie much earlier in time and, for the most part, are rooted in the Americas – North and South. As the meeting point between the two, Central America's wildlife had its beginnings in both, but via two very different evolutionary paths. And that's because for most of recent time, the Americas have been separate.

Around 65 million years ago, they were not. Then, as now, North and South America were linked by a land bridge, which allowed a drift of ancient species between the two; most significantly perhaps, North seeded South with a few primitive forms of mammals. Around 50 to 55 million years ago, everything changed. The inexorable movement of the earth's plates dragged South away from North and, when the connection was finally severed, South America entered a period of isolation that would last until the birth of the Central American land bridge. There may have been fleeting connections with North America, Antarctica and perhaps even Africa, but essentially South America was an island continent.

That isolation created a unique evolutionary landscape for its few passengers. Marsupials and xenarthans (sloths, anteaters and armadillos) diversified into an astonishing array, which included saber-toothed marsupial carnivores and elephant-sized ground sloths. Into the mix, rodents and monkeys rafted or island-hopped to South America, either from North America (which doesn't have primates today, but once had their progenitors) or more likely West Africa. Regardless, once here they flourished, giving rise to entire families of primates found only in the New World and the unique Neotropical rodents called caviomorphs – pacas, agoutis, capybaras and guinea pigs. Similarly, South America was the evolutionary laboratory for many bird families (toucans, antbirds, potoos, hummingbirds and cotingas among them), as well as a swag of more ancient groups like iguanas, basilisks, poison-dart frogs and cichlids.

The story in North America was very different. Isolated only for brief moments in geological time, North America repeatedly collided with Eurasia and exchanged whole new groups of

Why is there so much wildlife in Central America?

The world's tropical forests are the most species-rich terrestrial habitats on the globe. Estimates are still guesswork because so many species probably remain undiscovered, but it's thought that they contain somewhere between 50 and 80% of the world's biodiversity; they have the most species and also the most individual organisms. But *why* are tropical forests so packed with life?

There are many reasons, but the most fundamental begins with sunlight and rain. Because both are almost constant here, plants are exceptionally diverse and abundant. Plants, of course, sustain life. Via photosynthesis, they convert sunlight, water and carbon dioxide into sugars – conveniently digestible food for herbivores, which in turn feed the carnivores. The more plants, the more plant-eaters and the more eaters of plant-eaters. Plants also provide living space – no matter which level you scan in the forest, hundreds of organisms will be living on, in or under it. In the search for wildlife, it's easy to disregard plants, but if not for them, we wouldn't see anything.

mammals with no relatives in South America. So alongside a few marsupials (not nearly as diverse as in South America), North America had horses, tapirs, camels, peccaries, deer, cats, dogs, bears, weasels, raccoons, shrews, hares, squirrels and mice. When the Panamanian land bridge arose around three million years ago, the stage was set for a colossal exchange.

That's precisely what happened. Known to biologists as the Great American Interchange, South American groups went north and vice versa. Among mammals, the northern groups were generally more successful. Perhaps because South America's fauna had evolved in isolation for so long, they had less of a competitive edge, but even so, some species survived for many millions of years after the union (South American ground sloths persisted in southern North America until 10,000 years ago). And many still do, which is why in Central America today, there are ocelots hunting opossums, sloths and howler monkeys alongside squirrels; and armadillos and agoutis live among deer, peccaries and tapirs.

Migrations

Today, the interchange of species between north and south is largely restricted to a few species able to exploit the habitat changes wrought by humans (see Humans & Wildlife, p.20). However, seasonal migration is a feature of wildlife communities the world over and strategically positioned Central America sees a cyclic exchange of species on two tiers. More obvious of the two, seasonal arrivals of long-distance migratory birds from temperate North America can be spectacular. Generally from August and lasting until as late as May, millions of warblers, tanagers, flycatchers, raptors and others arrive in Central America during the northern winter or pass through on their way further south. Many of them spend more than half the year here and are more correctly considered tropical species who merely go north to breed. 'Classically' northern groups – sandpipers, plovers and terns – may stay even longer here, but ultimately, all breeding birds head north. Finally, Central America also receives a few South American migrants like sulphur-bellied flycatchers, yellow-green vireos and plumbeous kites, which breed here or further north in the first half of the year and then return south before the onset of the rainy season.

Less epic, but no less important, many species make short-distance movements to track the shifting availability of food. Cycles of fruiting and flowering ebb and flow on the slopes and the species that follow these resources are known as altitudinal migrants. Members of the parrot, trogon (including quetzals), hummingbird and cotinga families are among those that summer in the highlands and descend to the lowlands over the wet winter. Less dependent on elevation but equally subject to seasonal change, many waterbirds move in pursuit of the sporadic flooding of marshes and lakes. Seasonal differences here are not stark enough to prompt large-scale mammal movements such as those of Africa and Alaska, but the only species which forms large herds, the white-lipped peccary, travels extensively. Like many migratory birds, it is declining as its habitat is fragmented. ■

Watching the kettles

For a bird spectacle with truly mind-blowing numbers, look up. From August to December, North American raptors migrate south into Central America in their millions; indeed, the 2001 fall count at Costa Rica's Kéköldi Indigenous Reserve fell just short of three million, one of only three sites in the world to top a million raptors in a season (the others are Veracruz, Mexico and Eilat, Israel). As well as Kéköldi (which runs a hawk-counting program that accepts volunteers; see u www.anaicr.org), the best sites in Costa Rica are: RNVS Caño Negro, PN Tortuguero, BriBri Indigenous Reserve, PN Cahuita and RB Hitoy-Cerere and. The Canopy Tower in Panama's PN Soberanía provides a great view of the migration, and watch for kettling hawks along the north coast near ·Almirante; October is the best month for both diversity and numbers.

HUMANS & WILDLIFE

The ancestors of this Maya boy used wildlife extensively for food. Today, hunting for the pot is regulated and while it's declining in Costa Rica and Panama, it is still a significant factor in wildlife declines.

OF all the species that flooded into Central America when the land bridge arose, we are one of its most recent arrivals. In fact, except for the furthest reaches of the Arctic and a few island chains, the Americas were the last landmasses on the planet to be settled by people. Exactly when it happened is still vigorously debated. We do know that humans had definitely arrived in Alaska by around 12,000 years ago, crossing from Eurasia perhaps by boat or, more likely, simply by walking (at the time, the Bering Strait was an ice-free land bridge around twice the size of Texas). Once in America, people spread through it at an apparently astonishing rate, reaching Chile – 10,000mi (16,000km) south of Alaska – a thousand years after arriving. A closer look at the figures reveals that's only 10mi (16km) a year, a distance foraging humans could easily cover in a day, though why they would be compelled to move so steadily southwards is still unclear. Further clouding the issue, recent discoveries from Chile point to a much earlier occupation of America, suggesting people crossed the Bering Strait (or boated in to South America from somewhere else entirely) perhaps as far back as 35,000 years ago.

Whatever the route and its timing, as far as we can tell, people have only been in Central America for only about 11,000 years. Compared with Africa, which has felt the presence of hominids for at least seven million years (albeit different species to modern humans), our footprint on the Americas is only moments old. However, the effects on ancient fauna may be among the most devastating on earth. Around the time people first entered Alaska and advanced southwards, a wave of extinctions went with them. In fact, the Americas lost around 80% of their megafauna (great mammals like mammoths, ground sloths, native horses and giant camels, and the

Extinction and expansion

Despite humankind's very substantial ecological footprint on Central America, relatively few species have been lost forever – at least that we know of. Three endemic mammals and birds (Caribbean monk seal, Little Swan Island huita and Atitlán grebe) are now extinct, but there may be other, less obvious species which disappeared before they were even discovered. Of course, dozens more Central American species are in serious trouble and, while they may not appear on the global extinction lists, they are probably doomed in the region. Among them, the giant anteater is widespread in South America but is probably extinct here. Like most species, the anteater's chief problem is the destruction of its habitat.

Ironically, that destruction actually benefits some species. The spread of people has always been accompanied by a handful of creatures able to exploit human-wrought changes to habitat. And Central America has its share: The versatile coyote is spreading southwards at a few miles each year and generalist birds like great-tailed grackles and smooth-billed anis are radiating north. However, just like the more immediate demise of sensitive species like anteaters, the long-term consequences for biodiversity may be just as damaging. Grackles and anis displace many less common birds and the 10 species of wild dog endemic to South America might similarly suffer if the coyote makes it across the Darién Gap. In fact, after habitat destruction, invasive species such as coyotes and grackles are the single greatest cause of extinctions on the planet.

predators that hunted them including American lions and saber-toothed cats).

The still-controversial deduction from the pattern concludes that, unlike in Africa, America's large mammals were evolutionarily unprepared for humans and made all too-easy targets. Equivocally, the overkill hypothesis overlaps with the end of the last Ice Age which, equally, may have been a factor. Given that America's megafauna had endured the waxing and waning of 22 earlier ice ages, the predatory efficiency of our ancestors seems the more convincing argument, but in all likelihood it was probably a combination of both.

Conquest and consequences

Whatever the reason, Central America was probably as much a human highway as a place to settle until very recently. By 7000 years ago, the open grasslands that had dominated for most of the Pleistocene had given way to dense forest, driving the herds of plains herbivores to the north and south. People would have followed, leaving behind small communities tied to the coast and around lakes where foraging was fairly reliable. At least, that's what the pattern of archaeological finds suggests, but it may simply reflect where they're easy to locate – the rainforest doesn't preserve or give up artifacts easily.

In any case, Central America's human population remained tiny and thinly spread until the rise of agriculture, beginning around 5000 years ago and culminating in the great empire of the Maya. At the height of the Maya, even tiny Belize had about 10 times the population it has today and there must have been significant effects on wildlife. As well as being sophisticated farmers who cleared large areas of forest for their crops, the Maya hunted everything from iguanas to jaguars. They harvested marine turtles on the coast, fashioned armor from tapir hide and kept collared peccaries and turkeys for food. They even adorned themselves in quetzal feathers plucked from the living bird; to kill one was a capital offence (whether the sacred birds survived after being released is unknown). The Maya probably didn't exploit any species to extinction, but by the arrival of the Spanish the decline of wildlife had already begun.

Ironically, the conquistadors probably provided some respite. War and diseases decimated Central America's native population, reducing it from an estimated six million to no more than an estimated few hundred thousand. Although the Spanish and their technology would ultimately prove disastrous for wildlife, their numbers remained small during the colonial era and it would be a couple of centuries before European agriculture made a significant impact on the landscape. In contrast to the enormous human cost of Central America's depopulation, forest quickly reclaimed abandoned human settlements and wildlife numbers underwent a period of recovery. Predictably though, it could not last, and the spread of industrial forestry and farming has had the greatest impact on wildlife. Today, with a population nearing 40 million, Central America's greatest conservation challenge is ongoing loss of habitat. Ultimately, whether it can be curtailed will depend on the decisions made by the people who live here. ∎

CONSERVATION

FOR most travelers who spend time in Central America's wild areas, the sense of wilderness is compelling. Compared with the popular parks of North America or Southern and East Africa, the degree of development is modest and, so long as you dodge the most popular parts of well-visited sites like Monteverde, the number of people is few. But, as in many areas of the world, Central America's patchwork of protected areas is increasingly fragmented and isolated by the demands of humanity. Loss of habitat is the single greatest factor driving the depletion of biodiversity around the world and Central America's record is patchy. Suffering somewhat from its overuse as a conservation alarm bell, deforestation nonetheless continues to be the region's principal problem. Each year, Central America collectively fells around 2700 square mi (7000 sq km) of forest, an area a little larger than Delaware. Much of it is lost to commercial forestry, but by far the main culprit is farming: Contributing about equally, relatively few large-scale commercial crop and cattle ranches vie for land with hundreds of thousands of 'peasant' subsistence farmers.

The result is that natural habitat is increasingly found only in protected areas. Outside its parks and reserves, Costa Rica has less than 5% of its original forest cover; Belize, which boasts the region's highest figure, has only 20%. Taken alone, the statistics are indeed dire and they're the ones most often quoted, but they're somewhat deceptive because they exclude protected areas – those areas set aside specifically to counter the problem.

The conservation challenge

As a formal discipline, conservation in Central America is a very recent one. The oldest national park here is Panama's PN Altos de Campana, established in 1966, and most of the region's countries only implemented a parks system from the 1970s onwards. But since then, the number of protected areas has blossomed and today they collectively protect an area around the size of West Virginia (see Parks & Reserves, p25).

Setting aside parks is clearly the critical first step, but it is the ongoing protection of such areas that presents long-term problems. By the standards of developed nations, most Central American nations are poor and their governments simply do not have the money for conservation. Many parks still suffer from a lack of enforcement; illegal activities such as logging, hunting and especially farming are impossible to control when the areas are huge and the rangers are few, underpaid and under-resourced. Increasingly, like many threatened areas around the world, the answers in Central America lie with the vested interest argument: When poor local communities accrue benefits from conservation, they will embrace it.

The most obvious – though not always the most successful – connection between the people and conservation is the enormous ecotourism industry. Tourists who come for the parks and reserves are supporting not only the people that work in them, but all the other industries associated with their needs –

everything from restaurant-owners to taxi drivers (see 'The changing face of conservation' below). The main criticism leveled at the ecotourism industry in Central America has been its level of foreign ownership: If the money from tourism is funneling out of the country, then local people never see the benefits, nor any reason to embrace conservation. The problem is complicated by the 'bandwagon effect': Everything from cafés to laundromats is tagged with the 'eco' label in the hope of attracting the tourist dollar, but most have little – if any – connection to conservation. Increasingly, governments and the progressive private sector here are providing local people with the links to conservation that will also put food on the table. One project, called the Path of the Panther, is working to unite these efforts on a massive scale.

Path of the Panther

If the scale of conservation challenges facing Central America seems epic, so too are some of the answers. Born of the need to think huge, a consortium of conservation organizations and governmental agencies has embarked on an extraordinarily ambitious conservation proposal. Technically called the Mesoamerican Biological Corridor, its essence is better captured by its Spanish name, Paseo Pantera (Path of the Panther). With a range than runs from southern Chile to Canada – the widest north-south range of any American terrestrial mammal – the puma (or mountain lion) is the project's poster-animal. Known in some parts of their range as panthers, pumas require large areas and just as important, *connected* areas, but their once-contiguous distribution is now a series of fragmented stepping stones. The goal of Paseo Pantera is to reconnect them. Beginning in southern Mexico and running to Panama, the proposal would link protected areas by a series of biological corridors, creating an uninterrupted chain of wildlands running for 1100mi (1770km) and comprising 30% of Central America's landmass. If it succeeds, Paseo Pantera would restore the biological connection between North and South America that existed before European colonization.

Of course, the puma is merely one species among thousands that would benefit. But for it to succeed, one species in

---

The changing face of conservation

In his book, *Jaguar*, about the fight to establish Belize's Cockscomb Basin Wildlife Sanctuary (see pp70–1) Alan Rabinowitz tells of the (then) police chief of Orange Walk intentionally running down a jaguar in his vehicle. In the account, the cop boasts of swerving to hit the cat then backing over it to ensure it didn't escape so he could souvenir the skin. That was in 1984. Perhaps an experience I had in 2002 indicates how attitudes to conservation are changing in the region. In Dangriga, the closest main town to Cockscomb, a taxi driver told me how he'd unwittingly hit a margay while driving some tourists to the reserve. The little cat was knocked out, but obviously still alive so he raced it to the town's vet where, after a day recuperating, it was taken to Belize Zoo. Ultimately, it didn't survive its injuries, but to the taxi driver, the fact that he could show his children a photo of the cat and tell them how he tried to save it was evidently reward enough.

Cynics might reasonably observe that the police chief and the taxi driver differ because one has a vested interested in wildlife (the taxi driver's main clientele is tourists coming for Cockscomb) and the other does not. But of course, that's the point.

Luke Hunter

More than any other factor, habitat destruction is the primary cause of extinctions. Clear-felling, as shown here, leaves a wasteland where virtually no wildlife persists.

particular *must* benefit – us. The core areas of Paseo Pantera are those already protected, but to connect them requires land occupied by people, most of whom depend on it for their subsistence. The project will bear fruit only if those people can continue to utilize their land and prosper from their involvement. As much as a plan to protect biodiversity, Paseo Pantera has become a blueprint for incorporating humans into the network.

The key is to ensure that local communities capture a share of the revenue generated by protecting or restoring natural habitat. Among the inventive ideas, communities would be paid for 'ecosystem services' arising from their land; in other words, landowners would be rewarded for actions such as protecting watersheds and for carbon sequestration (the reduction of greenhouse gases captured as carbon dioxide by forests on their land). It may sound nebulous, but community forestry concessions totaling only 284,050 acres (115,000 hectares) in Belize's Maya Forest have carbon sequestration values worth around $63 million a year. Other sources of potential income are more obvious. Tourism is already the region's fastest-growing industry involving local people, a trend Paseo Pantera's proponents hope to augment; there is a plan for a continuous hiking trail running from southern Mexico to the Darién Gap, in which traversing rights would return revenue to the communities whose land is included in the route. Bio-prospecting, the lucrative search for pharmaceutical products arising from wild animals and plants, is increasingly a process in which local communities are paid for pharmaceutical discoveries made on their land; in some cases bio-prospecting may be undertaken by the communities themselves.

Paseo Pantera's achievements to date are impressive. All seven Central American nations and Mexico are signatories to the plan and each has implemented projects towards its goals. Collectively, they enjoy about $100 million in international support. Still in its infancy and with some obstacles that may ultimately prove insurmountable, Paseo Pantera nonetheless stands as one of the most genuinely visionary conservation initiatives on the planet. ■

PARKS & RESERVES

COMPARED with the century-old system of protected areas in North America or Africa, Central America's network of parks and reserves is very young. Most countries have formally implemented a protected areas' scheme only in the last few decades, but in that time their achievements have been impressive. Around 11% of the region falls under some sort of statutory protection that forbids the extraction of resources (except for seasonal harvests, eg, subsistence fishing, in a few). That includes everything from 'strict' nature reserves (which may be closed to all but researchers) to natural areas managed mainly for recreation, eg, some of the 88 coastal and marine reserves. Altogether, the region boasts some 330 protected areas; Costa Rica's tally of 85 is the highest per country, but Panama's 30 parks protect almost twice as much natural habitat.

Popular national parks usually have well-marked trails and signage. Here an umbrella plant dwarfs a sign in the Panama sector of PI La Amistad.

These figures don't include various parks that allow the exploitation of natural resources. Predictably, the main one is timber, and areas set aside for logging are called forest reserves (reservas forestal). These cover a vast area – almost one-fifth of the country in Belize's case – but despite the colossal damage wrought by tropical logging, they can be an important piece of the conservation patchwork. Where logging is selective (as it is in more enlightened nations) or harvested areas are permitted to regenerate, forest reserves can sustain important populations of wildlife. They also connect strictly protected areas – critical for species with large home ranges, such as big cats.

Strict nature reserves and forest reserves are generally off-limits to travelers, but most other parks in Central America are tourist-friendly. The best-conserved and easiest to visit are usually national parks or biological reserves. Most are equipped for visitors, but the level of development in Central American parks is far less than in, say, North America or Southern Africa; most have little more than a network of walking trails and camping or dorm-style lodging. Many parks have a cluster of privately owned lodges on their boundaries and there are many excellent private reserves, which usually boast more upmarket accommodations as well as very skilled guides; the best are covered in the Parks and Places chapter, and the Resources Guide. ■

Abbreviations

Except for the Belize section, this book uses the Spanish names and abbreviations for parks.

Biological Reserve *Reserva Biológica (RB)*	Marine National Park *Parque Nacional Marino (PNM)*	Protected Zone *Zona Protectora (ZP)*
Biosphere Reserve *Reserva de la Biosfera (RDLB)*	National Park *Parque Nacional (PN)*	Strict Nature Reserve *Reserva Natural Absoluta (RNA)*
Forest Reserve *Reserva Forestal* *(RF National)*	National Wildlife Refuge *Refugio Nacional de* *Fauna Silvestre (RNVS)*	Wildlife Refuge *Refugio Nacional de* *Vida Silvestre (RNVS)*
International Park *Parque Internacional (PI)*	Private Reserve *Reserva Privada (RP)*	

WILDLIFE-WATCHING

*Tips and hints on the art
of watching wildlife*

WHEN TO GO

The wet season usually means frequent rain, but rain can fall at virtually any time of year over much of the region.

EVEN though Central America is entirely in the Northern Hemisphere, the normal seasonal labels don't apply here. Its proximity to the equator produces consistent temperatures year-round and the seasons are better divided according to rainfall. The rainy season runs from around April to November (a little later in Belize) and is also the cooler period by a few degrees, enough to be called invierno (winter). The dry season from November to April is called verano (summer), but for much of Central America it's only a little less rainy.

Because rain is so plentiful here, wildlife generally doesn't count on its arrival as it does in truly arid areas like Africa or Australia. Nonetheless, rainfall is the single most important factor affecting wildlife behavior and movements, and while the shift between seasons in the tropics can be subtle, it would be a mistake to think that it doesn't influence the viewing. Each season has its attractions (pointed out in detail for each location in the Parks and Places chapter) and certain species and events are more likely to be seen at particular times and locations.

Most people come in the dry season, when the days are generally hot and sunny (punctuated by the occasional brief but heavy downpour), and trails are usually easier to negotiate. Many trees exploit the clear weather by flowering – their pollen stores are safe from deluges, and insect and avian pollinators are active for longer periods. This is the most rewarding time for birdwatchers, with the arrival of wintering migrants from North America and a few from South America, and many resident species nesting towards the end of the Dry. In a few localized areas, such as Costa Rica's Guanacaste province and northern Belize, a prolonged dry season sees wildlife congregate around dwindling water supplies; waterhole vigils sometimes produce rare mammal sightings, and waterbird flocks can number in the thousands.

When rains arrive, there is a rapid flush of new life. Many trees grow new leaves and the forest floor is crammed with new seedlings competing for space and light; both provide fresh food for arboreal and terrestrial browsers. The peak of the rainy season sees the greatest availability of fruit, and a single tree can host dozens of fruit-eating birds and mammals. Cloud-forest birds migrate to lower altitudes to exploit the abundance and to avoid cold, rainy conditions higher up. On the forest floor, insect abundance peaks, providing rich pickings for coatis, antbirds and lizards, and on the coast, marine turtles are returning to nest. During the wettest months, flooding can occur in some areas and certain parks may be inaccessible (see Parks and Places for details).

Remember that enormous geographical variety is packed into a tiny landmass here – you can travel from montane cloud forest to coastal mangroves within a few hours. Organize your trip to make the most of this variation, but don't expect to predict the timing perfectly. Speak to other travelers about destinations they have just left, and don't be afraid to change your itinerary when things happen unexpectedly. ■

Hurricanes

Hurricane season is roughly from June to November in Central America, but hurricanes affect only the Caribbean coast and are largely restricted to Belize; even there, chances of encountering a deadly hurricane are very low. Tropical storms are much more likely during this period and can dampen wildlife-watching with heavy rain lasting a few days.

HOW TO LOOK

Looking at the right time and place

Visitors are always amazed at the apparent ease with which professional guides locate and identify their quarry. While most of us can't hope to replicate their skills in a brief visit, a few pointers can hone your approach. The Wildlife Gallery and Parks and Places chapters give details for specific species.

Boardwalks, observation towers and blinds (or hides) are a feature of many popular wildlife-viewing destinations and can greatly enhance the experience.

Time of Day This is possibly the most important factor determining animal movements and behavior. Dawn and dusk tend to be the most productive periods for diurnal mammals and many birds. They're the coolest parts of the day and also produce the richest light for photographs. The middle of the day is usually too hot for much action, but this is when many raptors 'thermal' and when reptiles are most obvious. Night-time is when most mammals are active as well as owls, numerous reptiles and interesting smaller creatures such as tarantulas (see the Spotlighting section in this chapter). Read up beforehand on desired species so you know what they are likely to be doing at different times.

Weather Intrinsically linked to time of day are the prevailing weather conditions. High winds and rain drive many species into cover so concentrate your search in sheltered areas. Tropical thunderstorms are often followed by a flurry of activity as insect colonies and frogs emerge, and thus attract their predators. Overcast days may prolong hunting by normally crepuscular predators, and extremely wet nights might see nocturnal species still active at dawn because they were forced to shelter during their normal active period. Sunny, warm weather is best for seeing snakes and lizards; try nights just after rain for frogs.

Food Sources Knowing what your quarry eats will help you to decide where to spend time. A flowering bri-bri might not hold much interest at first glance, but knowing that it's irresistible to hordes of hummingbirds and butterflies may change your mind; similarly, fruiting trees attract toucans, guans, monkeys and squirrels. Short grass around water sources or along roadsides pulls in white-tailed deer and red brockets, occasionally followed by big cats. Garbage dumps around national parks and lodges may not be the most pleasant places to spot animals, but opossums, skunks and gray foxes forage there at night. If you're staying in remote villages, chicken coops often attract small predators including margays and ocelots. ∎

Watch your step

Perhaps not for the squeamish, mammal feces, especially those of carnivores and primates (including people), can be fruitful for spotting tiny wildlife. A procession of stingless bees, metallic ottitid flies and over 50 species of dung beetle compete frantically for freshly-laid deposits, and in turn attract predatory beetles, which feast on the dung-eaters and their eggs. Even bird droppings are worth watching – glasswing butterflies, incongruously beautiful in the setting, feed on them for the nitrogen they contain.

The Spanish for sloth is 'perezo-zo' (sleepy bear) and a sleeping sloth can be difficult to spot among the foliage.

Water Most animals drink daily when water is available so water sources are worthwhile places to invest time, but only where standing water is limited (as in Costa Rica's Peninsula de Nicoya during the dry season): Elsewhere, water may be too abundant to be very rewarding. Good times to stake out water sources are morning, late afternoon and just after sunset. White-tailed deer, collared peccaries, monkeys, coatis and large 'gamebirds', such as curassows and guans, are frequent visitors to waterholes.

Habitat Knowing which habitats are preferred by each species is a good beginning, but just as important is knowing where to look in those habitats. Animals seek out specific sites to shelter, to feed, to search their surroundings and so on. Hollows in trees, caves, clearings in the forest – all will be preferred by certain species. Check acacia trees for the nests of their ant defenders as well as a few bird species. Palo verde trees are non-descript but make very important nest trees for many birds during the dry season in north-western Costa Rica. To see tent-making bats, look for palms or banana leaves that are drooping downwards and the emerging, curled leaves at the center of heliconia plants that are often home to disk-winged bats. Ecotones – where one habitat merges into another – can be particularly productive because species from both habitats overlap. Finally, don't forget to think of human structures as wildlife habitat – bat roosts and motmot nests are found in Maya ruins, and geckoes congregate under porch lights.

Searching for wildlife

As much as knowing where and when to search, finding wildlife is all about recognizing patterns and shapes. Camouflage and shadows frequently conceal something that may only be revealed if you're looking for a hanging tail or the curve of a sleeping body. Pay attention to the behavior of other animals – they are often your best indicator of what's around. Animals fixedly watching something are worth investigating. Look for the unusual; some monkey species are so commonly seen, you'll ignore them after a while, but an entire troop vocalizing and looking in the same direction is a sign of possible danger. Vultures circling may simply be thermaling but if you see them descending to the ground or clustered in trees, it probably indicates a carcass. Don't forget to use your other senses. Monkeys often give themselves away by dropping fruit or branches, and a tamandua ripping open a termite nest sounds

Walking on the wild side

Boat trips excepted, most wildlife-watching in Central America takes place on foot; there are very few places suitable for African-style game drives by vehicle. To get the most from walking, begin early in the morning and step quietly to listen for wildlife sounds. It is very important to walk slowly and stop often; people often hit the trail with its end as the goal, but you'll see far more by taking your time. Avoid wearing strong scents and bright colors (though hummingbirds often come to investigate the latter) and keep still when you see something – many animals won't notice you if you remain motionless. Large mammals are notoriously challenging to see, so concentrate on the smaller delights at your feet, such as marching columns of leafcutter ants and bright red poison-dart frogs. Look up; in cities, people rarely raise their eyes above ground level, but in forests, this is where most of the action happens.

Canopy capers

Although not widespread in Central America, there are a number of options for getting up into the canopy where so much of the forest's wildlife action takes place. Hummingbirds, butterflies and other nectar feeders visit flowering epiphytes, parrots and woodpeckers fly past at eye level, and arboreal mammals and reptiles might reveal themselves; occasionally, shy ground-dwellers, such as cats and tapirs, are spotted moving below, unaware of people above them. The best canopy experiences are various combinations of suspension bridges (often advertised as 'skywalks') or towers. Costa Rica's RBBN Monteverde and Hotel Villa Lapas (near PN Carara) have excellent skywalks and Panama's Canopy Tower in PN Soberanía offers excellent rooftop viewing for guests. Adjacent to PN Braulio Carillo (CR), the unique Rain Forest Aerial Tram carries visitors through the canopy in open-sided cable-cars; see **w** www.rainforesttram.com. More for adrenaline than wildlife, zip-lines are beginning to proliferate on private land around popular destinations such as RBBN Monteverde.

like splintering wood. Follow your nose: Some guides can smell a herd of peccaries before they see them.

Using calls

Animals communicate with one another by an astonishing variety of vocalizations (or calls). For wildlifers, these can provide useful information for locating the callers. Long-range calls, such as those of howler monkeys, can help you decide which direction to begin searching, and alarm calls often warn of a predator on the move. Although it takes considerable experience to discern vocalizations, loud explosive calls, such as the barks of capybaras and monkeys, are generally alert signals; birds usually signal alarm by persistent high-pitched or raucous calls.

Calls can be mimicked to attract wildlife, especially birds. Pishing – making the sound 'pish' – will entice many small bird species. Sucking the back of your hand to make a squeaking noise may do likewise and can also attract small predators, such as gray foxes. Playing recordings of vocalizations on a portable tape or CD player is another technique that's particularly effective for bringing forest and woodland birds into the open. Whether playing back calls or mimicking them, use discretion – they disturb natural behavior and can provoke stress, territorial displays and occasionally aggression.

Beyond looking

Most wildlife-watching involves 'collecting' sightings and many wildlifers keep a list of everything they see – a practice known as 'listing' or 'ticking' among birdwatchers. Over time, lists also reveal which regions and habitats are richest in species and when. Even comparing one day's viewing with the next might reveal the effect of weather, time of day and many other factors not immediately apparent. Many field guides or park brochures include a list of species to help you keep track.

Beyond keeping a list, look a little closer. Try to identify individual animals and their sex. Even for very common species, complex behavior and interaction goes on constantly; observing a monkey troop, for example, is a great way to understand dominance patterns. The most interesting behaviors momentarily cease when animals are on the alert, such as the first few minutes after you arrive. Wait a little while for animals to relax and resume their normal activity – the rewards can be terrific. The Wildlife Gallery chapter provides a few clues. ∎

Where the party's at

The fact that Neotropical birds are so abundant and diverse leads one to wonder why the forest can seem so silent and empty at times. The answer to this mystery is that in the nonbreeding season many forest birds forage in bird parties (mixed-species flocks). After hours of fruitless searching, you can suddenly be inundated by a flurry of activity as all kinds of colorful birds arrive: Hopping along branches, rummaging in leaf litter and prising off bark. Then, before you can identify them all, it's over as quickly as it began. Bird parties usually consist of insectivorous or seedeating species, and often target fruiting trees. Other parties follow swarms of army ants (antbirds are renowned for this), feasting on the insects and other small animals they disturb. In the breeding season, some male birds gather to display and advertise for mates (such groupings are known as 'leks') – another good tip for spectacular birdwatching.

EQUIPMENT

Binoculars are essential, but despite the extra weight keen birders should also consider bringing a spotting scope, rather than queue up to look through someone else's at a rarity.

Binoculars and spotting scopes

Binoculars are the most important piece of equipment for wildlife-watching. They help to spot and identify animals (especially birds), and to view species and behaviors where a close approach is impossible. There are hundreds of models to select from, but some basic facts simplify the choice.

Firstly, what do those numbers mean? The first number is the magnification while the second refers to the diameter in millimeters of the objective lens (farthest from the eye) and indicates its light-gathering efficiency. Thus, 10x40 and 10x50 have the same magnification (times 10, ie, an object 100m away will appear 10m away), but the 10x50 admits more light, improving the brightness and clarity of the image, particularly in poor light. Higher magnifications and, in particular, larger objective lenses both add to the size and weight of binoculars. 'Compacts' (usually 8x20 or 10x25) fit into a top pocket, but performance can be poor in low light, whereas 10x50s are cumbersome on walks but clear in all light. Intermediate models such as 7x35 or 8x40 are a compromise between the two.

A spotting scope is a telescope designed for use in the field. Scopes give higher magnification and better clarity than binoculars, but usually require the stability of a tripod for effective use. They are mostly used by birdwatchers – professional guides and most organized wildlife tours should have scopes.

Flashlights and headlamps

A flashlight (torch) or headlamp is indispensable for spotlighting animals on night walks and boat trips. A flashlight is usually fine, but a headlamp frees up your hands for using binoculars or a camera; for photography, look for a lamp which sits at the side of the head rather than on the forehead so you can shine past a bulky flash. Headlamps are available at most camping stores. Models powered by batteries carried on a belt at your waist offer the longest battery life. Rechargeable models are available, but may be of limited use in remote areas.

Clothing

Clothing should be lightweight and fast-drying. Muted, natural colors are best, but avoid camouflage patterns – these may provoke trouble with local military or immigration authorities. Generally, shorts and light shirts will be most comfortable, but trousers (full-length cargo pants are ideal) provide protection from insect bites, especially after dark. A rainproof and windproof jacket (the sort that can be rolled up and carried in a belt-bag) is indispensable for sudden downpours. Waterproof boots are a good idea, and Teva-style sport sandals are useful for frequent river crossings. Central America gets about 12 hours of sun every day and the sun is right above you, so bring a hat, especially for river trips. An additional warm layer helps in cool mountain climates; travelers camping in high-altitude cloud forests will need even warmer gear and should be prepared for temperatures below freezing above 9800ft (3000m). ∎

Battling the elements

High humidity and rainfall can lead to fungus and faults in cameras, binoculars and scopes. Cram your camera bags with silica gel and treat them with spray-on sealant. Bring large trash-bin liners to cover your gear in sudden showers (some camera backpacks have a built-in equivalent) and pack a range of zip-lock bags; they make useful waterproof housings in an emergency. And, very important, clean your gear after each day in the field.

IDENTIFYING ANIMALS

Field guides

Field guides are usually pocket-sized books that depict the mammals, birds, flowers etc of a specific area with photos or illustrations. Identification pointers are usually provided for each species; sometimes there are also brief natural histories with notes on breeding, behavior, diet and so on. Guides to animals are usually organized in taxonomic order, a system that shows relationships between species and is usually consistent between guides; plant guides sometimes rank wildflowers by color.

Ideally, you should add your own observations, notes and sketches to what you read in field guides, but the excitement of wildlife-watching and the overwhelming variety of animals often make this impractical. Don't assume that because the book says species X is found here, it must be species X you're looking at. If you find something unusual – birds in particular often wander outside their usual range – take notes and refer to other books when you get a chance. Depending on how much you value the book's appearance, consider color-coding pages so you can flip to a section easily. Some people remove the ID plates from guides for use in the field (you'll see this often in Costa Rica). This reduces weight in your pack and is useful if you're already familiar with the local wildlife, but the text often contains the finer points for discriminating similar species.

Field guides are a handy tool that have made an incalculable contribution to the popularity of wildlife-watching. Rarely, though, are they the last word on a subject, and further reading of weightier texts can provide valuable detail not covered in your field guide – refer to the individual activity sections later in this chapter, and the Resource Guide for suggested reading.

Although jaguars are sometimes sighted by chance, you are far more likely to see footprints or scratches in a trunk (shown here) where el tigre has been sharpening its claws.

Tracks and signs

Even when you don't see animals they leave many signs of their presence. Spoor (tracks), scats (droppings), pellets, nests, scrapes and scent-marks provide information about wildlife and may even help to locate it. Tracks are easily spotted on muddy trails, on dirt roads and around riverbanks and waterholes; it won't take you long to recognize interesting ones. Spoor of big cats and tapirs is unmistakable and agouti tracks are fairly obvious. Identifying species by their spoor is mostly a specialist task but will be made easier if you are able to eliminate possibilities. For example, pumas are far more widespread than jaguars and are the most likely source of large-cat tracks outside conservation areas. Other signs suggest where to focus your searches. 'Whitewash' on cliff faces usually indicates nesting raptors, and clusters of pellets may signify an owl's roost. Porcupines deposit a dung pile outside their daytime tree hollows. A freshly opened termite mound may signal a nearby tamandua, and many species of bats shelter in distinctive leaf tents that are easily found with practice. There are hundreds of such signs and signals which, even if they don't lead you to the culprit, can enhance your enjoyment of wildlife immeasurably. Use a field guide to refine your skills; some are listed in the Resource Guide. ■

> **Trapping tracks**
> If you're staying overnight in an area, set up a 'track trap' by simply raking smooth a section of trail or laying down a bed of sand; an inspection early the next morning will reveal what's passed the night before. Pick a likely site, such as a fruiting tree, a waterhole or even a garbage dump.

GETTING AROUND

Aerial trams provide excellent views over the canopy, but their usefulness for watching wildlife depends on factors such as time of day and noise.

Doing it yourself

In most cases, the easiest way to get to parks and reserves in Central America is by car, which gives you tremendous flexibility to do your own thing. You can drive your own vehicle from North America or hire one once there. Hiring is often expensive – although you can get better deals for longer periods – and car-hire companies generally prohibit you from crossing country borders. Major routes are paved, but more remote ones aren't. Regardless, there are plenty of potholes, narrow roads and roaming livestock to keep you on your toes; drop your speed substantially if driving at night (see the boxed text 'What's the hurry?' below). A 4WD gives you access to more places and will help you negotiate muddy roads in the wet season; for some sites, it's mandatory. A few places are accessible only by boat or plane but their popularity usually means there are reasonably affordable options available. Local buses are excellent value but they move pretty slowly, especially once you're in the mountains, and they don't serve more remote areas. Many tour companies use more comfortable, Greyhound-style buses. Taxi drivers are willing to go virtually anywhere, but they're expensive and most don't have meters; establish the fee before you leave. Hitching is not recommended for safety reasons though of course many thousands of travelers do it without incident every year.

Guides and tours

The majority of foreign visitors to Central America go wildlife-watching with organized tours, which are available in every possible permutation and combination. They vary from day trips leaving from the major centers, to extensive, multisite tours. Before you decide anything, try to establish how much time the various tours spend in parks and how much time traveling between them. Many arranged tours, whether day trips or longer, often cover an enormous amount of ground – at the cost of quality time in reserves. Generally, spending more time at fewer sites is far more rewarding for wildlife-watching than trying to visit many parks.

The standard of tours is generally high and guides pride themselves on their ability to find and identify hundreds of species, particularly birds. For serious wildlife enthusiasts, specialist companies guarantee excellent guides, but of course they

What's the hurry?

Every year countless wild animals are killed on roads, both outside protected areas and, less often, within them. If you're driving yourself, you can avoid contributing to the needless tally simply by slowing down. In rural areas, raccoons, armadillos and jaguarundis often dart unexpectedly across the road at dusk or night-time and, during the day, ctenosaurs and snakes bask on roads. All of them make frequent roadkill, yet all are easily avoided by dropping your speed a few mph – and you'll also better dodge potholes and stray livestock. Inside parks, the limited network and quality of roads means speed is less of a problem but drivers still manage to hit animals at night on thoroughfares through parks – at Río Bravo, for instance – or long, level entrance roads as at Cockscomb Basin WS in Belize. Take your time and, as well as giving animals time to get off the road, you might also boost your chances of spotting a big cat.

Although most parks in the region are accessible by road or boat, there are only two ways to get to Cana in Panama's PN Darién: walk or fly.

are more expensive. Private reserves usually have their own well-trained guides though in many cases, you can arrive as part of a tour with your own guide. Similarly, most upmarket lodges situated near reserves have resident guides but you usually pay extra for any tours – they are generally not part of the accommodation package.

At the more popular sites, it's often possible to obtain a guide at the park gates or ranger station. You can pay per hour (an excellent option for exploring places like PN Tortuguero by boat) or pay for a set tour, which usually runs for a few hours; this is an easily arranged option in many parks – among them PN Carara, Crooked Tree WS, Community Baboon Sanctuary, PN Manuel Antonio, RBBN Monteverde and EB La Selva. Try to arrange it the previous day or a few hours ahead of time; guides are usually sourced from the surrounding communities and need some warning.

Using guides in this way is highly recommended. Being so practised at finding and identifying wildlife, they will almost certainly boost your species count, and in some cases, will know where to go for special requests. They also serve to introduce you to an area after which you're better equipped to explore on your own; hire a guide for a few hours in the morning, then spend the rest of the day alone. And finally, by using local guides, you'll help the communities on the boundaries of protected areas, in turn giving them a reason to support the park.

Parks and reserves

Government-run parks and reserves usually require fees for both entry and accommodation, but rates are generally extremely reasonable; they are much cheaper than North American parks. At some sites, you can also buy meals – which helps the park generate a small profit. Keep in mind that the money generated from fees is often the only revenue available to run parks and contributes to their ongoing protection.

Most reserves offer some form of accommodation; camping is the most common option and is permitted in most. A number of sites have more expensive, dorm-style rooms and a handful offer private rooms or cabañas. More luxurious lodges and hotels are common on the perimeter of parks. Privately-owned reserves usually have upmarket accommodation and don't permit camping. The Parks and Places chapter lists the options for specific sites. ∎

> **Saving on entry fees**
> Some parks offer good deals on entry fees if you're staying more than a day but it's rarely advertised. If you're staying just outside a park for a while and plan to pass through the gates on consecutive days, be sure to ask if it has a multiday pass.

CLOSE ENCOUNTERS

Feeders are an effective way of attracting hummingbirds and are set up at many private lodges and reserves. Here a long-tailed hermit takes a sip.

CONTRARY to their portrayal by Hollywood, tropical rainforests are not crawling with human-devouring snakes, giant killer spiders, lethal parasites and deadly armies of ants. Most such stories are myths and there are few species that are actually lethal to people; most encounters are with harmless but irritating insects that bite and sting. By taking some simple precautions you can avoid unpleasant situations. Stick to trails and watch where you put your hands and feet. Don't walk barefoot at any time (especially after dark when scorpions and some snakes are active), and leave handling snakes to professionals and morons. Never pick up amphibians, especially brightly-colored ones, which may contain deadly toxins in their skins. Some mosquitoes carry malaria or yellow fever and precautions should be taken to avoid mosquito bites; prophylactic medicine may be advised and long sleeves and trousers are recommended after dark. Ticks are widespread and are easily picked up while walking, especially through pasture areas. Again, long, lightweight trousers are useful. Lonely Planet's *Healthy Travel Central & South America* includes comprehensive coverage of these issues.

Feeding wildlife

Most parks prohibit feeding wildlife with good reason: Animals learn very quickly where to get a hand-out and may become pests at campsites. Some species, particularly monkeys and coatis, resort to aggression once they lose their natural caution around people and have to be destroyed by rangers, or are killed by cars while begging along roadsides.

Having said that, authorities often turn a blind eye to feeding less dangerous camp-followers, such as birds and small mammals. Indeed many private lodges have feeding stations to attract these species. There is great appeal in sharing your biscuit with birds or squirrels, but be aware you may be fostering a dependency or affecting an animal's health. Additionally, the artificial concentrations of animals attracted to hand-outs can result in increased fighting and a greater likelihood of disease transmission. At the very least, you are altering an animal's natural behavior – it's unavoidable where humans and animals coexist and generally not critically serious for small species, but it's probably something to avoid if you can.

Animal welfare

Although it's less prevalent here than in other areas of Latin America, you may occasionally encounter animal skins, live birds and other questionable wildlife products for sale in markets or villages. Similarly, a few wildlife species, such as marine turtles and pacas regularly appear on menus at restaurants. The hunting of wild animals has always been an important source of food for the rural peoples of Central America, and some countries permit locals to take certain widespread species such as deer, agoutis and gamebirds. In Belize, Costa Rica and Panama, such hunting is restricted to certain areas and seasons,

Up close and personal
Close-up views of wildlife are much more likely in areas where hunting is banned. Animals are far less likely to flee, there are more of them around and there is usually a greater diversity of species. It usually means that strictly protected areas, such as national parks, are more rewarding for wildlifers than those which allow utilization (like forest reserves).

and is intended for subsistence rather than commercial gain. Even so, the effects of hunting for the pot may be significant. A study comparing Costa Rica's RF Golfo Dulce (where hunting is permitted) with the neighboring PN Corcovado found that game species were between four and sixteen times less abundant in the hunted area. Additionally, because the hunters' most favored quarry – peccaries, pacas, agoutis and deer – was also the preferred prey of big cats, jaguars and pumas were absent from Golfo Dulce. Finally, because hunting is very difficult to control, strictly-protected species, such as Baird's tapirs and wild cats, were sometimes shot opportunistically.

There is no easy answer to the problems posed by hunting, legal or otherwise, but for visitors, the rule of thumb is clear: Don't buy wildlife products. That includes live animals. It is very tempting to buy them with release in mind, but this only fuels the trade and most don't survive without specialist expertise guiding the effort. If you can convince a seller to give you an animal, take it to a ranger station, biologist or vet.

Don't feed the animals! As well as provoking aggression (see text) feeding can result in health problems and obesity, as in this coati.

There are a couple of schemes designed to yield a sustainable harvest of wildlife products. At RNFS Ostional, locals are permitted to collect and sell olive ridley eggs (see Wildlife Gallery), and a handful of breeding programs in Costa Rica and Belize aim to farm pacas. Sustainable use should be supported because it usually encourages local people to protect the resource, but bear in mind that true sustainability is the exception rather than the rule and legal harvests may open channels for illegal ones.

Disturbing wildlife

Given that you can't usually leave trails and roads unless you're with a trained guide, the prospects of seriously disturbing animals are slight. Usually the worst outcome of disturbance is that the subject will move out of sight – probably more serious for the viewer than the viewed.

Nonetheless, it's important to remember that the presence of people can intrude on wild animals and to minimize this where possible. This has already been covered in the sections on Using calls, earlier, and Spotlighting, later, in this chapter, but a few other pointers should be kept in mind. Be very cautious about picking up animals. Never pick up a young animal that looks 'abandoned'. It almost certainly is not and the mother is probably waiting for you to move away before she returns. People love handling harmless animals like lizards and frogs but this invariably causes the animal stress. 'Getting close to nature' is laudable but wild animals are simply never handled; in their experience, being picked up is life-threatening. In areas which experience a distinct dry season, like Costa Rica's Peninsula de Nicoya, avoid swimming in waterholes; you may frighten off wildlife relying on the holes as their only source of water. Also, don't always assume that your guide is doing the right thing. Sometimes, the pressure to deliver sightings to paying tourists encourages guides to approach animals too closely, to startle them into action and so on. If you're uncomfortable with something your guide is doing, don't be afraid to speak up or even report it to park authorities. ∎

Insect vacuum cleaners

It's not unusual to come home from a day's hike to find columns of army ants in your room or tent, especially if you've sprayed for flying insects. Don't be alarmed: The ants will mop up insects and food crumbs (spotlessly!), and will invariably move off for their overnight nest within a few hours of sunset. However, leafcutter ants have been known to cut up an entire Goretex jacket overnight!

BIRDWATCHING

Ocellated antbirds are obligate antbirds, ie, they feed almost exclusively in association with swarms of army ants. Army-ant swarms attract many forest birds and are worth seeking.

Members of the bizarre cotinga family are usually high on birders' must-see lists. This is a turquoise cotinga, most often seen in lowland forests of Costa Rica's Pacific slope.

CENTRAL America should be on the radar of any world birder – if you haven't already been there, then put it at the top of your 'must go' list. Few parts of the world cram so much avian diversity into such a small space: Belize's Caribbean swamps, coral cayes and lowland forests boast over 560 bird species; in legendary Costa Rica – a country the size of West Virginia – some 874 species have been recorded (that's more than the whole of Australia); and 944 species have been logged to date in Panama, where vast tracts of forest still hold healthy numbers of sought-after species such as harpy eagles. Whichever destination you choose, at the right time of year with some careful planning (and a lot of time in the field), a first-timer could expect upwards of 300 lifers in a three-week trip, including representatives of most Neotropical families and sought-after highlights such as resplendent quetzals.

How it's done

Read as much as possible before arriving: Familiarize yourself with new bird families and prioritize sites according to the species you most want to see. Most birders will want to seek out personal targets (eg, resplendent quetzal, harpy eagle, etc) and should work out a 'hit-list' for your trip: Decide which species (or families) are most important to see. A typical regimen could include seeing as many of the endemic Neotropical families as possible plus the regional and country endemics, and your personal favorites. Consider hiring local guides – many are tuned into the needs of birders and with excellent eyesight and hearing they will be an asset to you; you'll also support local employment and encourage interest in conservation.

Coverage will depend mainly on time and money, but be sure to work as many habitats and elevations as possible, and share your time between the Pacific and Caribbean coasts, and the mountainous divide. Although there is much overlap between Costa Rica and Panama, each offers better chances at certain species, eg, access to cloud forest is easy in Costa Rica's RBBN Monteverde, but only Panama offers the Darién wilderness.

Make sure you binoculars are waterproof, since you'll be visiting plenty of rainforest and that can mean rain at any time. Good light-gathering configurations include 8x40 and 10x40; the heavier 10x50 can cause neck strain after hours of looking into the canopy! Spotting scopes are weighty and cumbersome on forest trails, but brilliant for scanning treetops from lodge balconies. A tape recorder and directional mike can be used to call in skulkers, but this technique has been overused at some sites and may not be effective. At all times consider the welfare of the birds when using playback.

Top spots to go

If you've never been to Central America before, head straight for Panama. Work the excellent lowland rainforest near Panama City for an introduction to Central American birding and visit the special sites, especially world-famous Pipeline Rd in PN

Soberanía. You *must* go to Darién province – this is fast becoming recognized as one of the world's Top 10 birding destinations, and here remoteness, diversity, endemics and some species found elsewhere only in hard-to-get-to Colombia ensure some very special birding indeed. Darién also offers a shot at one hard to get even in Amazonia: The magnificent harpy eagle. To round out a Panama birding trip, visit PN Volcán Barú in the Chiriquí Highlands, home to another suite of endemics – these ones shared only with Costa Rica.

Mere mention of Costa Rica usually sets birders a-drooling for its legendary birds, national parks and tourism-friendliness. As with Panama, your efforts are best spread between several areas, namely the northeastern lowlands (eg, PN Tortuguero, EB La Selva), Pacific northwest (RNVS Caño Negro and PNs Palo Verde and Santa Rosa), the southwestern lowlands (PNs Carara and Corcovado) and central cordillera (RBBN Monteverde and PN Tapantí). Being more mountainous than Panama, Costa Rica offers a different suite of birds at higher elevations, and is better for some hard-to-gets in Panama (eg, volcano juncos).

But, of course, numbers aren't everything and a birding visit to Belize will be amply rewarded with seabird colonies on coral cayes and some species, such as ocellated turkey, keel-billed motmot and birds more typical of Mexico's Yucatán Península.

Nearly every country in the region has at least one endemic bird species (depending on taxonomy, Costa Rica has six and Panama 12), and many more are endemic to two or three countries only (eg, 61 species are shared by only Costa Rica and Panama). It would be an exceptional trip that logged all of these, but the fun's in trying, right?

Field guides and checklists

The whole of Central America is covered by three excellent field guides: *A Field Guide to the Birds of Mexico and Northern Central America* (which includes Belize) by S Howell and S Webb; *A Field Guide to the Birds of Costa Rica* by G Stiles, A Skutch and D Gardner; and *A Field Guide to the Birds of Panama* by R Ridgeley and J Gwynne (the 1989 edition also covers the birds of Costa Rica, and if you are going to both countries you could save weight by carrying only this one). Savvy birders get the plates removed, laminated and ring bound for waterproofing and ease of use in the field – this way you could lighten the load in your day pack, especially if you take notes in the field and leave the main text back at base.

Reputable checklists include *Checklist of Costa Rican Birds*, published by the Asociación Orintológica de Costa Rica; *Lista de las Aves de Panamá*, published in several parts by the Panama Audubon Society; and *Annotated Checklist of the Birds of Belize* by H Lee Jones and AC Vallely, and *Birds of Belize: A checklist* by BW and CM Miller.

Also very valuable are trip reports published by birders that have been to a location – several basic ones are available for free on the Web. See the Resource Guide (pp218–20) for useful Web sites, but **w** www.camacdonald.com/birding/birding.htm is a good starting point for background information, some trip reports and birdlists. ∎

Take a load off. Birders enjoying a rare opportunity to ease neck strain while looking into the canopy.

DIVING & SNORKELING

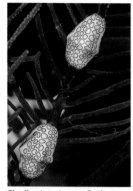

The flamingo tongue Cyphoma gibbosum *is a sea snail typically found on gorgonians and sea whips. The shell is actually white – the mantle provides the color.*

A diver feeds two nurse sharks off Belize's Ambergris Caye. Belize's clear reef waters provide exceptional underwater viewing.

CENTRAL America boasts some of the best diving and snorkeling on earth. The action is centered around offshore islands along the coast of Belize, where a 200-mile (320km) barrier reef (the world's second largest after Australia's Great Barrier Reef) contains three of the Western Hemisphere's four coral atolls. Here, warm seas, exceptional clarity and superb coral reefs make for an underwater extravaganza. For scuba enthusiasts, hundreds of reefs, spectacular wall dives, shipwrecks and Lighthouse Reef's famous Blue Hole provide interest for all levels of expertise. Many of the top diving sites are also suitable for snorkeling, and snorkeling trips are readily combined with manatee-watching and birdwatching. Whether you want to see cathedrals of colorful coral, navigate underwater caves or swim with hundreds of multicolored reef fish, Belize offers world-class diving and snorkeling for the novice to the veteran.

How it's done

You'll need internationally recognized certification for any scuba diving in the region. For nondivers looking for a course and experienced divers needing local knowledge and equipment, dive schools proliferate in the popular dive spots (see later) though the cheapest place to get your ticket is Honduras' Bay Islands (beyond the scope of this book). Regardless, as well as providing instruction and gear for hire, all dive schools arrange trips to nearby sites as well as to those further afield. It is important to assess carefully the gear and instructors you hire; although there are some excellent operators, others are not particularly good or safe. A few pointers can narrow the field for novices: Small groups (four to six people per instructor) are much better than large ones. Ask to see the instructor's card or even their logbook: 100 logged dives is not much, 500 is dive-master material. Make sure the gear looks well-maintained and clean; avoid patched or dirty equipment assiduously.

If you plan on snorkeling, you'll need only fins, mask and snorkel, which are widely available for hire at all dive centers. If you've never snorkeled before, it's hugely rewarding here and extremely easy to learn. The key is to breathe normally – anticipate a little resistance with the slight change in pressure even just a few inches below the surface. Also, don't panic when the snorkel fills with water as you submerge; simply blow it clear when you reach the surface.

Top spots to go

Belize's barrier reef extends from the northern tip of Ambergris Caye southwards to Honduras and offers more spectacular sites than a diver or snorkeler could explore in a lifetime. The most popular dive sites focus around Ambergris Caye and the three atolls (Lighthouse Reef, Turneffe Atoll and Glover's Reef).

Ambergris is Belize's largest offshore caye and the most popular; Belize's barrier reef lies less than a mile (1.6km) offshore and is packed with spur-and-groove reefs, reef cuts and swim-throughs with visibility up to 150ft (45m). Hol Chan Cut

Marine Reserve, four miles (2.4km) southeast of San Pedro, is a spectacular shallow dive suitable for snorkelers and intermediate divers. Since the reserve was proclaimed, marine life has proliferated: Schoolmasters, cubera snappers and 40lb (18kg) groupers are among the many creatures found here. For impressive displays of elkhorn, lettuce, boulder and staghorn coral, venture north to Cypress, a spur-and-groove reef and favorite haunt for novices and underwater photographers. For classic underwater canyoning, Tackle Box Canyons is your best bet.

Lighthouse Reef is renowned for the Blue Hole, a turquoise sinkhole rimmed by living coral and made famous by Jacques Cousteau's 1970 Calypso expedition. For advanced divers the descent reveals giant ghostly stalactites and the possibility of a shark or turtle encounter; snorkelers will find the vivid coral life around the perimeter of the hole fascinating. Some of Belize's most spectacular wall dives are at Lighthouse, including Half Moon Wall and Eagle Ray Wall.

Turneffe Atoll is easily accessible from Belize City and has enough sites to happily fill several weeks diving. Myrtle's Turtle is one of Belize's top deep-dive sites, and a night dive to Blue Creek can reveal giant spider crabs. For novice wreck divers, the Wreck of the Sayonara is a good starting point. Glover's Reef is less visited and harder to get to, but offers some superb diving and snorkeling, including the Long Caye Wall, Emerald Forest Reef and, for the intrepid, Shark Point. For giant sponges check out Southwest Caye Wall.

Behind the protection of the barrier reef, snorkelers can hardly go wrong in Belize – there are hundreds of superb sites. Hol Chan Cut Marine Reserve, Mexico Rocks and Mata Cut off Ambergris Caye are excellent. From South Water Caye you can get to the reef only 130 yards (120m) from the beach, and remote Queen Cayes is also worth the trip. Resorts on Ambergris Caye, Caye Chapel, Caye Caulker and South Water Caye have private beaches with nearshore snorkeling areas.

Belize offers some of the region's finest snorkeling and diving for all levels of skill and interest.

While diving and snorkeling are not as spectacular in Panama and Costa Rica, these countries still offer some decent sites. Visibility is generally better during the dry season (during the wet, river runoff clouds the water). Panama's top spots are the Archipiélago de las Perlas and Isla de Coiba (on the Pacific side) and the Archipiélago de San Blás (on the Caribbean side). In Costa Rica head to the northern part of the Península de Nicoya; Playa Hermosa, Playa del Coco, Isla del Caño and Playa Ocotal. For snorkeling try Montezuma and PN Manuel Antonio. On the Caribbean side, head to PN Cahuita to dive or snorkel the country's largest coral reef – unfortunately, the reef is close to shore and has been affected by silting from local rivers. For those prepared to venture further afield, Isla del Cocos – 310 miles (500km) southwest of Costa Rica – is world class.

Field guides

Lonely Planet Pisces guides give you the lowdown on the region's top diving and snorkeling sites and help you identify some marine creatures. Check out *Diving & Snorkeling Belize* and the Pisces Guide to *Caribbean Reef Ecology*. *Diving & Snorkeling Cocos Island* offers advice for this remote destination. ∎

SEA TURTLE-WATCHING

THE seafaring life of marine turtles makes seeing them a challenge, and encounters while diving or snorkeling are a matter of luck. However, all sea turtles originally evolved from terrestrial species and they are still tied to land for that critical stage of their life cycle – nesting. The most rewarding way to see them up close is when the females come ashore to lay or when the hatchlings emerge, and Central America is one of the best places in the world for this. Of the world's seven species of sea turtle, five nest on Central American beaches and all can be seen by wildlife watchers prepared to put in a little time. Even better (though far more difficult to predict), a few sites host mass nesting events called arribadas, in which tens of thousands of turtles synchronize their laying in truly spectacular fashion.

Sea turtles are survivors from an ancient age, but to see why it's probably best to see them in their element. This is a hawksbill turtle.

Female turtles haul themselves ashore after dark to lay their eggs in pits they laboriously dig in the sand with their hind flippers.

How it's done

The nesting season varies according to location and species so the key to watching sea turtles is being in the right place at the right time (see the table for Turtle nesting seasons, later). Loggerheads lay on the Caribbean coast, olive ridleys lay on the Pacific coast, and leatherbacks, greens and hawksbills utilize both. The number of females coming ashore to lay at any one time depends on the species: Leatherbacks, loggerheads and hawksbills generally nest alone, greens arrive in groups and olive ridleys arrive singly, in small groups or in massive arribadas. An arribada is the holy grail of sea turtle-watching. Only two species engage in these, the Kemp's ridley (which does not occur in the region) and the olive ridley, featured in the Wildlife Gallery chapter. No-one knows exactly what triggers an arribada, but they're more likely to occur during the first and last quarters of the moon in the wet season. Females can apparently hold fully-formed eggs for weeks and delay nesting until the signals are right, though why they are timed so exactly is still a mystery.

Because all species of sea turtles are endangered, key nesting sites are protected and most turtle-watching in the region is regulated. Many sites, particularly in Costa Rica, limit the number of people visiting the beach on any one night and the numbers making up individual tours: Book early in the peak seasons. The restrictions are designed not only to minimize disturbance to turtles, but also to enhance the experience; the guides are generally useful sources of extra information.

Park rangers and guides will advise you of correct turtle-watching etiquette, but if you stumble across turtles on your own there are a few basic pointers to bear in mind. Turtles prefer to lay on dark nights (presumably to reduce their vulnerability to predators) so don't use flashlights or photographic flashes. Keep your distance (some locations have specified viewing areas) and remain quiet, particularly if a female has just emerged prior to laying; this is when they are most cautious and will abandon the effort if alarmed. Enjoy the slow pace: It can take a female an hour to dig and lay her eggs. If you find hatchlings, don't shine light on them: Because the horizon is slightly lighter than the ocean, they use light as their cue to find the water and become disoriented by artificial light-sources. Be wary of guides from hotels or agencies who do not follow these principles, and don't hesitate to report them to park authorities. Remember that both the Caribbean and Pacific coasts are hot and humid, even at night, and receive a lot of rain year-round; lightweight clothing and a rain jacket are recommended.

Top spots to go

Costa Rica Playa Grande in PNM Las Baulas de Guanacaste is the most important leatherback nesting site in the world. The prime nesting season is from October to March (especially November to January). Leatherbacks also nest at RNVS Gandoca-Manzanillo (April to May) and greens arrive between July and September; you can also see hawksbills and loggerheads in small numbers here. PN Tortuguero is the key nesting site for greens in the Caribbean; the peak season is from June to November (also keep an eye out for leatherbacks and, to a lesser extent, loggerheads and hawksbills). July to November (particularly September and October) are the top months for olive ridley arribadas at RNFS Ostional and Playa Nancite (PN Santa Rosa). Both sites also attract nesting leatherbacks and greens. All these sites are covered in greater detail in the Parks and Places chapter.

Belize In comparison to Costa Rica, Belize has only a few small nest sites of three species – but this is the best place for loggerheads and hawksbills, which are difficult to see elsewhere in the region. Chico NP on Ambergris Caye is Belize's most important nesting site for loggerheads and green turtles (both May to August). Hawksbills nest between May and October on beaches in the Sapodilla Cays in the southern barrier reef, and in the Manatee Bar area on the mainland near the village of Gales Point.

Panama For a more adventurous option, head to Isla Cana from the end of August through September to see thousands of nesting green sea turtles. This place is not developed and is a challenge to get to. Otherwise, try PNM Isla Bastimentos or the nearby Humedal de San San-Pond Sak where four species nest (April to August). ∎

Turtle hatchlings are tiny and vulnerable to a host of predators. This hawksbill was rescued from poachers on Panama's San Blas Islands.

Turtle nesting seasons

	Jan	Feb	Mar	Apr	May	Jun	July	Aug	Sep	Oct	Nov	Dec
Leatherback	**P**	P	P/C	**C**	**C**	C	C		P	**P**	**P**
Loggerhead					C	C	C	C	C			
Green					C	P/C	P/C	**P/C**	**P/C**	**P/C**	P	P
Hawksbill				P/C	P/C	**P/C**	**P/C**	P/C	P/C	P/C	P	
Olive Ridley	P	P	P	P	P	**P**	**P**	**P**	**P***	**P***	**P**	P

P = Pacific, C= Caribbean; bold indicates peak months, * indicates best months for arribadas

WHALE-WATCHING

WITH warm currents and protected bays, Central America's oceans provide an ideal habitat for whales and dolphins to breed and to hunt in productive, shallow waters close to shore. There are at least 30 species of cetacean (the collective name for whales, dolphins and porpoises) known from the region, some of which provide excellent viewing for marine mammal-lovers.

How it's done

Apart from patience and binoculars, cetacean-spotting doesn't demand much in the way of specialized skills or gear. Watch for the characteristic 'blows' of whales and for hovering flocks of seabirds, which indicate large fish shoals – irresistible to many dolphins. Except for occasional lucky glimpses from shore, most viewing takes place from a boat, and trips offering close-up viewing are now commonplace in the region. The lack of industry regulation means that harassment is a serious problem and many tour operators do not follow basic safety procedures, such as carrying life-jackets and radios – make sure your tour does. Fortunately, a handful of conservation-minded operators promote low-impact techniques; the best ones are listed below.

Spotted dolphins in the Gulf of Panama. This is one of the most common and widespread dolphin species in tropical waters, and often rides bow-waves.

Top spots to go

Whales and dolphins occur along both the Pacific and Caribbean (Atlantic) coasts. The main attractions at Pacific sites are humpback whales (December through March and late July through October) and various dolphins, including rough-toothed, spinner (dry season) and huge schools of pantropical spotted dolphins; the Caribbean side offers year-round viewing of bottlenose, spotted and tucuxi dolphins.

On Costa Rica's Pacific coast, Fundelfin (**w** www.fundelfin -costa-rica.org) and Divine Dolphin (**w** www.divinedolphin.com) are spearheading cetacean conservation and offer well-run tours in Drake Bay, where at least 22 species occur. Other like-minded operators include Planet Dolphin (**w** www.cox-inter net.com/wmhanks/planetd) at Quepos (the Quepos-Manuel Antonio area is overrun with operators, so choose carefully) and, on the Caribbean side, the Talamanca Dolphin Foundation (**w** www.dolphinlink.org) at Manzanillo.

The tail flukes of humpback whales have a diagnostic shape, and individuals can be recognised by scars and markings.

In Panama, you can watch humpbacks and their calves at the Refugio de Vida Silvestre Isla Iguana from June to November. And, although access is difficult and costly, at PN Isla de Coiba you may see humpback, killer and sperm whales as well as spotted and bottlenose dolphins. Ancon Expeditions (**w** www.anconexpeditions.com) offers tours to Coiba.

Belize has a small but growing whale-watching industry, which focuses mainly on bottlenose dolphins, spotted dolphins and short-finned pilot whales. Boat trips around the cayes often encounter dolphins (see The Cayes section in the Belize chapter) and the US-based Oceanic Society (**w** www.oceanic-society.org) offers expeditions with specialist guides.

There are no field guides specific to Central America, but some good, general guides are listed in the Resource Guide. ∎

SPOTLIGHTING

MANY Neotropical animals are active only after dark so in order to see them, you need to go looking at night. Spotlighting can reveal kinkajous, opossums, owls, pauraques and potoos, as well as nocturnal hunters like boa constrictors, fer-de-lances and tarantulas. As an extra enticement, it also offers the greatest chance of catching large mammals on the move including tapirs, ocelots and big cats.

How it's done

For most situations, a strong flashlight will do provided you avoid bulky models, which quickly become a burden. Even better, headlamps leave your hands free, but the beam is often weak; choose a powerful one. Portable handheld spotlights (some are rechargeable) are probably overkill; you won't need more than 500,000 candle-power, and you should choose a model with a cigarette-lighter adapter for vehicle-based searching. Be careful where you spotlight by car: You might be mistaken for a poacher so advise rangers before setting out. Camping and marine equipment suppliers usually carry a range.

Olingos sometimes visit hummingbird feeders after dark in RBBN Monteverde, but otherwise you'll need to scan the canopy for this one!

When searching, sweep fairly rapidly and look for 'eyeshine', a reflection from a light-gathering layer of cells on the retina of nocturnal animals (called the tapetum lucidum). When you spot something, avoid shining directly at it – spotlighting may momentarily disorient animals or reveal them to predators. Instead, angle the light to nearby surroundings. A red filter (cellophane works) over your light source minimizes disturbance when watching mammals at close range. Staking out sites that attract animals will increase your spotlighting success. Try sitting quietly near a fruiting or flowering tree (such as balsa) or water source in the dry season and keep your light off until you hear activity.

Top spots to go

You can successfully spotlight on foot in any protected area, but let park staff know what you're doing and where you're going. Simply wandering around a camp site or lodge grounds after dark will often be rewarding. If you're venturing further afield, keep to well-known tracks and keep an eye on the trail for fer-de-lances. It's advisable not to go alone. Corcovado's trails are among the best for night-sights and the waterpoints at Santa Rosa and Palo Verde can be very rewarding. Cockscomb and Río Bravo have long entrance roads suitable for vehicle-based spotlighting, which occasionally produces cat sightings; drive slowly for the best chances. The camp sites/accommodation areas of both these reserves are good for pacas, kinkajous, gray foxes and boa constrictors. Panama's Pipeline Road offers possible nightbirds, kinkajous, sloths and night monkeys.

Spotlighting doesn't guarantee sightings of rarities – and in fact some nights you'll see very little – but the payoff for long hours in the field can be great, such as this jaguarundi.

Excellent guided night walks are available at RBBN Monteverde (highlights include tarantulas and olingos) and the Community Baboon Sanctuary (kinkajous virtually guaranteed). Lamanai Outpost Lodge has superb boat-based night safaris, and Chan Chich is one of the few sites in Central America with night-drives by vehicle; jaguars are sometimes seen at both locations. ∎

PHOTOGRAPHY

WILDLIFE photography is a highly specialised field but the quality of today's equipment – even modestly priced, nonprofessional gear - means that excellent results are possible for anyone. The nonstop pageant of species on show in Central America provides superb opportunities for photography but, equally, the environment here throws up constant challenges. To come home with good shots, you need to go prepared.

Equipment

If you're buying your first camera, the selection is mind-boggling. Most professional wildlife photographers use Canon or Nikon, largely because of their formidable lens quality, but all cameras essentially do the same thing (though with varying degrees of complexity and technological assistance). Most modern cameras have a full range of automatic functions, but select a model that also allows full manual operation. Once you've mastered the basics, you'll probably find it limiting if you're unable to begin experimenting.

A West Indian manatee provides a tourist with a chance for close-ups in Belize.

More important than camera bodies are the lenses you attach to them – and for wildlife, think long. A 300mm lens is a good starting point though for bird portraits you'll require longer hardware. Lenses of 400 to 600mm focal length are probably out of the price range of most, though 'slower' lenses (lenses with a relatively small maximum aperture) such as a 400mm f5.6 are reasonably priced and also weigh a lot less; rainforest trails are uncomfortable places to wield heavy gear. Also consider taking a macro ('close-up') lens which allows you to fill the frame with tiny subjects, such as poison dart-frogs, anoles, insects and orchids. The chances for macro photography in the rainforest are endless, far greater than for portraits of big game.

Zooms are generally not as sharp as fixed focal length lenses (ie, lenses that do not zoom), but the difference is only important if you're thinking about publishing your pictures. Many makes offer zooms around the 100-300mm range which, when paired with a short zoom like a 35-70mm, decently cover most situations for recreational photographers. 'Super-zooms'

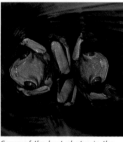

Some of the best photos in the rainforest are provided by its smaller denizens, rather than big mammals.

provide a comprehensive range of focal lengths in one lens. Canon's 35-350mm and 100-400mm, Nikon's 80-400mm and Sigma's 50-500mm or 170-500mm are worth investigating. None is cheap, but they yield publication-quality results in one versatile package. Given that most wildlife-watching in Central America takes place on foot, they also offer a lighter alternative to hauling around several lenses.

Most tropical habitats are fairly closed and dark, making even light and fast shutter speeds a rarity, and increasing the chances of spoiling shots by 'camera-shake' – particularly when using longer lenses. To get around the problem, use fast film such as 400 ISO (professionals will probably want to up-rate slower, less grainy emulsions), and carry a lightweight tripod or monopod – essential, particularly for macro and boat-based shooting. Canon's recently introduced 'image stabilizing' lenses (called 'vibration reduction' by Nikon) allow hand-held photography at speeds two to three times slower than normal; they're expensive but they perform extremely well in Central American conditions. Round out your equipment bag with a decent flash. Used as 'fill' (ie, in very soft bursts), a flash evens out patchy light and can illuminate subjects which would otherwise be too dark to shoot. Flashes are also very effective for dealing with shadows on back-lit subjects, which is invariably the scenario when shooting up into the canopy. Finally, come prepared for killer humidity and downpours; see the Equipment section earlier in this chapter for some pointers.

In the field

Before you go anywhere, know how your camera works. Visit the local zoo or park and shoot a few rolls to familiarize yourself with its controls and functions. Many good wildlife moments happen unexpectedly and pass in seconds; you'll miss them if you're still fiddling with dials and settings. For the same reason, when in reserves, leave your camera turned on (and pack plenty of batteries – they are expensive and scarce in Central America).

When wildlife is scarce look to rainforest plants like this passion flower for some worthwhile photo opportunities.

Most cameras will have shutter and aperture priority functions. In shutter priority mode, you set the shutter speed and the camera selects the appropriate aperture for a correct exposure; the reverse applies for aperture priority. These two functions are probably the most valuable for wildlife photographers, but you need to know when to use them. Shutter priority is excellent for shooting action. To freeze motion select the highest shutter speed permitted with the available light and the camera takes care of the aperture setting. On the other hand, if you're trying to emphasize depth of field in your shot, opt for aperture priority. Large apertures (low 'f-stops') reduce the depth of field – a useful effect for enhancing a portrait shot by throwing the background out of focus, and particularly so in forests where the backgrounds are often very busy. If, however, you're shooting a scene where you want everything in focus, such as thousands of nesting turtles on a mile-long beach, select a small aperture (high 'f-stops').

Composition is a major challenge with wildlife as you can't move your subject around; try different vantage points and experiment with a variety of focal lengths. If you're too far away to take a good portrait, try to show the animal in its habitat. A 400mm lens might give you a close-up of a booby's face while a 28mm will show the entire colony receding in the background – all from the same position. Try to tell a story about the animal or illustrate some behavior. Playful otters might be too shy to approach for a decent close-up, but could make a lovely subject if you included their river surroundings.

Above all else, when photographing wildlife, be patient. You never know what will appear at a flowering orchid next or when a snoozing sloth will suddenly make a move. You cannot always anticipate when an opportunity will arise but if you're willing to wait, you'll almost certainly see something worth shooting. ■

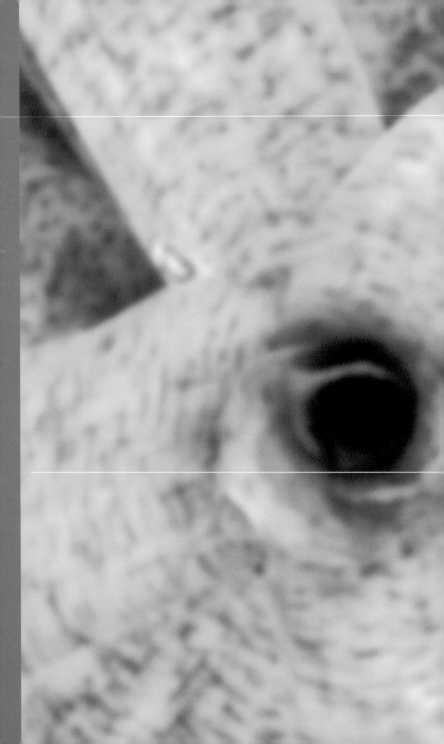

HABITATS

The Central American environment
and its wildlife

RAINFORESTS

Learn to recognise the distinctive Cecropia *tree: It is an important food source for many birds and mammals.*

THE most glamorous of all habitats, Neotropical rainforests are heaving with hundreds of bird species, and uncountable insects and other small animals. Incredibly rich in biodiversity and much studied yet little understood, rainforests support more animal species than any other terrestrial ecosystem. To enter the rainforest is to walk into a luxuriant world of growth and decay, where the humid air smells richly of dampness. Deep leaf litter makes a spongy carpet through which trees grow 10ft (3m) or more in diameter, with buttressed roots and trunks that barrel straight up to the canopy more than 100ft (30m) above your head. Massive interlocked branches support deep cushions of moss, and miniature gardens of epiphytic orchids and ferns. Shafts of sunlight piercing the gloom form pools on the ground that explode in a cloud of butterflies as you approach.

At times bustling with activity, at others silent, the rule in rainforests is much variety, but often comparatively small numbers of vertebrate species. Thus, mammals (apart from monkeys and agoutis) are usually few and far between and the largest aggregations of birds are constantly mobile feeding parties. The most productive part of the forest is where it adjoins another habitat, such as savanna, regenerating cultivation, or where a tree fall has created a gap in the canopy. Here sunlight reaches all levels, allowing a great diversity of plants to grow – often in a tangle of competing creepers, herbage and saplings providing food resources right down to ground level. Monkeys sun themselves, and birds and butterflies are at their most active; it's worthwhile to stake out a fruiting tree and watch the procession of birds and primates that visit over a day (and night).

The forest floor, with its cover of fallen vegetation, is a thoroughfare for large mammals – some which are equally at home in the trees. Insects, snails and spiders thrive in the rich layer of rotting vegetation, and in turn become prey for amphibians, reptiles and insect-eating birds and mammals. Trunks, branches and hollows are utilized as shelter, nesting and resting places, and highways to the bounty of fruits and blossom in the

Forest talk

The rainforest is an incredibly complex habitat and there is an abundance of terminology to describe it. Mostly, it's the province of specialists, but many local guides – and this book – employ the basic terms. Firstly, **primary** or climax forest is 'pristine' forest; it may never have been cleared (by logging or natural events like hurricanes) or if so, has been left for at least 150 years, around the time it takes for rainforest to mature. **Secondary** forest has been cleared more recently and is recovering; ultimately if left alone, it will become primary forest. Gallery or riparian forest is the specialized type that only grows along riverbanks or well-watered valleys, and, depending on its age, can be primary or secondary. Regardless of age or type, all forests have layers. The **forest floor** is obvious and with less than 2% light penetrating, typically has very few plants. Above it, the **understory** rises to no more than 13ft (4m) and is dominated by shade-tolerant species like dwarf palms. At the top, the **canopy** is an almost solid green ceiling that receives most of the light and thus is where the action occurs. Finally, a few isolated giants penetrate the canopy to create the **emergent** layer.

canopy. Birds, bats and primates disperse seeds in their droppings around the forest. Trees fruiting at different times ensure a year-round supply, and influence the movements of birds that follow their seasonal availability. Fallen fruit sustains ground-feeding animals, such as cracids, rodents and pigs.

Central America's lowland rainforest communities are among the richest on earth. Some are still extensive enough to support large mammals such as jaguars, tapirs and white-lipped peccaries, and peak avian predators such as the harpy eagle, but sadly much has been cleared. Rainforest can be experienced at many national parks, and remnants of the great swathes that once covered the region can be visited at Panama's PN Darién and various reserves contiguous with PI La Amistad in Costa Rica, such as PN Tapantí. ■

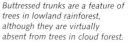

Buttressed trunks are a feature of trees in lowland rainforest, although they are virtually absent from trees in cloud forest.

Heliconias of many varieties grow in rainforests and attract a host of nectar-feeding birds, including many hummingbirds.

CLOUD FORESTS

Bromeliads are prominent among forest epiphytes – this one belongs to the genus Vriesia.

HIGH mountain ranges such as the Talamancas, which straddle the Costa Rica-Panama border, support a zone of distinct habitat called cloud forest that generally grows above 2300ft (700m). High altitudes of course mean lower temperatures and therefore increased condensation and rainfall; and warm air rising from the lowlands cools and rolls across the mountain slopes as dense mist most afternoons. It's a habitat dripping with water and atmosphere, at times silent, but often drenched with rain; and because a blanket of cloud blocks out the sun much of the time, evaporation is reduced and it can get very boggy underfoot. The transition from 'regular' rainforest to cloud forest is rarely abrupt, but as you climb higher the towering lowland forests give way to smaller trees growing close together and rarely topping 100ft (30m). The characteristic buttressing of lowland rainforest trees is almost absent; trunks and limbs are gnarled and invariably swaddled in moss, and seem bent by the weight of epiphytic bromeliads, orchids and ferns. The ground is so damp that thick cushions of moss grow everywhere and at the upper reaches of this zone the trees can be as small as 6ft (2m) high – so-called 'elfin' forest.

In Central America at least, no large mammals are restricted to this habitat, although the home ranges of tapirs, jaguars, pumas and white-lipped peccaries may extend into cloud forest; and ocelots and oncillas (a rare, little-known cat found in Costa Rica) may have their entire home range here. The most common mammals are squirrels, such as montane and some pygmy squirrels, and several amphibians and reptiles live only in this habitat, the most famous probably being the golden toad of Costa Rica's RBBN Monteverde.

Birds of course are abundant, and cloud forest in fact has a high rate of avian endemicity. Birders flock to look for three-wattled bellbirds, bare-necked umbrellabirds and the celebrated resplendent quetzal, all of which breed in cloud forest (or are presumed to: Nests of the umbrellabird and bellbird have never been found). These frugivores all range down to lower altitudes in response to food availability, but many birds, including specialized members of the tanager, warbler, tyrant-flycatcher, woodcreeper, thrush and other families live their entire lives in

Miniature forests in the canopy

Look into the canopy of any cloud forest and you'll see branches covered in dense cushions of moss several inches thick, and bromeliads, orchids and ferns poking through – flowering bromeliads and orchids adding a splash of color among the myriad greens. These miniature gardens are made up of epiphytes, plants that grow on others for support without causing them direct harm, although the twisted branches sometimes seem to groan under their weight. Epiphytes photosynthesize like their hosts, but trap moisture and nutrients in a network of roots – the epiphyte mat – that anchors them to the branch. Many epiphytic roots also contain fungi, which aid in their nutrient uptake and are also important for the host trees. And these treetop gardens also provide habitat for small animals, such as frogs, scorpions and spiders hunting insects and each other. Water that collects in bromeliads forms tiny pools, in which mosquitoes, crabs, frogs and salamanders breed; and from which birds such as toucans drink.

cloud forest. Many are closely allied to lowland species, and indeed many lowland species also range seasonally as high as the cloud forest. Thus, cloud forest feeding flocks may be composed of species common to lowland feeding flocks as well as some restricted to higher altitudes, such as spangled-cheeked tanagers. Groups such as bush-tanagers and tapaculos are well-represented in cloud forest, and the region's two species of silky-flycatcher are virtually restricted to this habitat.

The most famous of Central America's cloud forest reserves is RBBN Monteverde (see p102), but several other reserves, including PNs Chirripó (see p92) and Tapantí (see p114) are also worth visiting. Panama's PN Volcán Barú (see p138) is also easily accessible, and cloud forest at the summit of Cerro Pirre in PN Darién (see p134) boasts a few endemic species of bird and mammal. ■

The cloud forest experience often involves walking in near 'white out' conditions, as well as periodic heavy rain.

The resplendent quetzal is the best-known and most eagerly-sought of all Central American cloud forest birds.

HIGH POINTS

The volcano hummingbird is one of a few hardy species that can survive on the highest mountains, as long as there is available food.

LIKE an immense backbone holding up the humid lowlands clinging to either side, Central America is bisected by an unbroken, mountainous spine. Beginning in Belize's Maya Mountains and running to Panama's remote Darién wilderness, a connected chain of *cordilleras* (mountain ranges) rises to more than two miles (3.2km) above sea-level at its highest point. Elevation creates a slew of different habitats which would not arise if the landbridge was level; imagine a Central America without the mountains and you would not have the suite of species which are found only above the coastal plains. Missing would be many dozens of birds including quetzals, three-wattled bellbirds and highland hummingbirds; secretive mammals like oncillas; and montane squirrels and reptiles such as cloud forest anoles and highland alligator lizards.

The effect of the mountains reaches even further. Many more species that *do* live on the lowlands could not do so without the consecutive waves of fruiting and flowering that follow one another along the gradient; when the lowlands of PN Santa Rosa are withering in the long dry season, the slopes of nearby Rincón de la Vieja are covered with food. It's why so many species, especially birds and butterflies, are known as altitudinal migrants. They track the oscillations of new growth up and down the slopes and cannot survive without them.

Although many of Central America's peaks – including several active volcanoes – top 10,000ft (3000m), there are no glaciers or permanent snow. Nonetheless, at the very top, the peaks and plateaus create habitat which seem far removed from the tropics, and subzero temperatures, buffeting winds and frosts present an additional challenge to wildlife and wildlife-watchers alike.

Scattered throughout the slopes, volcanoes and craters appear poorly suited to host wildlife, but the surrounding stunted forest is perhaps the best place to look for some highland bird specialties, such as volcano hummingbirds, magnificent hummingbirds, peg-billed finches and montane squirrels. With their constant warm emissions, volcanoes also function as

Cold-blooded brooders

With sometimes freezing winds and subzero temperatures, the uplands of Central America present a formidable challenge for the wildlife that lives there – none more so than for reptiles. Relying on ambient heat to maintain their body temperature, most reptiles find the cold highlands too hostile, which is why only two species occur at the very top – highland alligator lizards and green spiny lizards. How do they survive here? Like reptiles everywhere, they seek out prominent spots which warm up quickly; boulders, fallen trees and stumps are ideal, especially as they also retain their heat longer than the surrounding terrain. Lizards locate the sunniest parts of their chosen post and then flatten their bodies to increase their surface area. Basking is fine for adults but what about their eggs? There is nowhere on the highlands that is consistently warm enough to ensure that eggs – or more accurately, the embryos within – don't freeze. Highland lizards overcome the challenges of incubation by doing it internally. The eggs develop normally, but instead of laying them, the female retains them inside – a trait known as ovoviviparity. So long as she can keep herself warm, the eggs are fine; they hatch while still inside mom and live babies, rather than cold-sensitive eggs, are the result.

An aerial view of Volcán Póas, showing a crater lake, vegetation which has regrown around it and a vast scar where fumes have denuded the landscape.

important stepping stones for great clouds of thermaling raptors; the clear view overhead at most peaks makes for some great viewing.

Far removed from volcanic hot gases and occasional eruptions, the highest land in Central America is dominated by alpine bamboo, tussock grass and heath-like páramo. Mostly difficult to reach (PN Chirripó offers by far the easiest access in Costa Rica), this freezing, tundra-like habitat is restricted to the Talamancas (including the summit of Panama's extinct Volcán Barú) and home to birds such as volcano juncos, sooty robins, slaty flowerpiercers and white-collared swifts. Pumas and the ubiquitous coyote hunt endemic Dice's rabbits while the only reptiles which can live this high – green spiny lizards and highland alligator lizards – warm themselves on exposed rock until they have the energy to ambush insects. ■

The deer potato is a conspicuous upland species utilized by a host of wildlife. The red flowers are favored by hummingbirds and flowerpiercers, while the berry-like fruits are eaten by everything from rodents to coyotes. Even the roots are used: Baird's tapirs excavate and eat them.

DRY FOREST & SAVANNA

The double-striped thick-knee is closely related to the migratory shorebirds, although it is resident and primarily a bird of grasslands and savanna.

FIRST-TIMERS to Central America are often surprised to find landscapes reminiscent of Africa nestled among the rainforest. Like many African habitats, these areas experience a prolonged dry season – a rarity for Central American landscapes – and they feature a mix of acacia thorn-trees and palms among plants more recognizably American. In the region covered by this book, they occur only in Costa Rica's Guanacaste province and the northern plains of Belize, and are known respectively as tropical dry forest and pine savanna.

Tropical dry forest probably once covered most of Guanacaste, but is now reduced to a few remnant patches. The best place to see it is PN Santa Rosa, where the vegetation is a unique amalgam of tropical trees like mahogany and orange-barked 'naked Indian' trees among various bulls-horn acacias, evergreen oaks, cacti, agaves and a swag of deciduous species. It's one of Costa Rica's most biologically diverse habitats, and during the dry season when rivers peter out and many trees drop their leaves, the forest opens up to provide some terrific viewing.

Dry forest specialties include birds like Hoffmann's woodpeckers, rufous-naped wrens, streak-backed orioles and grasshopper sparrows, while dwindling summer waterholes attract doves, great curassows, crested guans and African-style processions of mammals. Ubiquitous generalists like white-faced capuchins, Central American agoutis, white-nosed coatis and coyotes are common, but dry forest is also home to more elusive Baird's tapirs, jaguarundis, pumas and even jaguars.

To botanists, Belize's pine savanna (known locally as Pine Ridge) is a very different habitat dominated by stands of Caribbean pines among great open savannas of palmetto palms. However, in common with Guanacaste's dry forest, the species mix is adapted to a mostly rainless summer and nutrient-poor soils, a combination which creates an even more open spread of trees. Like in Santa Rosa, that translates to increased prospects for wildlife-watching. As well as being home to birds

What makes a savanna?

In some areas, the transition between rainforest and savanna occurs in a matter of meters, begging the question, what makes a savanna? A swag of environmental factors can give rise to savannas, but they have one thing in common – extremes. Very dry areas are the most obvious savanna country; rainforest trees mostly can't survive where there is a prolonged dry season. But equally, very wet areas can be covered in savanna; saturated soils leave less room for oxygen, making them suitable for only a few species of hardy grasses and shrubs. Whether wet or dry, savannas rely on another environmental extreme to persist – fire. Whereas most rainforest species cannot tolerate fire and indeed, very rarely experience it, savanna plants are adapted for regular burns. In fact, without fire, savannas lose species diversity, becoming near monocultures overgrown with a few types of grass or trees. The ever-changing timing and intensity of fires favors various savanna species differently so that no one type dominates. Finally of course, people create savannas. Clearing forest and setting fires can convert rainforest to grassland more effectively than any natural agent and indeed many Central American savannas are counterfeits – not so long ago, they were forest.

such as plain chachalacas, double-striped thick-knees, acorn woodpeckers, vermilion and Yucatán flycatchers, laughing falcons and open habitat sparrows (including grassland yellow-finches, and Botteri's and rusty sparrows), Pine Ridge provides critical breeding habitat for endangered yellow-crowned parrots (part of the yellow-headed amazon superspecies, of which the yellow-crowned parrot is probably best regarded as a full species).

The mammalian fauna has a North American flavor, but many tropical species also occur – they are merely less obvious. Pumas are the top carnivore (though jaguars wander into pine savanna from surrounding areas of rainforest such as at Río Bravo), but species more easily seen include white-tailed deer, common opossums, kinkajous, coyotes, gray foxes and jaguarundis. ■

PN Santa Rosa during the dry season. The prevalence of deciduous trees in the tropical dry forest gives rise to a land-scape more reminiscent of temperate North America than the tropics.

Many Central American savan-nas, like this one in PN Rincón de la Vieja, are the result of clearing by humans. Even so, they can be very fruitful places for spotting wildlife.

WETLANDS

The American pygmy-kingfisher is the smallest of the six Central American kingfisher species.

WATER sustains all life: Hundreds of species of fish and invertebrate equipped with gills draw oxygen from water and live all or part of their lives in it; it is a source of prey for many air-breathing animals that wade, swim, fly or perch; a refuge for animals that also spend much time on land; and essential for the daily drinking or bathing routine for many large animals.

The shallow margins of waterways are packed with life: Sunlight filtering through the shallows promotes the growth of algae, which is fed upon by huge numbers of tiny crustaceans and single-celled animals. These support fish, tadpoles and the young of many insects, all of which in turn become prey for larger aquatic species and air-breathing predators such as otters, crocodiles and birds. Larger fish living in deeper water feed crocodiles, anhingas and ospreys. A host of birds – herons, storks, ibises, spoonbills and egrets – feed in ways sufficiently different to allow mixed flocks to live and breed side by side; ducks likewise feed by different strategies and great flotillas build up where pickings are rich, such as at Costa Rica's RNVS Caño Negro. Floating on the surface are mats of water lilies, under which shelter invertebrates and fish; jacanas and limpkins walk over the top, feeding on insects and snails. But not all aquatic animals are carnivores: The world's largest rodent, the capybara, lives exclusively in freshwater swamps, where it feeds on aquatic vegetation.

Vegetation forms a succession from the floating mats to shore which over time can alter the course of rivers by choking and silting up bends that eventually are claimed by land plants and animals. Where water levels remain more or less constant, dense ranks of reeds and grasslike sedges mark the transition to dry land. Bitterns, crakes and rails live almost exclusively in these grass forests. Where running water is slowed and trapped by vegetation, otters hunt for fish, crabs and shellfish. Drowned trees and large, overhanging branches along rivers and lakeshores make secure nest platforms for colonies of herons and cormorants, which sometimes form mixed colonies; sandbanks are basking sites for crocs, and roosts for gulls, terns and ducks; and kingfishers dig nest tunnels in steep banks. Where

The spread of the capybara

The Neotropics are home to a unique group of large rodents, the caviomorphs, which includes the agoutis, pacas and the largest of all – the capybara. Not only is it the world's largest rodent, it is also one of the most dependent on water and is never found far from freshwater. Capybaras can swim well and, in fact, have webbed feet; when threatened they can submerge completely (and like many rodents, capybaras are a popular prey item, although it is mainly large cats that take adults). They feed mainly on aquatic vegetation, although will on occasion venture into nearby croplands, and young capybaras can follow their mother into water soon after birth. Although the capybara is widespread in South America, its range just creeps into Central America in eastern Panama. However, capybaras appear to be expanding their range in Panama along cultivated river valleys and around the edges of dams; as a favorite prey of jaguars, it could be speculated that big cats may also hold their own wherever capybaras are common – even near humans.

banks are not too steep, mammals visit the water's margin to drink, wallow or bathe. Thus, by sitting quietly by a waterhole in Costa Rica's PN Palo Verde, you may be treated to a procession of monkeys, coatis, deer and agoutis trooping down to slake their thirst.

Watching wildlife in wetlands is usually highly rewarding from shore or boat, not least because you don't usually have to crane your neck to stare into the canopy! Nonetheless, it will test your powers of observation: Look on submerged logs for turtles, swallows and kingfishers; and among lily mats for caimans showing just eyes and nostrils above the surface. It's easy to glide past birds perched quietly and lizards basking on overhanging boughs, and herons may skulk under overhanging banks. And don't forget to look up occasionally for raptors. ∎

While looking for wildlife on waterways, such as Belize's New River (shown here), check foliage on the banks, look overhead for raptors and scan overhanging branches.

Wetlands attract an abundance of wildlife at any time of year, but especially when prey becomes concentrated in drying pools late in the dry season.

MARINE COASTS

Ubiquitous scavengers of coast and mangrove, fiddler crabs emerge with receding tides to forage for tidbits left behind.

NO other habitat is as challenging to survival as the zone where land meets the sea. Its inhabitants must be adapted to a daily pattern of inundation and, often, a pounding by the waves, followed by exposure to baking sun for hours at a stretch. But this is classic edge habitat, a zone rich in resources exploited by human and animal predators alike. From the soup of plankton that originates in the warm surface waters and starts a feeding chain to rocky shelves supporting hardy mollusks and crustaceans, the shallow waters above the continental shelf support some of the greatest diversity of life on earth.

Coral reefs put on a show of living creatures rivaled only by rainforests for spectacle. Best appreciated underwater, a dazzling display awaits anyone who dons snorkel and mask (see the Diving & Snorkeling section, pp40-1): Fish in every shape and color, from neon blue to Day-Glo orange; crustaceans, some camouflaged with weed; and the corals themselves, solid blocks of lime constructed over millennia by tiny organisms into many forms, such as brain and staghorn corals. Fine examples of coral reefs can be explored at many sites on the Belize coast, and fringing several Panamanian island groups, such as Bocas del Toro and Isla de Coiba.

Where rivers empty into the sea, suspended silt deposited over millennia has formed expansive mudflats rich in nutrients and small animals such as mollusks and crustaceans. In places the fine but fertile mud supports underwater meadows of seagrass grazed by the West Indian manatee, and sheltering a suite of fishes and crustaceans different to those of coral reefs. At low tide mudflats attract a host of birds, such as herons and the many thousands of shorebirds that pass through the region on migration each year, many overwintering. Highly productive mudflats can be seen in Panama City at Puerto Viejo; and on Turneffe Atoll in Belize.

Away from the estuaries, sandy beaches pounded by surf are one of the most demanding of environments and consequently

Mangroves

Forming a buffer between sea and shore, mangroves are trees unique for their ability to withstand daily inundation in saltwater. Some have distinctive 'prop' roots, which elevate them above normal tide limits, as well as other roots (pneumatophores) which stick up through the suffocating mud like asparagus spears and extract oxygen directly from the air at low tide. Mangrove seeds are carried away by the tides and take root wherever conditions are suitable, but usually on sheltered points and in calm backwaters. Silt accumulates around the roots and eventually forms a deep ooze in which crustaceans and fishes burrow. Zones of different mangrove species develop – those less able to withstand salt grow closer to land, trapping more debris and eventually allowing land plants to grow. Commonly regarded as 'swamps' and subject to widespread clearing for coastal development, mangrove forests are now recognised for their great commercial importance: Their extensive root systems calm wave action and slow coastal erosion, and shelter hatchling fishes and crustaceans. Many bird species feed and roost in mangroves, including waders, kingfishers and some raptors; and the crab-eating raccoon habitually forages near the water's edge here, especially where its range overlaps that of the northern raccoon. Extensive mangrove forests grow on the Belize coast and in Panama's Darién Province, especially near Punta Patiño (see p137).

support the smallest number of life forms. A few shorebirds pick over the incoming tide and hermit crabs scavenge from dead animals washed up on the sands. However, large animals, such as tapirs, use beaches as thoroughfares in PN Corcovado, and female marine turtles haul themselves up the sand to dig nest chambers and lay their eggs. You're more likely to see the turtles at night on a turtle-watching tour (see the Sea turtle-watching section, pp42-3), but on an early-morning walk the next day tracks in the sand might show just how many turtles use a single beach – and how many predators visit beaches to dig up the eggs, among them coatis and coyotes. Jaguars regularly predate adult turtles (although you would need extreme luck to see this), and once the young turtles hatch, many other visitors appear at the feast, including vultures, herons and frigatebirds, as well as predatory fish waiting in the shallows. ∎

The twice-daily inundation of mangroves ensures a constantly replenished food supply. Here, a yellow-crowned night-heron hunts for crabs and small fish caught in the shallows on a dropping tide.

Mangrove trees are the only plants able to colonize sub-merged sandbars, but they may ultimately provide footholds for a host of other plant species.

OCEANS & ISLANDS

Frigatebirds circle high on thermals and fly far out to sea, only returning to land to roost or to breed. Here a male magnificent frigatebird inflates his throat pouch to attract a mate.

THE warm, sunlit waters at the oceans' surface are populated by countless millions of microscopic animals and plants drifting at the whim of currents and winds. Some live their entire life cycle in this state, others are the drifting larvae of larger animals, but this planktonic soup ultimately sustains all life in the oceans – including some of the largest animals that ever lived, the humpback whales that migrate to Central America's Pacific coast every year. Plankton feed on each other and are eaten by small fish that in turn fall prey to schools of tuna, pods of dolphins and marauding sharks. Herded near the surface by underwater predators, small fish are also taken from above by birds such as petrels, tropicbirds, frigatebirds and terns. Several remote islands (see Seabird Islands, p122) are breeding havens for these wide-ranging seabirds, as well as for sea turtles that spend their entire lives at sea, only returning to land to lay their eggs.

Central America's coasts have comparatively few islands, the biggest being Panama's Isla de Coiba and Costa Rica's Isla del Cocos (see p122). Islands can be fascinating biological laboratories, places where wildlife often evolves apart from its mainland progenitors (see the boxed text below). From a wildlife-watchers perspective, they are worth visiting to see these distinct forms (especially for birders, because island subspecies are regularly 'upgraded' to specific status by taxonomists). For example, Bocas del Toro and nearby islands in north-west Panama were cut off from the mainland some 10,000 years ago. In that time the strawberry poison dart-frog has developed into a race distinct from the same species on the mainland and, even more dramatically, it has recently been re-alised that the three-toed sloths on Isla Escudo de Veraguas (the oldest and remote island in the archipelago) are in fact a distinct species – much smaller than three-toed sloths on the mainland and dubbed *Bradypus pygmaeus*.

Isla de Coiba and Bocas del Toro are examples of continental islands – islands that are essentially drowned mountains. Off the coast of Belize, the peaks of an entirely submerged mountain range have become fringed with coral reefs. In places,

Lost land bridges

The scarlet macaw, one of the most spectacular of neotropical parrots, has a fragmented range that peters out in southern Costa Rica, then restarts in northern South America. The only places it is found in Panama are Isla de Coiba and a small patch of the adjacent mainland. That macaws originated in South America and spread north once the isthmus was formed seems clear, so why is it not found in mainland Panama? The geological history of the land bridge is complicated, but Isla de Coiba – and a few other islands along Panama's coast – is all that remains of an ancient mountain range after rising sea levels cut them off from the mainland. Most wildlife is identical to that of the mainland, but some has been isolated long enough to evolve into distinct forms: For example, Coiba has an endemic species of agouti and howler monkey. Further evidence of this lost land bridge is provided by an endemic bird, the Coiba spinetail, which is found nowhere else in Central America, but appears nearly identical to the rusty-backed spinetail of South America. And the gray brocket deer, a South American species, occurs in Central America only on San José island, south of Panama City.

enough sand and organic material has built up to allow vegetation to grow. Although the underwater life is often spectacular, most terrestrial animals have arrived after the formation of these cayes and atolls, and very few have speciated away from their mainland equivalents see pp74-5), although Half Moon Caye has an endemic lizard. The richness of terrestrial species also decreases with distance from the mainland, although seabirds are not usually constrained by distance and many cayes have thriving colonies.

Costa Rica's largest island, Isla del Cocos, is a volcanic island some 310mi (500km) from the mainland that formed at least 500,000 years ago and possibly one million years ago. Cocos has never been connected to the mainland, but apart from seabirds three distinct bird species and several reptiles occur there; all have arrived (some at least as passengers on drifting vegetation, but others possibly wind-assisted) and evolved during that brief geological span. But Cocos is being ravaged by introduced animals such as deer and pigs, which inevitably upset the ecological balance attained after millions of years. ■

Belize's barrier reef is the second-largest in the world, and acts as a buffer against the Caribbean Sea along almost the entire coastline.

The gull-sized royal tern is commonly seen plunge-diving for fish at sea or loafing on mudflats at low tide.

HUMAN ENVIRONMENTS

Many rural landscapes provide terrific opportunities for bird-watching, but also have the potential for genuine ecotourism. In between ticking off species, even something as simple as buying a meal or drink from the local community can help plant the seeds for tolerating wildlife.

ALTHOUGH generally bereft of large animals, urban environments are utilized by some species opportunistically and in a few cases are the habitat of choice. There are good reasons for animals to partake of human hospitality: Our endeavors provide extra sources of food, shelter and breeding sites for creatures equipped to make the transition from natural to human-engineered environments. Birds usually fare better than mammals, because the latter are often sought for food or eradicated as vermin. Keen wildlife-watchers probably won't want to linger in Central America's large cities, but inevitably you will have time to kill between tours, buses or flights and, since this is the Neotropics, you're virtually assured of seeing some some wildlife wherever you are. For example, city parks often support squirrels and roosts of bats; black vultures search for scraps near markets; and hummingbirds visit feeders in suburban gardens.

Watch along roads and highways for birds using roadside fixtures, such as fences and telegraph poles, as perches and nest sites. The toll of wildlife taken by traffic inadvertently benefits opportunists, such as vultures and coyotes, and because animals are less wary of vehicles than pedestrians, these may allow a close approach and photo opportunities through vehicle windows. Where land is cleared for cultivation or ranching, the end result is comparatively poor plant and animal communities. Most large animals quickly desert these areas, or if unable to move far, die out. Nonetheless many birds and small mammals (particularly rodents) readily adopt agricultural land as an extension of natural habitat, such as savanna. And a few actually benefit from the change by exploiting an abundant food source, eg, peccaries may raid cereal crops and white-tailed deer thrive where patches of grassland abut woodlands. Others inevitably come into conflict with humans, such as when the odd jaguar learns that stock is a ready food source; or are hunted to local extinction for food, as has happened to Baird's tapirs and white-lipped peccaries in many parts of Central America. The management of conflict between wildlife and human interests is an increasing problem for conservation agencies.

Beans and biodiversity.

In terms of bird diversity, just how significant is the difference between shade-grown coffee and so called 'sun coffee'? In a nutshell, the answer is: huge. Studies throughout Latin American have shown that about 90% fewer bird species are found in sun coffee plantations than in traditional, shaded plots. Only a few versatile species like grackles and sparrows can utilize sun coffee plots whereas in El Salvador, for example, at least 520 species have been counted in shade-coffee areas. Many of them are migratory species using the bird-friendly farms like stepping stones as they head south. Indeed, as sun coffee farms have spread, the populations of some migrants have dropped; Baltimore orioles now avoid formerly favored routes because they are dominated by treeless plantations. The bottom line is, as far as birds are concerned, converting shade coffee to sun coffee is essentially deforestation. As so much rainforest is now under coffee, the only hope for most birds is that the plots remain shaded.

Much highland rainforest has been cleared to make way for coffee plantations, one of Central America's most valuable commercial crops. Traditionally, coffee was grown in low-density holdings with patches of natural vegetation that provided important wintering habitat for migrating birds, but in recent decades large-scale industrial plantations have eaten up many of these small plantations, stripping them of their remaining natural vegetation and depriving migratory birds of habitat. However, the enlightened owners of several fincas (such as Fincas Lérida and Hartmann adjacent to Volcán Barú, Panama) grow coffee under shade trees that maintain bird habitat (see boxed text). These plantations combine ecofriendly cultivation techniques and, recognizing the ecotourism potential, also actively encourage visits from birders. ∎

Like these Neotropic cormorants taking it easy in Belize, several seabird species have learned to wait for returning fishermen to scavenge scraps.

Once the centerpiece of populous cities, Mayan temples today are places to look for bat roosts, basking reptiles and the nests of some notable birds like keel-billed motmots.

PARKS AND PLACES

The best wildlife-watching
destinations in Central America

BELIZE
The tropics in a nutshell

Highlights

- Searching the walls of unexcavated Mayan pyramids at the Caracol ruins for nesting keel-billed motmots
- Watching manatees in 6ft (1.8m) of clear water at Swallow Caye, knowing they will inevitably surface for air
- Waking up to booming Yucatán black howler monkeys endlessly staking their territorial claims at the Community Baboon Sanctuary
- Watching nesting jabiru in the dead logwood trees at Crooked Tree WS
- Spotlighting greater fishing bats as they cruise over Lamanai's New River Lagoon in search of prey
- Finding fresh jaguar tracks and scratching trees at Rio Bravo
- Hearing the teeth-clacking threat display of white-lipped peccaries at close range in Cockscomb's rainforest
- The sight of magnificent frigatebirds pirating the catches of the red-footed boobies at Half Moon

A little larger than Massachusetts, Belize is Central America's smallest country after El Salvador and while it cannot claim the species counts and endemics boasted by Costa Rica and Panama, its diversity belies its dimensions. Partly, that's owed to its location: As the northernmost Central American country it has a blend of habitats – and wildlife – reflecting both tropical and temperate influences.

In the north of the country, dry sandy plains are covered with open woodland savannas of Caribbean pine, oaks and palmetto palms where endangered yellow-crowned parrots and north American colonists like coyotes and white-tailed deer are at their most obvious. Extending into Belize's coastal plain, the 'pine ridge' forests ultimately give way to mangroves, which provide cover for American crocodiles and nest sites for a wealth of herons, egrets and other waterbirds. Belizean coastal waters harbor the Caribbean's largest population of West Indian manatees, also found in the country's extensive inland lagoons where permanent water attracts huge dry season flocks of resident and migratory birds. Surrounding the lagoons, swamp forest is the preferred nesting habitat for endangered jabirus – the largest nesting population in Central America is found here.

Of course, it's the rainforest that draws many wildlife watchers to Belize. The great crucible for biodiversity, large tracts of rainforest cover much of northern and western Belize where it forms part of the huge Selva Maya (Maya Forest) extending into Guatemala and southern Mexico. In the south of Belize, rainforests still exist in great expanses in the lowlands of the Maya Mountains and further south in Toledo. Founded almost exclusively on forestry, Belize has seen repeated cycles of logging and regeneration so that few areas are 'pristine', but even so, an estimated 70% of the original rainforest is intact. Much of it is protected in reserves; indeed, almost 50% of Belize's area falls under some protection, an extraordinary figure for any nation, let alone one usually called 'developing'. That figure includes 'forest reserves' in which logging still takes place, but increasingly, it's a selective enough process that big cats, spider monkeys and great curassows still occur there alongside literally thousands of less specialized animals. And, unlike most Central American countries, the private conservation sector has flourished; indeed, the country's single largest reserve, Rio Bravo, is privately owned.

Belize boasts the world's only reserve set aside specifically for jaguars, although it probably won't deliver a sighting of the secretive big cat. But be assured, this tiny tropical nation will deliver encounters with a truly extraordinary array of wildlife. ∎

Not to be confused with the national park of the same name, the Blue Hole is a 400ft sinkhole in the middle of Lighthouse Reef and one of Belize's most popular dive sites.

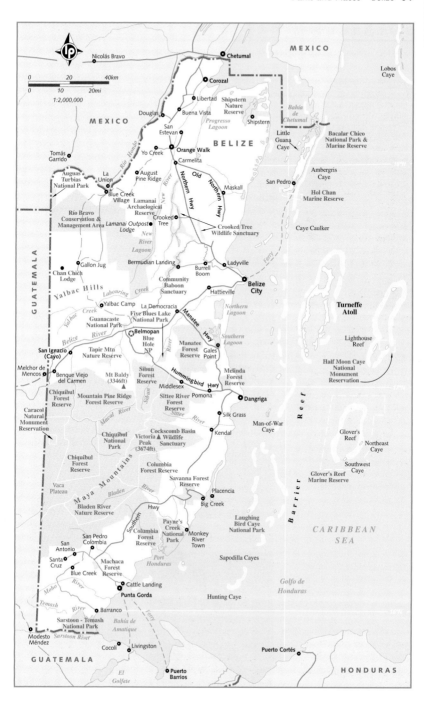

COCKSCOMB BASIN WILDLIFE SANCTUARY

World's first jaguar reserve

Wildlife highlights
Jaguars, pumas and ocelots occur, but are very elusive. Much better chances for seeing Baird's tapirs, both peccary species, red brocket, Neotropical river otters and tayras. Deppe's squirrels and gray foxes are very tame here. Unrestricted self-guided night-walks hold chances for pacas, kinkajous, boa constrictors, fer-de-lances and tree frogs. Very rich birdlife with more than 300 species recorded, most around the park HQ.

BELIZEANS usually call Cockscomb 'The Jaguar Reserve', intimating to hopeful wildlifers that sighting the big cat is a given. People do spot **jaguars** here but, like everywhere, they are exceptionally elusive; less than a half-a-dozen visitors a year actually see one. The sanctuary's nickname actually arises from its status as the world's only reserve specifically set aside for jaguars (though, of course, they occur in many others), a blood-and-tears triumph chronicled by researcher Alan Rabinowitz in his terrific book *Jaguar*. The handmade cage-traps Rabinowitz used to catch the big cats are displayed at park HQ, perhaps this is as close as you'll come to seeing one, but for seeing less secretive species in abundance, Cockscomb is one of Belize's top spots.

Cockscomb's trails range from very accessible short walks near the headquarters to the 26mi (42km), four-day hike to Victoria Peak, Belize's second-highest point. The latter requires prior arrangement with the Belize Audubon Society (☎ 223-5004) and was closed at the time of writing owing to damage by Hurricane Iris (it will eventually be reopened), but don't think you have to cover lots of ground to see wildlife here. Everything from jaguars to **boa constrictors** can be spotted within earshot of park HQ.

Many of the trails follow South Stann Creek and its tributaries, revealing a mix of forest and water-loving wildlife. The River Path, especially at the picnic area, consistently produces sightings of **Neotropical river otters** as well as **sungrebes, great egrets** and six **heron** species including resident **agami herons**. Waterbird prey, **cichlids** and tiny **billum fish** are abundant here; swimming is permitted and rewarding underwater views can be had if you pack a snorkeling mask, especially of the many multicolored cichlids (search areas of calmer water where leaf litter accumulates). The fish market also attracts four **kingfishers** (**ringed, Amazon, green** and, less commonly, the tiny **American pygmy**), which you can see in action by sitting at the river's edge with binoculars. If the picnic area gets busy, benches overlooking a small tributary of the South Stann along the Curassow Trail can be just as productive.

Overhanging Cockscomb's waterways, groves of bri-bri trees (recognizable by their smooth bark and shading, spreading crown) have much sought-after flowers and fruits. Ten species of **hummingbird** are regular diners, while occasional, rarer visitors include **brown violet-ears band-tailed barbthroats** and **scaly-breasted hummingbirds**. Hordes of insects are also nectar feeders, and bring in dozens of **flycatchers** – there are about 40 species here – as well as

Poster-child for Cockscomb, jaguars are actually very difficult to see here. The best chances come from night walks or slow drives along the entrance road.

rufous-tailed jacamars, and white-necked and white-whiskered puffbirds. The bri-bri's long podlike fruits are filled with a sweet, fluffy white pulp, spawning the alternate name of icecream bean and irresistible to fruit-eaters, such as **rainbow-billed toucans**, **plain chachalacas**, **crested guans**, **white-nosed coatis**, **Deppe's squirrels** and, sometimes, **great curassows** and **Central American spider monkeys** (both are rare in Cockscomb). **Yucatán black howlers** (which were reintroduced to Cockscomb after succumbing in 1978 to the lethal cumulative effects of hunting, yellow fever and Hurricane Hattie) also visit the trees to supplement their mainly leafy diet. One troop occupies the River Path-Curassow Trail-Rubber Tree Trail loop, while other accessible ones are seen on the Gibnut Loop, Tinamou Loop and Wari Loop.

Night visions

For an entirely different view, stake out a bri-bri at dusk (comfortably done at the large specimen shading the River Path picnic table). Nectar-eating bats (such as **common long-tongued** and **little yellow-shouldered bats**) are thought to be equally significant bri-bri pollinators as hummingbirds, and **kinkajous** and **Mexican porcupines** relish the fruits. On the ground, **pacas** mop up fallen fruit and Cockscomb is probably Belize's finest site for viewing these customarily shy rodents.

There are no restrictions on walking around at night at Cockscomb, meaning you can venture further afield than the nearest fruit tree, but avoid long or strenuous routes (familiarize yourself with the trails during the day) and watch underfoot for **fer-de-lances**, which are fairly common. As well as small fry like **red-rumped tarantulas** and **glass frogs**, night sights include **ferruginous pygmy-**, **spectacled** and **mottled owls**, **common nighthawks**, **pauraques** (especially on the entrance road), **red brockets** and both species of **peccary** (the last three also often seen at dawn and dusk). In the kaway tree swamp on Wari Loop (kaways are obvious by their broad, buttress roots, which support them in the soggy soil), there are easily seen **red-eyed tree frogs**, **marine toads**, **boat-billed herons** and, not so easy, **Baird's tapirs**. Night also holds the best chances for cats; **jaguars** and **ocelots** are the species most likely to be seen (neither very often, of course) and, sometimes, **pumas**. All three species readily walk along the entrance road late at night. Attacks by Belize's cats are virtually unheard of, but if you're spotlighting on foot, go with a friend. ■

Location 21mi (34km) south of Dangriga. Bus to Maya Center, then 7mi (11km) hike or taxi (ask at Maya Center) to the park entrance.

Facilities Trails, small museum at park HQ.

Accommodations Camping, dorms and cabanas.

Wildlife rhythms The dry season (January to April) is much easier for access/exploring and for seeing wildlife. Many trees flower and fruit during the Dry, attracting many species, including numerous nesting birds. Migrant birds arrive from about December onwards.

Contact Belize Audubon Society (☎ 223-5004; fax 4985; e base@blt.net).

Watching tips

Tame gray foxes hang around park HQ (especially near the new kitchen) and are virtually guaranteed scroungers after dark at the rubbish bins behind the office. Nine-banded armadillos and striped hog-nosed skunks also sometimes turn up at the bins.

CROOKED TREE WILDLIFE SANCTUARY
Belize's waterbird paradise

Wildlife highlights

One of the prime water-bird sites in the country with large dry-season flocks of many species, and smaller numbers of rarities such as jabirus. Also around 170 resident bird species including excellent raptors; snail kites and lesser yellow-headed vultures are present in large numbers. Black howlers are commonly seen from the waterways, while Morelet's crocodiles, green iguanas and striped basilisks are among the more obvious reptiles.

NAMED for the twisted logwood trees lining a tangle of interconnected lagoons, creeks and swamps, Crooked Tree is one of Belize's most important wetlands for birds. With a reliable supply of water year-round, it draws arrivals from the seasonally parched areas of northern Belize, as well as from southern Mexico and the Guatemalan Petén. Joining North American migrants in sometimes spectacular dry-season congregations, and with chances at seeing an additional 170 resident species, Crooked Tree is a must for observing wildlife on the wing.

Water in the Dry

Without a doubt, Crooked Tree is best visited in the Dry. At its peak around April and May, the watermark can be two-thirds under the wet-season level, leaving much reduced permanent pools and dwindling swampy patches, which are rich focal points for wildlife. Unless the entire lagoon system dries up (it's only happened once in recorded history), you'll need a boat regardless of when you visit. Tours are available at the village or, if so equipped, you can launch your own. To arrange either, check in at the visitor center, located just after the causeway over the large Northern Lagoon where most trips begin. The wide expanse of the lagoon and its swampy edges typically produce sightings of three duck species: **blue-winged teals**, **black-bellied whistling-ducks** and, less abundant, **muscovy ducks**. **American coots**, **northern jacanas**, **black-necked stilts**, **least** and **Baird's sandpipers**, and the more common **heron** species (**great egret**, **snowy egret** and **little blue heron**) are also obvious here. Scan the trees along the edges for **black-cowled orioles** and **red-lored parrots**, and check overhead for **lesser yellow-headed vultures**, the most abundant vulture species here (in contrast to almost

Black Creek ultimately joins up with the Belize River, which runs through the middle of the Community Baboon Sanctuary. If you have your own boat, it is possible to explore both reserves without leaving the water.

everywhere else in Belize where very similar black or turkey vultures predominate). **Snail kites** occur throughout Crooked Tree and it's possible to see hundreds hunting over the lagoon.

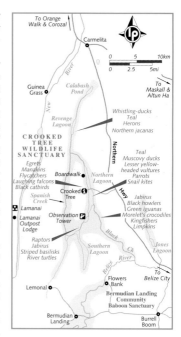

If you miss anything in the lagoon, head north for the swamps on the way to Revenge Lagoon. The species mix is similar, but dry-season flocks of some (such as teals and whistling ducks) can number in the thousands. The other direction (if you're in your own boat, it's a good idea to hire a local guide or take a GPS) sees the waterways narrow, providing habitat for a more diverse catalog of sightings. Both Black Creek and Spanish Creek are very rewarding. Leaving the main lagoon, scrubby mimosa bushes provide cover for **purple gallinules**, **least grebes**, **sungrebes**, **boat-billed herons**, **green herons** and abundant **black-crowned night-herons**. All of Belize's five **kingfishers** can be spotted here (**American pygmies** are the least common) and **limpkins** are unusually conspicuous.

The further south you travel, the higher the canopy becomes, as the mimosa bushes give way to stands of logwood trees and patches of more open pine savanna. Check the pines for endangered **jabiru** (a few pairs nest here, from December until around May) and the logwood forests for **Yucatán black howlers**. Both habitats provide perches for **gray-necked woodrails** and numerous raptors including **crane hawks**, **black-collared hawks**, **gray-headed kites** and ubiquitous **snail kites**. **Peregrine falcons** are seen here fairly often and **ospreys** are very common. If you're out around dusk, look for **tarpon** breaching to hovering insects – the ospreys do and sometimes favor patient boaters with thrilling close-up catches. Reptilian residents include **green iguanas** (guaranteed on the high walls of freshwater bamboo scattered along the creek), **striped basilisks**, **Central American river turtles** (called hickatees here) and shy **Morelet's crocodiles** – check bare patches on the bank beneath the logwoods for basking crocs first thing in the morning.

And for the land lubbers ...

If you get sick of boating, Crooked Tree village has a trail network, bird observation tower (a few miles south) and an elevated boardwalk (a few miles north). Both the tower and boardwalk provide views of many of the same birds you see on the water, but combining some time there with the trails will add a suite of more terrestrial species to your list. Among the hundreds of possibilities, a sample of those seen often includes **clay-colored robins**, **northern bentbills**, **Couch's kingbirds**, **rose-throated becards**, **barred antshrikes**, **yellow-billed caciques**, **laughing falcons** and both **red-capped** and **white-collared manakins**. In the pastures around the village, expect species such as **cattle egrets**, **groove-billed anis**, **spot-breasted wrens**, **great kiskadees**, **vermilion flycatchers** (in droves), **common tody-flycatchers**, **blue-black grassquits**, **blue-gray gnatcatchers** and **pale-vented pigeons**. ■

Location 33mi (53km) north-west of Belize City. Buses to Crooked Tree village.

Facilities Visitor center, museum, trails, boardwalk, bird observation tower.

Accommodations Numerous B&B options at the village (most allow camping), plus a couple of upmarket lodges.

Wildlife rhythms The dry season (especially April to May) sees peak congregations of waterbirds; many other migratory species also present (from January onwards).

Contact Belize Audubon Society (☎ 223-5004; fax 4985; **e** base@blt.net).

Watching tips
Black catbirds can be reliably spotted close to the visitor center, often in the trees behind the main building. Their distinctive cat-like mewing song is a giveaway.

THE CAYES

Islands teeming with life

SHELTERED by the second largest barrier reef in the world, Belize's cayes (pronounced 'keys') are the visible peaks of a submarine mountain range running the length of the country a few miles offshore. There are hundreds of cayes, most tiny and uninhabited, and they are visited mainly for the diving (see the Diving & Snorkeling section, pp40-1). But that's not all they have to offer for wildlife-watchers, and this section deals with the cayes' wildlife attractions.

Most of Half Moon Caye's boobies are white; this brown phase of the red-footed booby is common everywhere else but is a rarity in Belize.

Ambergris Caye

Almost connected to Mexico, Ambergris Caye is the largest and most populated caye and also boasts the most diverse wildlife. It has the largest protected area of any caye, Bacalar Chico NP, which preserves Belize's most important beaches for nesting **green** and **loggerhead turtles** (between Rocky and Robles Points). The mangroves around Laguna de Cantena host a large waterbird colony; over 1000 individuals of 10 species roost here, including **double-crested cormorants**, **wood storks**, **anhingas**, **white ibises**, **tricolored herons** and **reddish egrets**. About 40 mammal species have been recorded from the park, including **northern raccoons**, **collared peccaries** and **white-tailed deer**. Still relatively remote and undeveloped, Bacalar Chico can only be reached by boat; contact the national park office (☎ 226-2420) in San Pedro – Ambergris' only town.

Ambergris' birding is very good with around 200 species, including common **black catbirds**, **cinnamon hummingbirds**, **yellow-billed caciques** and, occasional Mexican specials, **Yucatán jays** and **orange orioles**. The Caribbean Villas Hotel (☎ 226-2715; e c-v-hotel@btl.net) has a small bird sanctuary with a worthwhile observation tower; they arrange excellent birding trips, as well as wildlife-watching tours by boat.

Caye Caulker

Caulker is biologically less diverse than Ambergris, but **white-crowned pigeons**, **rufous-necked wood-rails**, **black catbirds** and abundant **ctenosaurs** (also called **spiny-tailed iguanas**) are seen on the trail around South Point. Ubiquitous **brown pelicans**, **magnificent frigatebirds** and **laughing gulls** are easy to ignore, but they present superb photographic opportunities here if you stake out returning fishermen towards dusk; the birds hang above motionless in the Caribbean breeze waiting for scraps. An extremely tolerant pair of **ospreys** has nested on Caulker for the last decade, usually on the telephone pole at the eastern end of the airstrip. Caulker's birdlife is easily enjoyed on your own, but for excellent tours with a local naturalist, contact Dorothy and Jim Beveridge at Sea-ing is Belizing (☎ 220-4079, e bzvisuals@btl.net).

Caulker is also home to 'Chocolate' Heredia (☎ 226-0151, e chocolate@btl.net) whose boat trips venture to nearby uninhabited Swallow Caye looking for **West Indian manatees**. There are dozens of manatee tour operators in the cayes, but

Chocolate's are the best. A passionate crusader for manatee conservation, he guarantees sightings of the endangered sea mammals, sometimes within a few feet (it's illegal to swim with them, but they often approach boats if you're quiet). Chocolate is also responsible for a campaign to formally protect Swallow Caye as a reserve and he devotes a portion of his guiding fees to the project. As well as manatees, the tours enjoy regular encounters with **bottlenose dolphins** and they make a stop at Shark-Ray Alley for very tame **southern stingrays** and **gray nurse sharks**.

Half Moon Caye

Protected since 1982 as a national monument, the main draw-card of Half Moon Caye is its massive **red-footed booby** colony, the only one in Belize. Around 1500 pairs nest in the ziricote thicket on the western side of the island, where a tower provides excellent views. Nesting begins around mid-December and most chicks will have fledged and left the island by late August; to see small chicks, March to April is best. Curiously, virtually all of Half Moon's boobies are white; the occasional brown adult you see is the most common form throughout the rest of the Caribbean. **Magnificent frigatebirds, white-crowned pigeons, mangrove warblers** and **ospreys** also nest on the island and, in winter, the caye acts as critical landfall for around 80 North American migrants.

Half Moon is also home unusual reptiles, including large **Allison's anoles**, found nowhere else in Belize, and Belize's only endemic, the **Belize atoll gecko**. Other reptiles include ubiquitous **brown anoles** and **ctenosaurs**, and **green iguanas** (introduced by 18th century islanders for food) and **green anoles**, a Cuban species that evidently hitched a ride across in the 1960s (it's conspicuous at the observation tower). Half Moon Caye is 45mi (72km) from the coast and can be visited on (rather rushed) day tours or live-aboard dive trips. Camping is permitted; bring your own food and water. Contact: Belize Audubon Society (☎ 223-5004; fax 4985; e base@blt.net).

Turneffe Atoll

Comprising more than 200 mangrove-covered islands, Turneffe is home to Belize's largest population of **American crocodiles**. The three inner lagoons are less saline than the ocean, providing preferred habitat for the crocs, especially in Central Lagoon. Crocs nest in the mangroves, along with **Caribbean doves** and colonies of waterbirds – **magnificent frigatebirds, double-crested cormorants, white ibises, anhingas** and many **herons** and **egrets**. Up to a dozen pairs of **ospreys** also nest here. The entire eastern side of the atoll is strewn with productive mudflats, which attract impressive congregations of waders, especially over winter; expect **whimbrels, ruddy turnstones**, numerous **sandpipers** (especially **spotted, semi-palmated** and **western**) and six species of plover. Turneffe is a very popular dive site, easily visited with dive companies; the US-based Oceanic Society (w www.oceanic-society.org/pages/expb.html) conducts participatory research trips on **American crocs** and **bottlenose dolphins** at Turneffe's Blackbird Caye. ∎

RÍO BRAVO CONSERVATION & MANAGEMENT AREA

Rainforest giant

Wildlife highlights

Exceptional birdwatching, with more than 390 recorded species, including very conspicuous ocellated turkeys and some easily-seen endangered species such as yellow-crowned parrots and jabirus. Wintering migrants include more than 60 North American species. White-tailed and red brocket deer are common and white-lipped peccaries, Mexican porcupines, pacas, kinkajous and gray foxes are encountered often. All five of Belize's cats are seen relatively regularly. Boat tours at night usually see Morelet's crocodiles by spotlighting as well as nocturnal birds.

SITTING at the convergence of Belize's northwest border with Mexico and Guatemala, Río Bravo is part of the largest tract of tropical forest north of the Amazon. Known as La Selva Maya (the Maya Forest), it spans the three countries in an unbroken swathe larger than the whole of Belize. Río Bravo represents a small fraction of the total, but as the single largest protected area in the country, its conservation value is immeasurable. It shelters vigorous populations of the most land-hungry species like **jaguars**, **pumas**, **Baird's tapirs**, **ornate hawk-eagles** and **great curassows**, as well as protecting thousands of less demanding ones. Its birdlife is especially rich; large areas ensure habitat for a medley of resident species, but just as critical, Río Bravo provides winter refuges for dozens of migratory bird species from as far north as Alaska.

Río Bravo's unwieldy full name reveals the reserve's twin aims – conservation of nature and utilization of its resources. The latter translates primarily into sustainable forestry, centered on the Hill Bank Station. In addition to managed pine savannas, it gives rise to a combination of primary and secondary forest – a diversity that, in turn, brings about exceptionally varied birding. For a decent shot at the near-400 species that occur, visit both Hill Bank and La Milpa (which has excavated Maya ruins as its focus).

Hill Bank's disturbed habitat is actually preferred by **double-toothed kites**, **laughing falcons**, **Yucatán jays**, **Yucatán flycatchers**, **blue-black grassquits** and abundant **tanagers**, **warblers** and **orioles**. Nearby pine savanna hosts resident **yellow-crowned parrots** (they frequent the station on foraging trips) and the scrubby forest along the old airstrip is good for **rufous-browed peppershrikes**, **gray-throated chats**, **rufous-breasted spinetails** and resident **northern cardinals**. Hill Bank sits on the New River Lagoon, home to dozens of waterbird

The pine-dominated forest at Punta Gorda on the southeastern boundary of Río Bravo. A half-hour walk in any direction leads to entirely different habitats, with a corresponding change in the wildlife mix.

species including **pinnated bitterns**, **grey-necked wood-rails**, **soras**, **uniform crakes** and **jabirus**, as well as **mangrove swallows** and **gray-breasted martins**. Guided night-trips by boat have a chance at **northern potoos**, close-up views of **limpkins**, snoozing **kingfishers** and assured **Morelet's crocodiles**.

Hill Bank also has old growth forest, but the best tracts are around La Milpa. Visit here for **great curassows**, **trogons** (four species), **tody** and **blue-crowned motmots** (common around the ruins),

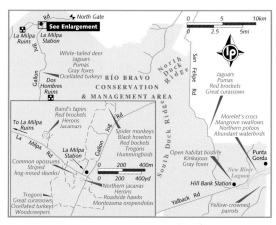

strong-billed, **barred** and **ivory-billed woodcreepers**, **rufous pihas**, **lovely cotingas**, both Belizean **manakins** (**white-collared** and **red-capped**) and **rufous-tailed jacamars**, to select a few. **Ocellated turkeys** are abundant and night-walks see **mottled owls**, **black-and-white owls**, **Yucatán poorwills**, **Yucatán nightjars** and **common pauraques**.

Belize's best-kept cat secret

For mammal-watchers, the most obvious species at Río Bravo is **white-tailed deer**; they're impossible to miss at the cleared edges along Gallon Jug Rd. The deer in turn draw out their predators and, in the words of local guide Freddie Gomez, 'Río Bravo may be the best-kept cat secret in Belize'. Freddie runs a shuttle service in the area (best arranged through Lamanai Outpost Lodge or Chan Chich) and his sightings list for 2001 on the road included eight **jaguars**, two **pumas**, two **ocelots**, and once, late at night, a **margay**. Freddie drives the road a few times every week so he's bound to see more than the casual visitor, but it's worth driving slowly or even walking the road at dawn and dusk for a chance. If you are lucky enough to see a cat in the distance, don't speed up; most species disappear regardless, but the jaguars here are fairly used to vehicles and often hang around if approached slowly. Jaguars are also seen weekly on the San Felipe and Yalback Rds at Hill Bank.

Less elusive mammals include **gray foxes**, **white-nosed coatis** (the former common in the open habitat near Hill Bank and both often seen on roads), **Yucatán black howlers** and **Central American spider monkeys**; both primates are regularly spotted near the La Milpa ruins. At dusk, **common opossums** emerge onto the open area in front of La Milpa Station; sit with a flashlight on the veranda and you might also see large **striped hog-nosed skunks**. The little pond on the La Milpa Rd sees occasional visits from **Baird's tapirs** and **red brockets**; your best chances come from being in place before dawn breaks (wait silently and bring bug repellent!). Hill Bank's night river trips also sometimes see tapirs and, more often, **pacas**, **kinkajous**, **Mexican porcupines** and **gray four-eyed opossums**. ■

Location 58mi (93km) southwest of Orange Walk.

Facilities Walking trails (guided and self-guided), night boat trips, canoes, research excursions (mainly archaeological, but also nature-oriented).

Accommodations Dorms and cabanas at La Milpa and Hill Bank.

Wildlife rhythms Most migratory birds are easily seen in winter (September to March). Hill Bank station has frog-watching excursions in the rainy season (June to December), which survey up to 15 species.

Contact Program for Belize (☎ 227-5616; fax 227-5635; e pfbel@btl.net).

Watching tips
The fields north of Río Bravo are extremely fruitful for raptors. In a morning's roadside birding you could easily see white-tailed hawks, zone-tailed hawks, roadside hawks, short-tailed hawks, gray hawks, laughing falcons, American kestrels and the ubiquitous turkey vulture.

COMMUNITY BABOON SANCTUARY

Baboons abounding

Wildlife highlights
The best place in Central America for Yucatán black howlers. Night-walks are good for nocturnal mammals especially forest rabbits, kinkajous and common opossums. River trips see super-abundant green iguanas, as well as many waterbirds, mainly common species of heron, egret and kingfisher. Birdlife is abundant but dominated by species that are tolerant of humans, such as brown jays, anis, cattle egrets and certain hummingbirds and parrots.

Location 26mi (42km) west of Belize City (see map p73). Buses to Bermudian Landing stop at the visitor center.
Facilities Trails, guided night-walks, canoe trips (day and night). Small museum and restaurant at visitor center.
Accommodations Camping at the visitor's center. Numerous cabanas and camping options in the village.
Wildlife rhythms Howlers are generally most active and most vocal at dawn and dusk.
Contact Visitor center (☎ 220-2181; e baboon@blt.net; PO Box 1428, Belize City).

Watching tips
Nature Resort next to the visitor center has cashews planted around its cabanas, irresistible to rufous-tailed hummingbirds and little and long-tailed hermits when in flower (late January to February). In March to April, the fruits attract multitudes of Aztec parakeets and yellow-crowned and white-crowned parrots.

IN Belize, **Yucatán black howler monkeys** are known as baboons (they're not closely related) and this sanctuary is the only protected area established entirely for their conservation. It's also a wholly community-based initiative. Founded in 1985 at the village of Bermudian Landing, landowners voluntarily pledge to manage their land in monkey-friendly fashion. Forested strips are maintained along the Belize River and along property boundaries to create corridors for howlers, and important food trees such as figs and hogplums are never felled. The scheme has spread to surrounding villages and now includes over 100 landowners. Black howlers occur throughout Belize, but to observe them utterly indifferent to people, the Community Baboon Sanctuary is impossible to beat.

Howlers are often visible from the main road, but a maze of trails provides the best views. The routes traverse private property, so stop by the visitor center at Bermudian Landing for an introductory guided tour; the sanctuary operates on the very modest fees and, besides, the tours are excellent. The guides will find the most habituated troops, some of which approach to within a few feet – a privilege unique to the sanctuary. Other commonly seen species on the trails include **forest rabbits**, **ctenosaurs** (known as spiny-tailed iguanas here), **brown jays**, **groove-billed anis** and, sometimes, domestic dogs; remember, sanctuary and village are essentially the same thing so pets, distant stereos and a little litter are part of the experience. After the tour, you're free to explore on your own.

With an estimated 1800 black howlers, the Sanctuary protects the densest population of any howler species anywhere; a few areas have more than 250 individuals per hectare. It makes for outstanding viewing, but places a premium on space and this is probably the most aggressively territorial population of howlers on the planet. Groups are larger than elsewhere – essentially because there isn't the room to spread out – and their roaring calls proclaim land rights *constantly*. Although concerns of over-population have been raised, the black howler is a suprisingly adaptable species; small groups here have lived successfully in a single food tree for over a year.

Howlers aside, canoe trips down the Belize River deliver views of numerous **herons** and **egrets**, **mangrove swallows**, **Neotropic cormorants**, **sungrebes**; **green**, **Amazon** and **ringed kingfishers** (the latter have nest holes in the banks here); and **green iguanas** by the hundred; canoes can be arranged at the visitor center or just next door at Nature Resort (☎ 614-9286, e naturer@btl.net). Both also conduct guided night-walks, and the promise of nocturnal mammals including **kinkajous** (called 'night-walkers' and almost guaranteed), **nine-banded armadillos**, **Mexican porcupines**, **common opossums** and, occasionally, **pacas**. Although it's not widely advertised, you can take nocturnal canoe trips, which very occasioanlly produce **ocelots** and **jaguarundis**. ∎

BELIZE ZOO & TROPICAL EDUCATION CENTER

Captive audience

GIVEN the wealth of parks and reserves in Belize, it may seem a little incongruous to include a zoo in this chapter. But apart from being the only place where you can reliably see the most elusive species, Belize Zoo is also one of the most active conservation players in the country. Although zoos everywhere invariably list conservation and education in their mission statements, only a fraction of them actually practice it. Belize Zoo does so by the busload. One of their programs sees every Belizean school-kid come though the gates at least once to view the wholly indigenous inhabitants (no exotic species are kept at the zoo). Creative interpretive signs in the animals' 'voices' explain to the kids why it's wrong to hunt them, catch them for pets or clear their habitat.

The zoo offers views of around 40 native species, including all five **cats**, **Baird's tapirs** (inset), **tayras**, **pacas** and numerous charismatic and rare birds such as **jabirus**, **ornate hawk-eagles**, **mottled owls**, **scarlet macaws** and **great curassows**. The enclosures are mostly large and dense with natural vegetation, providing authentic views of the animals in their environment, but also allowing them to take refuge if the crowds become too much.

For photographers, it's essentially the only real chance to shoot **pumas, jaguars** and other secretive species; a small fee gets behind-the-scenes angles guided by one of the keepers.

About a half-mile (1km) away, on the other side of the Western Hwy, the zoo also operates the Tropical Education Center (TEC). Sitting on 84 acres (33.5 hectares), the TEC has interpretive trails through pine woodland and savanna habitat, plus bird observation decks – excellent for resident species like **plain chachalacas**, **yellow-crowned parrots** and **violaceous trogons**, as well as migratory **warblers**. The TEC's facilities are mostly set up for school and research groups, but accommodations (including camping) are available to casual travelers; book ahead and bring your own food unless otherwise arranged. A rewarding combination is to stay at the TEC after one of the Zoo's terrific guided night-tours (which reveal nocturnal species like **margays**, **kinkajous** and **boa constrictors** on the move) and then walk the trails and birdwatch from the decks early the next morning. The TEC is also the hub of the zoo's research activities; ask the staff about their programs on wild **scarlet macaws** and flyways for **migrating birds**.

For many wildlife-watchers, zoos are dreary at best and an aberration at worst. But in visiting this one, be assured that your entrance fee is contributing to far more than simply keeping the animals housed. ∎

Wildlife highlights
Great close-up views of Belize's most secretive and endangered wildlife in captivity, including five cat species and Baird's tapirs. Birdlife includes 20 captive species plus many others, which range freely in the zoo grounds and are very tame. Species at the TEC include various trogons, parrots and many migrants. Night-walks promise chances at seeing nocturnal mammals such as gray foxes, opossums and armadillos.

Location Western Hwy, 29mi (47km) west of Belize City. Buses stop at the entrance.
Facilities Trails, bird observation decks and reference library (TEC); small gift shop at Zoo (food is not sold).
Accommodations Camping, dorms and cabanas at the TEC.
Wildlife rhythms Early in the morning is best for catching many species at their most active and to avoid the crowds. The zoo is busy on weekends.
Contact Belize Zoo (☎ 220-8004; e belizezoo@blt.net). TEC (☎ 220-8003; fax 8010; e tec@btl.net.

Watching tips
Take a self-guided night-walk on the TEC's trails for a good chance at spotting gray foxes, common opossums and nine-banded armadillos.

CHAN CHICH LODGE

Jaguar central

Wildlife highlights
Possibly Belize's best site for seeing jaguars. Easily visible Yucatán black howlers, white-nosed coatis, Central American spider monkeys and white-tailed deer. Extremely diverse bird fauna; around 390 species with a mixture of tropical forest, grassland and wetland birds. Night-drives and night-walks produce nocturnal specials such as kinkajous, mottled owls and potoos.

Location 130mi (209km) west of Belize City.
Facilities 9mi (14.5km) of walking trails, guided walks (day and night), night-drives, horse riding and canoeing.
Accommodations Luxurious (and expensive) lodge with 12 cabanas.
Wildlife rhythms Winter is best for migratory birds and is also the dry season, better for getting around to different habitats; it's also the tourism high season.
Contact Chan Chich Lodge (☎/fax 223-4419; USA ☎ 1-800-343-8009; fax 508-693-631; e info@chanchich.com).

Watching tips
A pair of ornate hawk-eagles has a terrifically visible nest on Sac Be Trail. For a chance at seeing lovely cotingas, stake out the suspension bridge at dawn or dusk.

ADJACENT to Río Bravo, this luxury lodge sits in the lower plaza of unexcavated Mayan ruins. More importantly for wildlifers, it's in the middle of one of the largest private reserves in the country, which has sometimes spectacularly visible wildlife. A visit to Chan Chich doesn't come cheaply, but of course your dollars buy two things: ongoing preservation of the area as wilderness and some of the finest wildlife-watching in Belize.

Chan Chich is part of La Selva Maya, the largest intact tropical forest north of the Amazon (see the Río Bravo account, pp76-7). Large tracts of forest protect a huge array of wildlife, but for some species they are essential. Topping the list is the **jaguar** and Chan Chich probably has the highest rate of sightings in Belize – an astonishing 60 to 70 a year. Jaguars here regularly use the trails around the lodge and they are seen even more often on the Gallon Jug Rd. Don't panic if you encounter a jaguar on foot – they are the only big cat with no record for targeting people as prey. Conversely, don't approach or disturb them, especially a female with cubs. Their unblemished reputation is for *unprovoked* attacks; a jaguar is quite capable of killing a person, if given a motive.

Even in Chan Chich, observing jaguars should be considered exceptional, but seeing other mammals is far more likely. **Yucatán black howlers**, **Central American spider monkeys**, **Deppe's squirrels** and **white-nosed coatis** are common, and try Gallon Jug's open habitat for **gray foxes**, **white-tailed deer** and occasionally **jaguarundis**. The guided night-walks and night-drives (a rare treat in Central America) produce **kinkajous**, **red brockets** and **white-lipped peccaries**. The drives will also boost your chances for another shot at jaguars.

Cats aside, Chan Chich means 'little bird' and the diversity of habitats produces an exceptional birdlist of species of all sizes. **Ocellated turkeys** are impossible to miss around the lodge, where other regulars include **crested guans**, **masked tityras**, three **euphonias** (**yellow-throated**, **olive-backed** and **scrub**), **purple-crowned fairies**, **red-capped manakins** and nesting **Montezuma oropendolas**. Try the suspension bridge for a mix of forest, riverine and open habitat species: both **Louisiana** and **northern waterthrushes**, **green jays**, **bat falcons**, **barred** and **collared forest-falcons**, **yellow-bellied flycatchers**, **dusky antbirds** and at least three **trogons** – **black-headed**, **slaty-tailed** and **violaceous**. The Gallon Jug area is rich in grassland species like **scissor-tailed** and **fork-tailed flycatchers**, **orchard orioles**, **giant cowbirds**, **white-tailed kites**, **gray hawks** and **short-tailed hawks** while, to the north, Laguna Verde and Laguna Seca have the usual wetland complement of **northern jacanas**, **herons** and **kingfishers**. Capping off an extraordinary variety, the night activities pick up **mottled owls**, **common pauraques**, and **northern** and **great potoos**. Night drives will give you another chance for **jaguars**, and an even better chance for smaller cats, such as **ocelots** and **jaguarundis**. ■

LAMANAI ARCHAEOLOGICAL RESERVE & OUTPOST LODGE
Luxury on the lagoon

SITTING on the 28mi (45km) long New River Lagoon, the Lamanai Archaeological Reserve conserves the Maya Lamanai ruins, once a prosperous city of perhaps 50,000 residents, but now largely covered by forest. Long better suited for wildlife than Maya, the city is mostly visited for the handful of excavated buildings, but it is a fruitful kick-off point for wildlife-watching in the region. However, to really get the most out of Lamanai's wildlife and assuming you have the cash, the nearby Lamanai Outpost Lodge offers a whole lot more.

Lamanai can be reached by air and road, but boating along the New River is by far the most rewarding option. A dozen **heron** and **egret** species can be spotted (try canoeing down Dawson Creek for **agami herons**), as well as **least bitterns, pied-billed grebes, anhingas** and all five of Belize's **kingfishers. Lesser yellow-headed vultures, snail kites** and **ospreys** are abundant, and striking **black-collared hawks** are virtually assured. Between December and May, **jabirus** nest here; there is a very visible nest in a dead fig tree at the northern entrance of the main lagoon. Most tours from Orange Walk arrive by boat and the lodge offers early morning and afternoon lagoon trips with excellent guides.

On dry land, the jungle at the Archaeological Reserve will swell your list by many dozens. The fig trees around the three main temples are especially good, both for fig-eaters and, because fruit-eating insects swarm around fig trees, insectivores; **royal flycatchers, yellow-crowned parrots, tody motmots, violaceous trogons, keel-billed toucans** and **collared aracaris** are all easily seen. The abandoned British sugar mill in the south of the reserve produces more retiring forest specials like **great tinamous** and **collared forest-falcons**. Birds are definitely the main attraction here, but **Yucatán black howlers** are also common.

Lamanai means 'submerged crocodile' and for superb views of them (**Morelet's croc** is the only species found here), the lodge's spotlighting safaris on the lagoon are terrific. Nocturnal **Yucatán nightjars, common pauraques** and **northern potoos** are regulars, as are hunting **greater fishing bats**. Other mammal sightings are fewer, but include **northern tamanduas, kinkajous, Mexican porcupines, white-nosed coatis, northern raccoons** and – exceptional but on the rise – **jaguars, ocelots** and **margays**.

For a unique hands-on experience, the lodge's Field Research Center has crocodile-catching trips and mist-netting for birds with professional biologists. Lamanai is also an unexpected center for tarantula diversity. Alongside ubiquitous **red-rumped tarantulas**, three entirely new species have been discovered here: the **pygmy tarantula, Gutzke's tarantula** and, one that bears Lamanai's name, *Crassicrus lamanai*, the **cinnamon tarantula**. All Belizean tarantulas are completely harmless to people and very reclusive, but Lamanai's guides and researchers can find them. ∎

Wildlife highlights
Around 385 species of bird. The best place in Belize for greater fishing bats in action. Kinkajous, northern tamanduas, Mexican porcupines and white-nosed coatis are common. Excellent night safaris occasionally see one of the cat species, as well as owls, potoos and nightjars. Tarantulas are exceptionally diverse.

Location 36mi (58km) south of Orange Walk (by road).
Facilities Only at Lamanai Outpost Lodge: guided nature, birdwatching and ruins walks, lagoon tours (day and night), canoeing and research excursions (by prior arrangement).
Accommodations None at Archaeological Reserve. Lamanai Outpost Lodge is a full-service lodge with 17 luxury cabanas.
Wildlife rhythms December to June is best for migratory birds, including nesting jabirus.
Contact Archaeological Reserve, Department of Archaeology (☎ 822-2106; fax 882-3345; e celbelize@btl.net). Lamanai Outpost Lodge (☎ 223-3578; USA ☎ 1-888-733-7864; e outpost@lamanai.com; w www.lamanai.com).

Watching tips
Bat falcons habitually perch on the lodge's radio mast looking for prey. They can be spotted all day, but for chances of an aerial hunt, watch them at dawn and dusk. At the reserve, a large boa constrictor lives around the Jaguar Temple.

OTHER SITES – BELIZE

Blue Hole NP

Named for its signature cenote (a drowned limestone sinkhole), Blue Hole sits in the foothills of the Maya Mountains and, although small, it's surrounded by far more extensive wilderness (the reason jaguars and Baird's tapirs are occasionally seen here – if you're very lucky). But more likely, you'll see dozens of bird species (the park has 200-plus) and perhaps Deppe's squirrels, white-nosed coatis, red brocket and peccaries. You can also visit St Herman's Cave, an impressive cavern once used by the Maya, but today home mainly to colonies of common long-tongued bats, short-tailed bats and, in winter, cliff swallows.

12mi (19km) SE of Belmopan Belize Audubon Society: ☎ *223-5004; fax 4985;* e *base@blt.net*

Chiquibul NP

Remote, huge and little-visited, Chiquibul is Belize's largest protected area and covers a huge slice of the Maya Mountains that includes Belize's highest point, Doyle's Delight (not Cockscomb's Victoria Peak, as often stated). It's also the site of Caracol, a 36,000-building Maya city and Chiquibul's most accessible sector, though reaching even here requires some serious 4WD. Caracol has a modest trail system where, among the 300 known birds (the list is still growing), you might view some montane rainforest rarities such as tawny-throated leaftossers, spectacled foliage-gleaners and spotted woodcreepers. Keel-billed motmots are common and nest in the pyramid walls, ocellated turkeys forage around the complex and there is a small breeding population of scarlet macaws. Climbing the main pyramid, Ka Ana, is excellent for raptors, including white hawks. Visible mammals include black howler and spider monkeys and abundant Baird's tapirs, which sometimes graze at dusk in the main complex. Chiquibul (including Caracol) can be impossible to reach in the rainy season; tours are best arranged in the dry season (January to June) from San Ignacio.

81mi (130km) S of San Ignacio Department of Archaeology: ☎ *822-2106; fax 3345;* e *celbelize@btl.net*

Five Blues Lake NP

Five Blues – the name refers to the variable shades of the park's 200ft (60m) deep lake – is a very picturesque site with a well-developed trail system. Apart from the lake itself, the main attractions of the park are the numerous caves, sinkholes and exposed limestone cliffs that provide roosts for more than 20 bat species. Most of the caves require a guide and permits from the Department of Archaeology to explore in depth, but the trail to the Lake passes a sinkhole with thousands of lesser doglike bats visible at the entrance. Birding is usually rewarding with about 200 species on record; the limestone cliffs are good for raptor-spotting. The visitor center hires kayaks and mountain bikes to explore the park.

22mi (35km) S of Belmopan PACT: ☎ *822-3637; fax 3759;* e *pact@btl.net*

Guanacaste NP

Not to be confused with the much larger Costa Rican park of the same name, Guanacaste is a tiny reserve on the Western Highway very close to Belmopan. Its accessible location makes it an excellent day-trip, particularly for birdwatching. There's nothing here that doesn't occur elsewhere in Belize's parks but over 100 bird species are resident, including such notables as black-faced ant-thrushes, squirrel cuckoos, blue-crowned motmots, black-headed trogons and red-lored parrots. Mammals are fairly thin on the ground, but there's a chance you'll see agoutis and white-tailed deer.

2mi (3km) north of Belmopan-Belize Audubon Society: ☎ *223-5004; fax 4985;* e *base@blt.net*

Mountain Pine Ridge Forest Reserve

Belize's many forest reserves are primarily for logging and mostly difficult (if not forbidden) for tourists to visit, but Mountain Pine Ridge is the most tourism-friendly of the lot. Adjacent to Chiquibul NP, the fauna is essentially the same and most easily spotted around the three lodges in the park (details below) or around the D'Silva Forest Station where there is a trail system. The open grass-covered vistas of Bald Hills (the

soils here are apparently too poor to sustain forest) are excellent places to look for raptors on the wing and hold probably the best chance in Belize for orange-breasted falcons, king vultures and black-and-white hawk-eagles.

*45mi (72km) S of San Ignacio
Forest Department (D'Silva):
☎ 822-2630; fax 2333 Pine Ridge
Lodge: e prlodge@btl.net
Blancaneaux Lodge: e blodge@
btl.ne Five Sisters Lodge: e five
sislo@btl.net*

Northern and Southern Lagoon

Wholly distinct from the lagoons of the same name at Crooked Tree WS (see pp72-3), Northern and Southern Lagoon lie a few miles inland from the coast south of Belize City. The more accessible of the two, Southern Lagoon has Belize's largest inland population of West Indian manatees. The rainy season, when water levels are high, is the best time to see them (visibility permitting). Recent research is suggesting that the high level of boat traffic is forcing the manatees to other areas; check with your tour before it leaves that they approach manatees using poles (an example set by the better operators in the cayes). Both lagoons are also rewarding for waterbirds; Northern Lagoon's Bird Caye is an island of red mangroves used by breeding white ibises, double-crested cormorants, anhingas, and boat-billed herons.

27mi (43km) N of Dangriga

Payne's Creek NP

Usually visited on tours from Placencia, much of Payne's Creek is inaccessible marshland, even in the dry season. Most wildlife-watching takes place around Monkey River village, actually just outside the national park, but managed by the community as a contiguous protected unit. The best option is probably an overnight kayak trip along Monkey River. Black howlers, hundreds of green iguanas and dozens of waterbirds are guaranteed (including

high chances at pinnated bitterns), and Baird's tapirs are fairly common away from the village. The adjacent marine reserve protects breeding West Indian manatees and the mangrove-free beach is used by nesting hawksbill turtles, with a peak in June to July.

*13mi (21km) S of Placencia
(by boat)
Toledo Institute for Development & Environment: ☎ 722-2929; fax 2655; e tidetours@
belizeecotours.org*

Sarstoon-Temash NP

The second largest national park in Belize, Sarstoon-Temash is also its southernmost protected area. Abutting Guatemala along the Sarstoon River, it protects the largest and oldest red mangrove forests in Belize, as well as large wetlands which provide habitat for dozens of species of waterbird. Mammals include everything from jaguars to northern raccoons, but facilities are not yet in place for reasonable chances of viewing them. Sarstoon-Temash is managed by a coalition of surrounding communities who have only very recently begun development aimed at wildlife tourists.

*48mi (77km) S of Punta Gorda
(by road)
SATIIM, Kekchi Council of
Belize: ☎ 722-2320;
 e kcbtol@btl.net*

Shipstern NR

A mosaic of forest, coastal savannas, mangroves and saline lagoons, Shipstern is home to

Belize's largest breeding populations of two uncommon birds, white-winged doves and reddish egrets. Wood storks, great egrets and Neotropic cormorants also have significant colonies here (on the small islands in Shipstern Lagoon) and a further 215 bird species can be seen. Apart from primates (apparently wiped out in 1955 by Hurricane Janet), most of Belize's mammals occur and although elusive, the saline mudflats around the lagoon are excellent for their tracks. More than 200 butterfly species are found in the reserve; there is a nice butterfly breeding center at the park HQ providing close-up views of some of them.

*53mi (85km) NE of Orange
Walk
Belize Audubon Society:
☎ 223-5004; fax 4985;
 e base@blt.net ∎*

*Photo far left: Birdwatching at
Lamanai.
Center: Mayan ruins at Altan Ha.
This page: A male magnificent
frigatebird displays his wares.*

COSTA RICA
A crowded cornucopia

Highlights

- Watching a resplendent quetzal from Monteverde's viewing platform as they pluck wild aguacatillo fruits and alight nearby to eat them
- Looking down on huge American crocs at Carara's Río Grande de Tárcoles while scarlet macaws commute overhead
- Encountering jaguar tracks in Tortuguero's green turtle colony on the Caribbean coast
- Sharing crumbs with volcano juncos on Costa Rica's highest peak, Cerro Chirripó
- Central American squirrel monkeys within touching distance in Corcovado's rainforest, entirely indifferent to the observer
- Counting the procession of mammals coming to drink at Santa Rosa's waterholes during the long dry season
- Clouds of black-bellied whistling-ducks exploding into flight as a peregrine falcon sweeps over Palo Verde's Laguna Varillal
- Coming face-to-face with a tayra on the trails at Tapantí

A T slightly under 20,000 sq miles, Costa Rica is smaller than Austria or West Virginia, but this tiny country is literally crammed with life. Covering less than 0.01% of the earth's land area, it's home to over 4% of all living species – this may not sound like much, but it means that Costa Rica's biodiversity tally comes in at just over 500,000 unique species. It has almost as many birds as the USA and Canada combined, more reptiles than Europe and five times as many butterflies as Australia.

The reasons for this abundance are many, but it's partly to do with the country's extraordinary geography. The most mountainous of Central American nations, Costa Rica's central spine of cordilleras rises abruptly to over 2mi (3.2km) above the coastal lowlands on either side. This elevation creates a slew of different habitats, which if you took a countrywide cross section at the highest point, are crowded into a narrow bridge of land spanning only 80mi (129km) from coast to coast. So, in addition to the typical lowland habitats of wet, humid rainforest, swampforest and the dry tropical forest of Guanacaste, Costa Rica has constantly misty cloud forest, windswept elfin forest covered in beds of moss, and even Andean-like páramo on the plateau of the Cordillera de Talamanca.

Such high diversity promises superb wildlife-viewing: Marine turtles and migrating waders, crocodiles and mangrove-roosting parrots, cloud forest mammals and quetzals, and volcano hummingbirds and highland lizards. But its conservation also requires enlightened determination and fortunately, Costa Rica has one of Central America's most progressive systems of protected areas. Almost 30% of land is under statutory protection; much of

that is open to exploitation, particularly for forestry, but about 12% is set aside solely to preserve natural habitat and wildlife. This includes not only the rainforest – for most visitors, synonymous with the tropics – but also habitats that many have not even heard of until they arrive.

Many of the parks rank among the most accessible in Central America, and the options for exploring range from camping rough to staying at nearby luxury lodges with excellent guides. And there's an admirable system of private reserves here; still one of the most research-rich Latin American nations, Costa Rica's numerous biological stations regularly admit enthusiastic laypeople – a unique opportunity that is rare outside the region. Whether it's a guided tour, back-country hiking or volunteering at a research station, the opportunities in Costa Rica to experience the best of the Neotropics are difficult to surpass. ∎

Costa Rica is small enough to travel from beaches to cloud forest in a day, with a staggering diversity of wildlife in between.

SUGGESTED ITINERARIES

One week Costa Rica is a small country and well served by roads, which means you can cover a lot of ground quickly. But don't be tempted to rush around to many sites. Generally, spending more time at fewer parks is far more rewarding. Combine two nights at Monteverde with a three-day trip to either Corcovado or Tortuguero; if you take domestic flights, you could do all three with two nights at each. Otherwise, head to Chirripó which needs a minimum of three days/two nights and then head down to Corcovado for three nights. Return to San José with stops at either Carara or Manuel Antonio. In Guanacaste, spend two nights each at Santa Rosa, Rincón de la Vieja and Palo Verde. Stay a day less at one site to give you time to get to Mariño Las Baulas for nesting leatherbacks (October-March). Otherwise, base yourself in San José which is close to many suitable day trips or overnight stops; Carara, Manuel Antonio, Poás, La Selva and Tapantí are some possibilities.

Two weeks A fortnight gives you ample time to really explore a few of the best sites as well as make some worthwhile stops in between. Spend two nights each at Monteverde and Arenal then head to Guanacaste for Rincón de la Vieja (two nights), Santa Rosa (two nights), Palo Verde (two nights) and Lomas Barbudal (one night). Alternatively from Arenal, head to Caño Negro for a night, then head cross-country to Braulio Carrillo and La Selva for three nights and onto Tortuguero for three. Alternatively, substitute Tortuguero for three nights at Chirripó. Otherwise, with a hire car and internal flights, you can combine the best of very different habitats; three nights in Santa Rosa's dry forest, three nights in Tortuguero (Caribbean lowland rainforest), three nights in Monteverde's cloud forest and three at Corcovado (Pacific rainforest). Any days over can be filled with day trips from San José to Poás, Carara or Irazú.

One month A month gives you time to really cover Costa Rica's diversity. Six very different sites warrant at least three days each; Corcovado, Chirripó, Tortuguero, Monteverde, Palo Verde and Santa Rosa. With these as your scaffolding, fill in the gaps with shorter stops and side-trips on the way. From Tortuguero, a very accessible side-trip is Barra del Colorado and you could also head down the Caribbean coast for two nights at Cahuita. Carara and Manuel Antonio are easily visited (one/two nights each) driving between Corcovado and San José. From Monteverde, head to Arenal for a night and then onto Caño Negro for a night. From Palo Verde, head to Mariño las Baulas (one night) and down to Cabo Blanco for two nights. Otherwise a month could be spent making the 10-day trip to Isla del Cocos combined with any 20-day combination of the above. Fill in any extra time with day trips from San José. ■

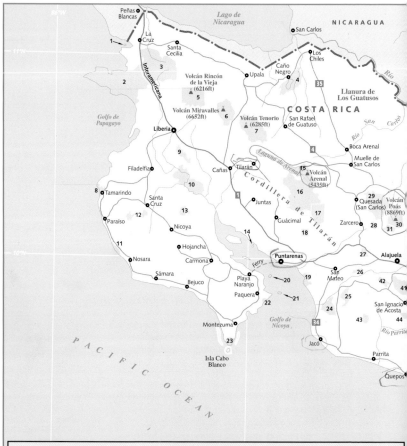

1 Refugio Nacional de Fauna Silvestre Isla Bolaños
2 Parque Nacional Santa Rosa
3 Parque Nacional Guanacaste
4 Refugio Nacional de Vida Silvestre Caño Negro
5 Parque Nacional Rincón de la Vieja
6 Zona Protectora Miravalles
7 Parque Nacional Volcán Tenorio
8 Parque Nacional Marino Las Baulas de Guanacaste
9 Reserva Biológica Lomas Barbudal
10 Parque Nacional Palo Verde
11 Refugio Nacional de Fauna Silvestre Ostional
12 Bosque Nacional Diriá
13 Parque Nacional Barra Honda
14 Reserva Biológica Isla de Los Pájaros
15 Parque Nacional Volcán Arenal
16 Reserva Biológica Bosque Nuboso Monteverde
17 Zona Protectora San Ramón
18 Refugio Silvestre de Peñas Blancas
19 Zona Protectora Río Tivives
20 Parque Nacional de Isla Guayabo
21 Reserva Biológica Islas Negritos
22 Refugio Nacional de Fauna Silvestre Curú

23 Reserva Natural Absoluta Cabo Blanco
24 Parque Nacional Carara
25 Zona Protectora Cerros de Turrubares
26 Zona Protectora Cerro Atenas
27 Zona Protectora Río Grande
28 Zona Protectora El Chayote
29 Parque Nacional Juan Castro Blanco
30 Parque Nacional Volcán Poás
31 Reserva Forestal Grecia
32 Reserva Forestal Cordillera Volcánica Central
33 Parque Nacional Braulio Carrillo
34 Estación Biológica La Selva
35 Refugio Nacional de Fauna Silvestre Barra del Colorado
36 Zona Protectora Tortuguero (Corredor Biológico)
37 Parque Nacional Tortuguero
38 Zona Protectora Acuíferos Guácimo y Pococi
39 Reserva Forestal Cordillera Volcánica Central
40 Parque Nacional Volcán Irazú
41 Zona Protectora Cerros de Escazú
42 Zona Protectora El Rodeo
43 Zona Protectora La Cangreja
44 Zona Protectora Cerro Caraigres

45 Zona Protectora Río Navarro y Río Sombrero
46 Reserva Forestal Los Santos
47 Zona Protectora Cerro Nara
48 Parque Nacional Manuel Antonio
49 Parque Nacional Tapantí
50 Reserva Forestal Río Macho
51 Parque Nacional Chirripó
52 Zona Protectora Cuenca Río Tuis
53 Zona Protectora Río Pacuare
54 Reserva Biológica Barbilla
55 Zona Protectora Río Banano
56 Parque Internacional La Amistad
57 Reserva Biológica Hitoy Cerere
58 Parque Nacional Cahuita
59 Refugio Nacional de Vida Silvestre Gandoca – Manzanillo
60 Parque Nacional Marino Ballena
61 Reserva Biológica Isla del Caño
62 Reserva Forestal Golfo Dulce
63 Parque Nacional Corcovado
64 Refugio Nacional de Fauna Silvestre Golfito
65 Jardin Botánico Las Cruces
66 Zona Protectora Las Tablas
67 Parque Nacional Isla del Cocos

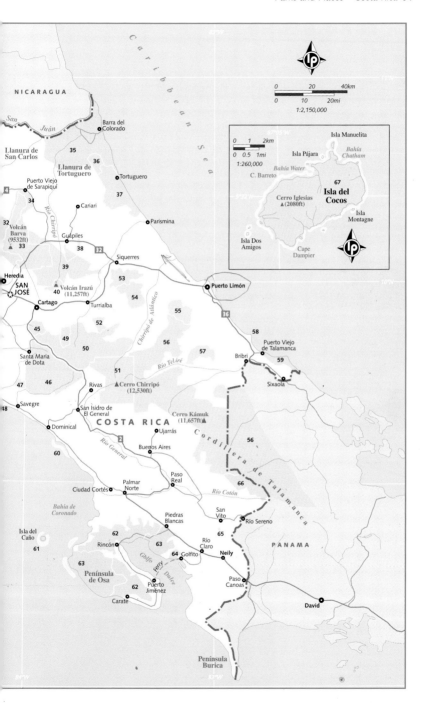

NICARAGUA

Caribbean Sea

0   20   40km
0   10   20mi
1:2,150,000

Isla Manuelita

Bahía Chatham

Isla Pájara

Bahía Water

C. Barreto

0   1   2km
0   0.5   1mi
1:260,000

Cerro Iglesias
▲ (2080ft)

67

Isla del
Cocos

Isla Montagne

Isla Dos Amigos

Cape Dampier

San Juan

Barra del Colorado

Llanura de San Carlos

35

36

Llanura de Tortuguero

Puerto Viejo de Sarapiquí

34

Río Chirripó

Cariari

32

Volcán Barva
(9532ft)

33

Guápiles

38

32

Siquerres

39

Tortuguero

37

Parismina

Heredia

SAN JOSÉ

40

Volcán Irazú
(11,257ft)

Cartago

Turrialba

52

45

49

50

Santa María de Dota

47

46

48   Savegre

51

Rivas

53

54

55

56

57

58

Puerto Limón

36

Puerto Viejo de Talamanca

Bribri

59

Sixaola

Chirripó de Atlántico

Río Teliré

▲ Cerro Chirripó
(12,530ft)

San Isidro de El General

COSTA RICA

Dominical

60

Ujarrás

2

Buenos Aires

Cerro Kámuk
(11,657ft)▲

Cordillera de Talamanca

56

Ciudad Cortés

Palmar Norte

Paso Real

Río Cotón

66

Río General

Piedras Blancas

San Vito

Río Sereno

PANAMA

Isla del Caño

61

62

Rincón

63

Golfo Dulce

Ferry

63

62   Puerto Jiménez

Carate

Península de Osa

64   Golfito

Río Claro

65

Neily

Paso Canoas

David

Península Burica

Bahía de Coronado

RNVS **CAÑO NEGRO**

Life of the black lake

Wildlife highlights
One of the best wetland sites in Costa Rica. Abundant waterbirds, especially during winter when migratory duck congregations can be enormous. Very well-represented groups include kingfishers, herons, egrets, ibises and rails. Anhingas and Neotropic cormorants are extremely numerous. The only reliable Costa Rican site for Nicaraguan grackles and lesser yellow-headed vultures. Both sloths, white-faced capuchins, mantled howlers and proboscis bats are very common. Easily seen reptiles include spectacled caimans, green iguanas and striped basilisks.

LESS than 8mi (13km) by road from the Nicaraguan border, RNVS Caño Negro is part of a wetland chain that connects Costa Rica to Nicaragua's massive Lago de Nicaragua. The reserve's centerpiece is Lago Caño Negro, a shallow, freshwater lagoon that covers more than half of the reserve during summer. In the dry season, it shrinks to a network of smaller pools, providing winter refuge for a host of resident waterbirds and their migratory counterparts. Surrounded by seasonally inundated marshes and ribbons of riverine forest, a boat trip into Lago Caño Negro ensures constant bird activity and some close-up encounters with Costa Rica's more common mammals and reptiles.

Most people visit Caño Negro on organized tours, which depart from Los Chiles. In fact, these tours head down the Río Frío and most stop just short of the refuge's boundary, avoiding the park's entrance fee and hence contributing nothing to protecting it. Some are also entirely inappropriate for wildlife-watching: The boats are large and noisy with up to 50 people per trip and a few of the guides have the habit of trying to raise a response from anything sighted by whistling, yelling or, in some cases, chasing it. The Los Chiles option can be rewarding (the wildlife is essentially the same as inside the reserve), but be sure to ask about what you're getting. Alternatively, hire a local from the docks; you'll be guaranteed a far more peaceful wildlife experience and it encourages people in the community to protect the wildlife along the river.

Ducks almost unlimited

The alternative is to head to the tiny Caño Negro village where the park's HQ is based. It's less accessible than Los Chiles, but it ensures access to Lago Caño Negro, especially towards the end of the dry season when it's the focus for large congregations of winter migrants. **Muscovy ducks** are common, and flocks of **blue-winged teal** and **black-bellied whistling-ducks** number in the thousands. **Masked ducks** are visible year-round, but the dry season is best to see them in numbers. Likewise, all

Wild muscovy ducks – the progenitor of the common domestic breed – are easy to see during the dry season at Caño Negro.

four of Costa Rica's **ibis** family (not including the **white-faced ibis**, which is a vagrant) are resident, but they all move to the southern end of the lagoon as it dries up. From March to April head there to see dozens of **glossy, white** and **green ibises,** plus **roseate spoonbills** (this is also the best time and place for **limpkins** and **wood storks**). Caño Negro is excellent for **jabirus**, but not when most of the migrants are there; best seen during the summer, they usually leave before the start of the dry season to breed in PN Palo Verde (see pp 106–9) and further afield.

'Ticks' aplenty

Regardless of season, Caño Negro is host to a legion of permanent residents. All six Costa Rican **kingfishers** occur (**belted kingfishers** only between September and April) and herons are diverse and abundant. Expect **bare-throated tiger-herons, yellow-** and **black-crowned night-herons, boat-billed herons, cattle egrets, snowy egrets, green-backed herons, great blue herons, great egrets** and **little blue herons**; the numbers of some swell during the dry season, but all should be visible year-round. Caño Negro has Costa Rica's largest population of **Neotropic cormorants** and one of the largest of **anhingas**. (watch for the latter swimming with only their head and neck above the surface). Other likely 'ticks' on your list include **gray-necked wood-rails, northern jacanas, mangrove swallows, purple gallinules** and, with some luck, **sungrebes, spotted rails, gray-breasted crakes, least bitterns** and **pinnated bitterns**. **Great** and **common potoos** are common in the trees along the Río Frío, but you need hawk-eyes to spot one; local guides are nearly always successful, but if you're on your own drift along slowly and scan fairly high up on bare trunks or branches. Potoos are often in the open, but their intricate coloring and a motionless, upright posture can transform them into yet another dead branch.

This is also where you're most likely to see two local specialties – **Nicaraguan grackles** and **lesser yellow-headed vultures**. The former's range just creeps over the border from Nicaragua, and the vulture seems to have a dietary preference for dead fish and reptiles; both are very uncommon in Costa Rica away from the immediate area of the lagoon. Wetland-loving raptors are easy to spot overhead and include **snail kites, mangrove black-hawks, bay-winged hawks** and **black-collared hawks**, as well as occasional **peregrine falcons** during winter. Rare visitors, but best seen here in all of Costa Rica, **merlins** pass through between September and early November. The forested edge of the Río Frío is worthwhile habitat to search for **little tinamous, black-headed trogons, spot-breasted wrens, prothonotary warblers** and, in winter, **magnolia warblers**.

Green iguanas and **striped basilisks** are common and, in the lagoon, there are hundreds of **spectacled caimans**. **Mantled howler monkeys, white-faced capuchins** and both **sloth** species (but especially **Hoffmann's two-toed**) are the most common mammals; all of them are easier to spot along the Río Frío than at the lagoon. ■

Location 14mi (23km) south-west of Los Chiles.

Facilities Canoes and boats available for hire at nearby villages and park HQ. Walking trails seasonally (in the dry).

Accommodations Camping at park HQ; various accommodations in Caño Negro village and Los Chiles.

Wildlife rhythms The dry season is best for migrant birds and congregations are densest around March to April. Jabirus visit during the rainy season (August to December).

Contact SINAC (☎ 192; regional office (Los Chiles) ☎ 460-6484; fax 460-5615; e arayad@ns.minae.go.cr).

Watching tips
Scan the trunks of trees lining the water's edge for roosting proboscis bats lined up head-to-toe; it's thought the behavior mimics the vertical grooves of bark to confuse predators, and although they're common here, it certainly makes them difficult to spot.

PARQUE NACIONAL **CARARA**

Where dry meets wet

> **Wildlife highlights**
> Scarlet macaws are guaranteed and some of Costa Rica's largest American crocodiles. Over 400 bird species; especially visible and diverse groups include antbirds, parrots, trogons, manakins, herons and shorebirds. Nearby mangrove areas have high chances for yellow-headed caracaras, yellow-naped parrots and mangrove hummingbirds. White-tailed deer, red brockets, collared peccaries and Central American agoutis are easily seen on the trails and this is one of Costa Rica's better sites for tayras.

STRADDLING the transition between the dry forests of Costa Rica's northwest and the sodden rainforests of the southern Pacific lowlands, Carara is a biological melting pot of the two. Acacias intermingle with strangler figs, and cacti with kapoks, creating a heterogeneity of habitats with a wildlife blend to match. **White-tailed deer** occur alongside **red brockets**, and **fiery-billed aracaris**, **scarlet macaws** and **great tinamous** mix with **crested caracaras**, **white-fronted parrots** and **white-throated magpie-jays**. Surrounded by a sea of cultivation and livestock, it is also one of the few areas in the transition zone where wildlife finds sanctuary.

On the trail of tayras and trogons

There are only two trails in Carara. Close to the Río Grande de Tárcoles, the Sendero Laguna Meándrica is dominated by open, secondary forest punctuated with patches of dense, mature forest and wetlands. The mix makes for superb birding (even before the trail – elusive **orange billed sparrows** are common near the gate) and for constant activity, begin very early. Highlights include five **trogons** (including **Baird's**), **crimson-fronted parakeets**, **blue-headed parrots**, **golden-naped woodpeckers**, **rose-throated becards**, **gray-headed tanagers**, **long-tailed manakins** and abundant **rufous-tailed jacamars**. At least five species of **antbird** and **antshrike** are common; **black-faced antthrushes** are very confiding. Look out for **rufous-naped wrens** nesting in the bulls-horn acacias lining the road; pugnacious resident **acacia ants** that protect the tree from browsers also keep egg-predators at bay. Unusually, you can also see both **anis**: The **smooth-billed** is a Panamanian invader rapidly replacing the **groove-billed** in the region and Carara sits in the zone of overlap. About a mile along the trail, an oxbow of the Río Tárcoles forms a lagoon where, among others, **boat-billed herons** are very conspicuous; upwards of a dozen roost in the trees at the lookout. Birds aside, the wide trail also yields high visibility

White-tailed deer are common along the Sendero Laguna Meándrica.

of mammals; **red brockets**, **white-tailed deer**, **collared peccaries**, **Central American agoutis** and **tayras** regularly cross the road ahead of walkers.

The southern trail (actually two connected loops) takes in splendid primary forest which is, in fact, characteristic of most of the reserve. Chances are good here for **great tinamous**, **gray-headed chachalacas**, **blue-throated goldentails**, **riverside wrens**, **blue-crowned manakins**, and, at the second crossing of the Quebrada Bonita (there's a little bridge), **orange-collared manakins** lek and bathe in the creek. If you haven't already seen **scarlet macaws** by now, there's a superbly visible nest in a hollow dead tree about 330ft (100m) into the trail from the park HQ, between the first and second interpretive signs.

Croc encounters

Even without entering Carara, it's easy to see some of its most charismatic residents. Stop at the bridge over the Río Grande de Tárcoles and scan the sandbanks below for as many as 30 **American crocodiles**, including a few monsters (large crocodiles are now rare because of persecution and Carara is easily the best place in Costa Rica to see some old-timers). For really close-up encounters, various crocodile tours leave from Tárcoles. The tours are at least partly the reason the crocs are tolerated here, but they also hand-feed them (see 'Feeding wildlife' p 36, for a discussion of the problems arising from this activity).

Make sure you have binoculars to scan for birds. **Great blue** and **little blue herons**, and **great**, **cattle** and **snowy egrets** are common; and expect various waders including **black-necked stilts**, **lesser yellowlegs**, **semipalmated plovers** and **spotted** and **least sandpipers**. **Wilson's plovers** have their shallow nests in the sand here. At dawn and dusk, the bridge is directly in the path of a continuous, raucous procession of parrots. Commuting between their mangrove roosts at the river mouth and feeding sites inside the park, pairs of **scarlet macaws** are virtually guaranteed; the photo opportunities for flying macaws at eye-level are terrific. Other easily-seen species include **white-crowned parrots**, **red-lored parrots**, **mealy parrots** and large flocks of **orange-chinned parakeets**.

Minutes from Carara, two lodges provide high chances for additional species. Try Tarcol Lodge (☎ 297-4134, **e** mark@ranchonaturalista.com, **w** www.ranchonaturalista.com) at the mouth of the Río Tárcoles for **yellow-headed caracaras**, **mangrove swallows**, **yellow-naped parrots**, **mangrove hummingbirds**, **roseate spoonbills** and dozens of waders; resident numbers are swelled enormously by the arrival of migrants in November/December through to March; and **Pacific screech-owls** roost in the almond trees opposite the front gate. Villa Lapas (☎ 222-519, **e** info@villalapas.com, **w** www.villalapas.com) has a superb skywalk which, among other highlights, yields a direct view into a **kinkajou's** nest; occasionally the hole is occupied by a **Mexican porcupine**. ■

Location 55mi (88km) south of San Jose.
Facilities Trails, self-guided or guides can be arranged through park HQ.
Accommodations Camping is possible with prior permission at park HQ. Numerous lodges nearby and in Tárcoles village.
Wildlife rhythms The crocs are visible year-round, but best at low tide and during the dry season. Migratory shorebirds are most abundant in the winter (December to March), also when scarlet macaws and most other parrot species are nesting.
Contact SINAC (☎ 192; park HQ ☎ 383-9953; **e** raviles@ns.minae.go.cr).

> **Watching tips**
> About 14mi (22km) north of Carara on the Carretera Costanera Sur (National Route 3), Orotina town square virtually guarantees both roosting black-and-white owls and Hoffmann's two-toed sloths.

PARQUE NACIONAL **CHIRRIPÓ**
Costa Rica's zoological zenith

Wildlife highlights

Excellent for cloud forest and highland birds including resplendent quetzals, three-wattled bellbirds, highland tinamous and black guans. Andean-like páramo at the top guarantees volcano juncos, sooty robins, slaty finches and highland hummingbirds. Easily-seen mammals include Central American spider monkeys, white-faced capuchins and, at higher elevations, coyotes, endemic Dice's rabbits and occasional Baird's tapirs. Pumas use the savanna areas, but are extremely elusive. Unusual high-altitude reptiles – green spiny lizards and highland alligator lizards – are common.

An uncharacteristically flat section of the Sendero Principal; mostly it goes up!

Watching tips

Baird's tapirs gravitate to the various highland lagoons, mainly in the rainy season. Where the muddy edges show recent tracks, stake out the lagoon at dawn or dusk for a chance of seeing them. At night, coyotes visit the rubbish bins at Crestones Base.

COSTA Rica's mountainous spine runs the length of the country in four distinct cordilleras (ranges) of which the Cordillera de Talamanca is the highest, longest and most remote. Most of the Talamanca highlands are difficult to reach, but Costa Rica's highest peak, Cerro Chirripó at 12,530ft (3820m), is the focus for a much-visited national park. Like a tiny chunk of the Andes, at PN Chirripó rainforest gives way to temperate forests dominated by mountain oaks, fields of alpine bamboo and, at the very top, páramo (distinctive, cold-adapted vegetation, which resembles heath). Unique in Costa Rica, Chirripó is an entirely unexpected respite from the heat and humidity of the rainforest and is also the best place in the country to see the wildlife of the entire highland spectrum.

The only way up to Chirripó is by foot, and all the routes are long. Most hikers start at the park office in San Geraldo de Rivas and take the 8.5mi (14km) Sendero Principal to Crestones Base, the only accommodation near the top. You can also arrive from the north along the Sendero Herradura-Uran, a trip which takes four days and is undertaken only with guides – those from Costa Rica Trekking Adventures (☎ 771-4582, e trekking@racsa.co.cr) are Chirripó specialists and are outstanding.

Either way, the height gain is about 1.2mi (2km). In the first part of the hike, low-altitude cloud forest edged by encroaching fields and coffee plantations provides a mix of open habitat and rainforest wildlife. As you climb, numbers of **flame-colored tanagers, gray-capped flycatchers, blue-black grassquits** and the inevitable **cattle egrets** and **groove-billed anis** quickly drop off, to be replaced by highland specialties. Chances are good for **highland tinamous, black guans, green-crowned brilliants, three-wattled bellbirds, silvery-throated jays, buffy tuftedcheeks, mountain robins, black-faced solitaires** and **black-thighed grosbeaks. Emerald toucanets** are very common and **collared trogons** readily appear to imitations of their call, a descending *cow-ca* whistle (try at the Llano Bonito hut, about halfway up and also very good for **chestnut-capped brush-finches**). **Resplendent**

quetzals occur year-round, but are most abundant between March and May. Mixed flocks of **flame-throated warblers**, **collared redstarts** and **slate-throated redstarts** are often encountered, and coveys of **spotted wood-quails** cross the trail. **Central American spider monkeys**, **white-faced capuchins** and **red-tailed squirrels** are common and **tayras** are sometimes seen.

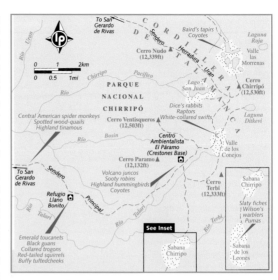

About 1.2mi (2km) from the Crestones Base, the oak forests suddenly open up – the result of successive fires. Dead trees are good for **woodpeckers** (including **acorn**, **hairy** and **golden-olive**), while **band-tailed pigeons** and flocks of **sulfur-winged parakeets** often fly over. This is also the last chance to see species whose range ends at the timberline; look for **timberline wrens**, and **peg-billed** and **large-footed finches**.

Crestones Base sits on a plateau covered by páramo proper, the northernmost stand of this freezing, tundra-like habitat anywhere in the Neotropics. Wildlife here is less diverse than on the lower elevations, but some high-altitude specialties are guaranteed. Abundant and tame **volcano juncos** sneak into the base to scrounge for crumbs, while slightly less confiding **sooty robins** are just as common outside. The red, tubular, bell-shaped flowers of deer potatoes attract highland **humming-birds** – **volcano**, **scintillant**, **fiery-throated** and **green violet-ears** – as well as **slaty flowerpiercers**, which puncture the base of the flowers for the nectar prize. Rare **slaty finches** can be spotted in the savanna areas while **Wilson's warblers** are notable for being the only winter migrant found regularly in páramo. Chirripó is just south of the extraordinary raptor migrations that see upwards of 2 million North American migrants flying along the Talamancas' Caribbean slope, but flocks of **red-tailed hawks**, **Swainson's hawks**, **broad-winged hawks** and **swallow-tailed kites** sometimes occur here. If you climb Cerro Chirripó, wildlife is sparse, but **white-collared swifts** hurtle about at 60mph (100 km/h) in the pounding wind.

Aside from birds, you'll see the only two reptiles that can live this high, **green spiny lizards** and **highland alligator lizards**; they're easily approached on sunny mornings. Mammals are scarce, but **coyotes** and their main prey, endemic **Dice's rabbits**, are abundant – you'll see the scats of both on the trails. Die-hards should stake out the Sabana de los Leones overnight for pumas, but the nights are freezing and you will be strongly discouraged unless you're with very experienced guides (Costa Rica Trekking Adventures works closely with the park authorities and can arrange this). ∎

Location 93mi (150km) south-east of San José.

Facilities Walking trails.

Accommodations Dorm-style rooms at Crestones Base; reservations essential. Be prepared for subzero temperatures and BYO food. Lodges and B&Bs in San Gerardo de Rivas.

Wildlife rhythms The rainiest period (September to November) is excellent for humming-bird and flowerpiercer activity. The dry (December to March) is the coldest season, but days are clear; this is the best time to catch nocturnal mammals on the move at dawn.

Contact SINAC (☎ 192; park office ☎ 770-8040; e cmcg@ns.minae.go.cr).

PARQUE NACIONAL **CORCOVADO**

Headland haven

Wildlife highlights

One of Costa Rica's finest sites, especially for mammals. Perhaps the only place in Central America where Baird's tapirs are virtually guaranteed. Northern tamanduas, red brockets, white-lipped peccaries and Central American squirrel monkeys are local specialties. Boasts the most recent record of possibly locally extinct giant ant-eaters. Three-toed sloths, Central American agoutis, mantled howlers and Central American spider monkeys are abundant, and chances are reasonable for kinkajous, crab-eating raccoons and tayras. Birdlife is extremely diverse and includes hard-to-miss scarlet macaws and very good chances for king vultures. Great curassows, fiery-billed aracaris, chestnut-mandibled toucans, turquoise cotingas and endemic black-cheeked ant-tanagers are other highlights.

PROJECTING into the Pacific like a bony thumb bent down towards Panama, the Península de Osa ranks among the wettest and most rugged of Costa Rica's lowlands. Until fairly recently it was also one of the most inaccessible, so the scourge of logging (and, particular to the area, gold-mining) arrived relatively late. With much of its original rainforest intact, the peninsula functions as the principal refuge for fauna of the southern Pacific coast, and PN Corcovado is its heart. Actually in two sections separated by the Golfo Dulce, access for tourists is restricted to the main sector on the peninsula proper where the spectacular wildlife includes many species whose northern range peters out here. Sirena Research Station is the goal of most wildlife-watchers, but however you see Corcovado, rest assured you'll return with a list of sightings difficult to surpass.

Destination Sirena

The best wildlife-watching in Corcovado is at Sirena, but you have to get there first. It's possible to fly or boat in (trips run from Bahía Drake and Puerto Jiménez), but most people hike in and are rarely disappointed. There are three trails, all of them long but not difficult. The best strategy is to take the better part of a day and spend much of it looking out for animals; the viewing on the hikes can be terrific. Two of the trails, from La Leona and San Pedrillo/Llorona, follow the coast and both alternate between coastal forest with scattered abandoned banana groves, and the beach itself. The trail from Los Patos passes through mature rainforest where the wildlife mix is rather different.

The coastal trails have two advantages: They're more open and the constant crashing of waves covers the sound of noisy walkers. **White-faced capuchins, red-tailed squirrels, collared peccaries, white-nosed coatis** and **northern tamanduas** are regularly seen on both, and more **pumas** have been spotted on the

Corcovado's rainforest grows right down to the coast and river edges – offering a rewarding window on its wildlife.

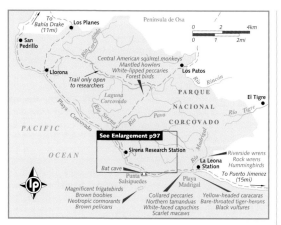

La Leona trail than anywhere else in the park (but sighting one is still a matter of enormous luck). Also on the La Leona trail, check the cave at Punta Salsipuedes for cave-roosting bats including occasional **greater fishing bats**; it's on the far side of the pebbly cove where the trail emerges onto the beach.

More so than mammals, the coastal trails produce an endless pageant of birds. **Scarlet macaws** are guaranteed; the tropical almond trees lining the coast are a favorite food. The various river crossings are good for **bare-throated tiger-herons**, **masked tityras** (especially Río Madrigal), and if you wade upriver a little (Teva-style sandals are useful), **riverside wrens**, **black-bellied wrens** and **charming hummingbirds**. When the tide is receding, **yellow-headed caracaras** routinely patrol the river mouths for fish caught in the shallow stretches.

The sections along the beach (bring sunscreen and drinking water) produce **mangrove black-hawks** by the dozen and numerous waterbird species, especially **magnificent frigatebirds**, **brown pelicans**, **Neotropic cormorants** and the occasional **great blue heron** combing the rock pools. The little rock island opposite Salsipuedes serves as a roost for hundreds of **magnificent frigatebirds** and **brown boobies**. Be sure to look overhead from time to time; among ubiquitous **black** and **turkey vultures**, Corcovado's beaches are excellent places to scan for thermaling **king vultures**.

Real rainforest fans should take the Los Patos trail. Lowland rainforest birds such as **great curassows**, **chestnut-mandibled toucans**, **fiery-billed aracaris**, **turquoise cotingas**, **rufous pihas**, **trogons** (including Baird's), **hummingbirds** and **woodcreepers** (**tawny-winged** is a local specialty) are plentiful; of course, many of these are also seen on the coastal trails. Encounters with mixed flocks are common and include species like **white-throated shrike-tanagers**, **white-shouldered tanagers**, **black-hooded antshrikes**, **great antshrikes**, **chestnut-backed antbirds** and, with some luck, endemic **black-cheeked ant-tanagers**. Mammals commonly sighted on the trail are similar to those on the coastal trails, but Los Patos is better for **primates** and **white-lipped peccaries**. Extremely unlikely but theoretically possible,

Location 205mi (330km) southeast from San José.
Facilities Walking trails, canoes for hire.
Accommodations Camping and dorm-style rooms at Sirena. Excellent, inexpensive meals can be bought here and the park actually makes a small but important profit if you buy food rather than bring in your own.
Wildlife rhythms Corcovado is very wet; the drier period (January to April) is better for exploring and for birdlife (when migrant species are present and it's less windy, so birds tend to be more visibly active). If you do visit in the wet, the start of the season (May to June) is when numerous trees fruit, attracting frugivorous birds and mammals.
Contact SINAC (☎ 192; regional office (Puerto Jiminez) ☎ 735-5036; fax 735-5276; e lbarquer@ns.minae.go.cr).

Endemic to Costa Rica's Pacific coast, granular poison-dart frogs are common along Corcovado's streams.

you might even see a **giant anteater**. Perhaps now extinct in Costa Rica, the last definite record was on the Los Patos trail in 1997; report it if you defy the odds!

For wildlifers frustrated at the difficulty of seeing rainforest mammals, a stay at Sirena Research Station is a must. The continual presence of researchers has habituated many customarily shy species to the comings and goings of people, and it makes mammal-spotting uncommonly easy. Topping the list, **Baird's tapirs** are practically assured. The airstrip after dusk pays off at least once daily and there is a little swamp favored by tapirs on Sendero Sirena just before the beach. Remarkably for such a normally elusive creature, tapirs are also seen on the beach itself during the day. They snooze under the overhanging vegetation at the high tidemark and occasionally even venture into the surf to defecate; it's a common tapir habit, ordinarily restricted to freshwater ponds where it may play a role in tapir communication.

Sirena is excellent for other herbivores, particularly **red brockets** (easily seen on Sendero Sirena) and both species of **peccaries**. The widespread **collared peccary** is outnumbered here by its rarer and larger cousin, the **white-lipped**, which is easy to see on Senderos Sirena, Los Espaveles and Guanacaste. Collared peccaries are often seen near the lagoon on Sendero Olla, but they're more likely to be spotted closer to La Leona and Los Patos. No matter where you are, **Central American agoutis** are abundant.

The profusion of meat on the hoof means there are predators aplenty, but unfortunately, they're not nearly as confiding. Sirena falls into a number of different **jaguars'** home ranges and at least one male and one female regularly include the airstrip in their territorial rounds; very early morning (midnight to 4am) walks by flashlight might be lucky. More likely to be seen while spotlighting at night are **kinkajous**, **striped hog-nosed skunks** (uncommon, but sometimes on the airstrip) and **crab-eating raccoons**, which in Costa Rica occur only on the Pacific coast and the extreme southern Caribbean coast; they're best seen around the mouth of the Río Sirena. **Ocelots** are probably your best chance for observing a cat but, again, they're difficult; most sightings have occurred on Sendero Olla, which is also good for **tayras** (the latter usually seen by day).

Poison darts and harmless rockets

Traversed by many streams and rivers, Corcovado is a hotspot for exquisitely beautiful poison-dart frogs. Two species here, the granular poison-dart frog and the Golfo Dulce poison-dart frog, are Costa Rican endemics and, indeed, the latter occurs only in and around Corcovado. A search of the leaf litter in the streams near Sirena readily turns up both species, as well as the more widespread green-and-black poison-dart frog. You might also find some other members of the family that have one important difference: they're not poisonous. Called rocket frogs because of their habit of launching themselves into streams when disturbed, they are essentially poison-dart frogs without the poisonous punch. Why the difference? It probably arises from their diets. Poison-dart frogs have a diet dominated by ants, very rich in alkaloids, which are thought to give rise to their formidable defenses. Rocket frogs also eat ants, but in far lower quantities and rely instead on their astounding leaps to escape predation. They also lack the dazzling warning colors of their toxic cousins, but it's safer (and kinder to the frog) to observe, rather than handle, any species you encounter.

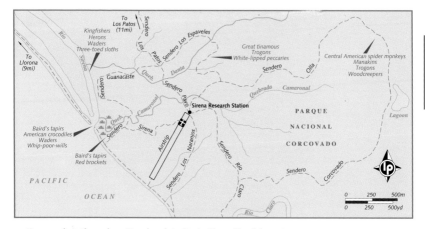

Corcovado is the only national park in Costa Rica with all four of the country's primate species. **Central American spider monkeys** are the most common monkey in the park (in contrast to virtually everywhere else in Costa Rica) and, along with **mantled howlers** and **white-faced capuchins**, can be encountered anywhere. Sendero Sirena is best for the fourth and most endangered species, the **Central American squirrel monkey**. Despite their status, they're easy to see here and are terrifically indifferent to observers, even within touching distance (but don't – they bite). Try Senderos Los Naranjos, Sirena, Los Espaveles and Guanacaste or walk a couple of miles along the trail to Los Patos.

Finally, for the mammalogist who has everything, Sirena has fair chances for the extremely hard-to-find **silky anteater**. Known in Spanish as the 'banana-tree angel' (serafín del platanar), they're reported with unusual regularity from the forests along the beach between the Río Claro and the station. Strictly nocturnal, silky anteaters spend the day curled up high in the treetops where they're essentially impossible to see; go spotlighting for a chance of finding one.

Of course, there is also plenty on show for birdwatchers at Sirena. The hike in will already have yielded an impressive list, but the trails around the research station are particularly good for **crested guans**, **spectacled antpittas**, **manakins** (**red-capped**, **orange-collared**, **thrushlike** and **blue-crowned**), **golden-naped woodpeckers** and very tame **great tinamou**. Less easily seen, but reasonably regular, are **red-breasted blackbirds**, **marbled wood-quails** and **red-throated caracaras**. Rehabilitated **scarlet macaws** and **chestnut-mandibled toucans** sometimes visit the station; if not, you can depend on seeing these species almost anywhere in the park. Night-walks reveal **black-and-white** and **spectacled owls** and, resting in the sand on the beach, **whip-poor-wills**. Take to the Río Sirena (canoes can be hired) for **kingfishers** (mainly **green** and **ringed**), **little blue**, **great blue**, **green** and **tricolored herons**, **bare-throated tiger-herons**, **snowy egrets**, waders including **ruddy turnstones** and **western sandpipers**, and common **gray-headed kites**. **American crocodiles** and **brown-throated three-toed sloths** are other riverside regulars. ∎

Watching tips

The abundant banana trees along the coastal trails are not indigenous to Corcovado (bananas are Asian in origin), but they can be magnets for wildlife because many animals eat them, including swarms of hermit crabs on fallen fruit. Look closer at the hanging leaves for tiny tenants: Rufous-tailed hummingbirds build their nests under overhanging banana leaves at the eastern end of La Leona trail and common tent-making bats and Thomas' fruit-eating bats snip the supporting veins of the leaves to create their awning-like tents.

ESTACIÓN BIOLÓGICA **LA SELVA**
Rain with patches of brilliance

Wildlife highlights
Intensely-studied lowland rainforest and adjoining secondary growth with a superb trail network and facilities for researchers. Bird highlights among more than 435 recorded species include three-wattled bellbirds, bare-necked umbrellabirds and great curassows; toucans and Montezuma's oropendolas common. Mantled howler monkeys, white-faced capuchins and Central American spider monkeys are all usually easy to see; collared peccaries abundant, tayras and Neotropical river otters seen regularly and ocelot sightings a possibility; 115 mammals known to occur.

APART from an excellent system of national parks, Costa Rica boasts a number of private reserves that also play an important role in preserving the country's biodiversity. La Selva is a research station run by the Organisation for Tropical Studies (OTS) where wildlife and habitats have been protected since the 1950s. Apart from being a first-rate birding destination, La Selva is contiguous with PN Braulio Carrillo and forms its northern extension; together the reserves protect a peninsula of lowland forest jutting into a sea of agriculture. PN Braulio Carrillo is a magnificent tract of forest just outside San José that is well worth exploring in its own right, especially for birds, but there is a high overlap in diversity between the two reserves and La Selva is featured here as an example of a successful private reserve (see the Resource Guide for other listings). Allowing visitors to La Selva is part of the station's philosophy, but access is strictly limited and by permission only, and researchers take priority for facilities at all times.

Heavy rain can fall at any time of year, but when the clouds roll back you won't have to go far to see birds and could easily spend a productive morning or afternoon birding around La Selva's admin center. **Scarlet-rumped** and **golden-hooded tanagers**, **banded-backed wrens** and **rufous-tailed hummingbirds** work the bushes around the reception area; **turkey** and **black vultures** glide overhead and **semiplumbeous hawks** often perch quietly near the bridge. **Montezuma's oropendolas** and **white-necked jacobins** frequent the fig trees back down the entrance road just beyond the guard post (the oropendolas are easily located by their call). **Central American agoutis** are common – try the edge of the small playing field by the river – and a handsome black-and-russet race of the **variegated squirrel** can often be seen in trees around the admin centre. Among the accommodation blocks you should see ground-feeders, such as **gray-chested doves, clay-colored robins** and **white-throated thrushes**; and **white-collared manakins** are usually in the low vegetation behind the Tortuga dormitory. **Rainbow-billed** and

La Selva's collared peccaries are very tame, but be cautious about approaching too closely.

Watching tips
Don't fret if a guided bird walk doesn't take you deep into the forest: There's usually excellent bird action around the admin centre and birds can be few and far between in primary forest.

chestnut-mandibled toucans are common in trees around the compound, while the daily procession of parrots overhead can include **white-crowned**, **brown-hooded** and **mealy parrots**, and fast-flying flocks of **orange-chinned parakeets**. **Three-wattled bellbirds** call tantalisingly from behind the patch of forest behind the accommodation blocks, but can be difficult to see – scan over the fence to the treetops in the adjoining property and be prepared to wait for one to show. Look for **great antshrikes**, **squirrel cuckoos** and **white-collared manakins** in the forest fringing Río Puerto Viejo and the webs of large **orb-weaving spiders** spanning the

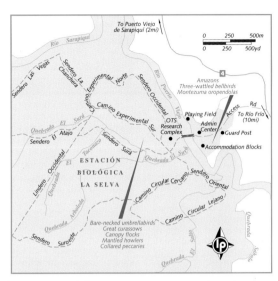

supports on the suspension bridge. Scan up and downstream for **spectacled caimans** and **black river turtles** that have hauled out onto logs; **Neotropical river otters** are also sometimes seen from the bridge, particularly late in the afternoon.

Guided birdwatching walks normally take visitors into the superb primary and secondary forest over Río Puerto Viejo. **Bird feeding flocks** often move through the OTS research complex, and **great curassows** and **tayras** sometimes wander into this area. Beyond the complex the forest is contiguous with PN Braulio Carrillo – you will experience some of this forest on a guided walk, during which you stand a good chance of encountering many of La Selva's birds, mammals and herps.

Mantled howlers are the most abundant primate – there are an estimated seven to 12 troops at La Selva – and some are usually encountered along the trails (from which you must never stray). **Central American spider monkeys** and **white-faced capuchins** are not so common, but the former can often be seen along Surá trail and the capuchins near Pantano Cantarrana. La Selva is also a great place to see **collared peccaries** at close range – they are common on Sendero Surá – and both **two-toed** and **three-toed sloths** are present, although the latter is more abundant; sightings in *Cecropia* trees near the admin centre are not unusual. **Coatis** are also common and La Selva's mammal fauna is rich so expect the unexpected – an **ocelot** was seen crossing the bridge one morning!

By wandering along the access road at night with a flashlight there's a chance of seeing a **striped hog-nosed skunk** (one has been seen regularly near the admin centre) and **pacas** (usually near the river in the dead of night). Other possibilities include **kinkajous**, **opossums** and nocturnal birds such as **vermiculated screech-owls**. Remember to wear protective footwear when walking around at night – poisonous snakes such as **fer-de-lances** are not uncommon. ■

Location 40 miles (60km) north-east of San José; 2 miles (3km) south of Puerto Viejo de Sarapiquí.

Facilities Marked trails, trained guides, self-guiding nature trail, visitor's center, bookshop.

Accommodations Dorms, cabins (no camping) and meals available for a fee by arrangement (see contact details below).

Wildlife rhythms Three-wattled bellbirds and bare-necked umbrellabirds are best sought during the dry season, when a dropping river level also makes for easier viewing of otters, caimans and turtles.

Contact Estación Biológica La Selva (☎ 240-6696; fax 240-6783; **e** nat-hist@ots.ac.cr; **w** www.ots.ac.cr) All arrivals must check in at Reception.

PARQUE NACIONAL **MANUEL ANTONIO**

A gentle introduction to paradise

Wildlife highlights
Excellent Pacific slope forest with some highly visible mammals and good introductory birding. White-faced capuchins are almost guaranteed, mantled howlers are common and this is one of the best places in Costa Rica for Central American squirrel monkeys. Several Costa Rica/Panama endemic birds, such as fiery-billed aracaris and riverside wrens, are readily seen among 270 recorded species, and brown pelicans and brown boobies nest on offshore islets. Large lizards – ctenosaurs, green iguanas and basilisks – are a specialty and humpback whales are sometimes seen in season.

FORESTED headlands and gently sloping beaches give Manuel Antonio an idyllic setting and it is understandably popular with visitors. In fact, tourism pressure has forced the park authorities to close the park on Mondays and restrict daily visitor numbers. The gates open at 7am and you are advised to queue up early to get the most of wildlife-watching opportunities; alternatively you could visit Manuel Antonio during the wet season and avoid the crowds. But easy access, well-marked trails and some eminently watchable mammals – including the endangered **Central American squirrel monkey** – amply repay a visit by even a seasoned wildlifer. Trained guides are available at the entrance, and although not compulsory, they are an asset for finding animals and you'll also support a local industry.

Visitor pressure means that all comers are funneled along the main access road, but you should have no trouble seeing animals along here and even as you queue up at the gate. **White-faced capuchins** are very used to people and normally troops feed and interact within a short distance of visitors – they could be encountered anywhere along the main access road and around Playa Manuel Antonio. You'll probably hear **mantled howler monkeys** soon after sunrise and, like the capuchins, they could be seen virtually anywhere inside the park and even along the road to Quepos – watch for them crossing the monkey bridges that a local conservation group has erected. **Central American agoutis**, **white-nosed coatis** and both **three-toed** and **two-toed sloths** are common and could be encountered along any trail (the guides are good at spotting sloths – you probably won't have any trouble seeing agoutis or coatis yourself). However, the movements of the park's star animal and Central America's rarest primate – the **Central American squirrel monkey** – are far less predictable. These attractive monkeys are more retiring than the capuchins and, although they might be seen near the park entrance in the early morning, they usually melt into the forest well before opening time. With luck a troop

Safe beaches backed by forested headlands with some easily-seen wildlife make PN Manuel Antonio a popular destination.

could be encountered during a morning's walk, and they often reappear in beachside trees and on the fringes of Manuel Antonio township in the early evening. Lucky encounters in the park itself could include a **northern tamandua**, and with a guide you'll have a good chance of seeing one or two **bat** species – especially **proboscis bats** – clinging to tree trunks near the trails. And cetacean-watchers should also head for Manuel Antonio – **pantropical spotted** and **bottlenose dolphins** are seen by tour operators most

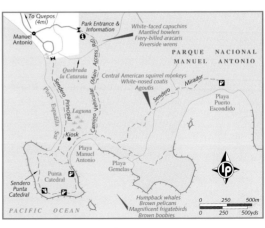

months, and **humpback whales** pass through on their regular migration route; other possibilities include **orcas** (killer whales) and **false killers** (both rare in these waters), and **rough-toothed dolphins**.

Manuel Antonio is not usually on the serious birders' trail of Costa Rica, especially because camping is now prohibited in the park (and therefore spotlighting and dawn birding are not possible). However, the bird list is respectable and a few Costa Rica/Panama specialties may be seen here. The usual suspects – **blue-gray** and **palm tanagers**, **great-tailed grackles**, **bananaquits** and **blue dancises** – loiter near the kiosk and park entrance. Canopy flocks should contain **scarlet-rumped** and **golden-hooded tanagers**; common representatives of Neotropical families include 15 different types of **hummingbird**; and watch for **double-toothed kites** feeding in association with **white-faced capuchin** troops. Among the regional endemics, keep a lookout for **fiery-billed aracaris** near the park entrance; **riverside wrens** fossicking near the first creek crossing along the main access road; **black-hooded antshrikes** are common in trailside vegetation; and **Baird's trogons** are occasionally reported. **Black-bellied whistling-ducks** often perch on exposed branches overlooking the vegetation-choked lagoon behind the kiosk area; it's hard to get a look into the lagoon, but herons, such as **yellow-crowned night-herons**, roost in trees around the edge. Out to sea you should have no trouble seeing **brown pelicans**, **magnificent frigatebirds** and **brown boobies**. Look in the mangroves lining the creek between Playa Espadilla Sur and the camp site in Manuel Antonio township for **spotted sandpipers**, **green herons** and **ringed kingfishers**. **Crab-eating raccoons** frequent these mangroves, and **northern raccoons** can often be seen loitering near camp sites at night.

Big lizards are something of a feature at Manuel Antonio: It's hard to miss the large **ctenosaurs** and **green iguanas** that bask near the kiosk at Playa Manuel Antonio and in the vegetation behind Playa Espadilla Sur. But the rustle of leaves is sometimes the best clue to locating the well-camouflaged **basilisks** that are also abundant, especially near the lagoon. ■

Location 170mi (275km) southeast of San José; 4mi (7km) south of Quepos.
Facilities Trail network, trained guides.
Accommodations Wide range, including camping, available in Manuel Antonio township. Note that camping is no longer permitted in the park itself.
Wildlife rhythms Humpback whales may be seen offshore between January and April, orcas are best sought March to April and rough-toothed dolphins are commonest May to July.
Contact Visitor center (☎ 777-0644; fax 777-0654).

Watching tips
Please don't feed the monkeys! Avoid the temptation to share your lunch with monkeys (or coatis) – it can cause long-term health problems for the animals and may end in a nasty bite for you.

MONTEVERDE

The Green Mountain

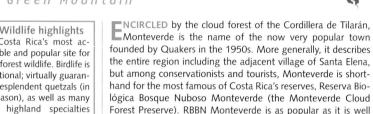

Wildlife highlights
Costa Rica's most accessible and popular site for cloud forest wildlife. Birdlife is exceptional; virtually guaranteed resplendent quetzals (in the season), as well as many other highland specialties such as black guans, bareshanked screech-owls, threewattled bellbirds, emerald toucanets and orange-bellied trogons. Hummingbirds are very visible, especially at the Hummingbird Gallery, which offers excellent photo opportunities. Mammals include easily-seen mantled howlers, white-nosed coatis, Central American agoutis, Alfaro's pygmy squirrels and variegated squirrels. Less often seen attractions include olingos, kinkajous and margays. About 750 species of butterfly occur, showcased at the Butterfly Garden.

ENCIRCLED by the cloud forest of the Cordillera de Tilarán, Monteverde is the name of the now very popular town founded by Quakers in the 1950s. More generally, it describes the entire region including the adjacent village of Santa Elena, but among conservationists and tourists, Monteverde is shorthand for the most famous of Costa Rica's reserves, Reserva Biológica Bosque Nuboso Monteverde (the Monteverde Cloud Forest Preserve). RBBN Monteverde is as popular as it is well known, and as one of the most accessible parks of the region it is visited by thousands of people each year. Few depart disappointed, but it is merely one of many rewarding options here for wildlifers wishing to see the fauna of the cloud forest.

RBBN Monteverde

Privately owned by the Centro Científico Tropical (Tropical Science Center, a Costa Rican non-government organization), the RBBN Monteverde soared to international renown following a 1983 feature in *National Geographic* magazine. The article and a subsequent documentary established Monteverde as *the* place to view one of Central America's most flamboyant birds, the **resplendent quetzal**, and with good timing you don't need to venture far into the reserve to see one. Only 800ft (250m) into the Sendero Bosque Nuboso, there's a viewing platform overlooking much sought-after quetzal food – a wild avocado tree. Quetzals are 'altitudinal migrants', moving up and down mountainsides as different tree species produce their fruit, and they arrive in Monteverde from about December onwards. When the crop of wild avocados is at its greatest in April and May, they breed here – the best time to view them; by July they'll have moved to lower elevations. If you can't locate a quetzal on your own (the benches along El Camino are also very good), Monteverde's guides are excellent. They've organized themselves into a local association (Asociación Guías de Monteverde) with photo IDs, and apart from quetzals, they're invaluable for finding and identifying dozens of other birds. The park office or any hotel in the region can arrange an accredited

RBBN Monteverde's trails are among the most accessible and best-maintained in the country.

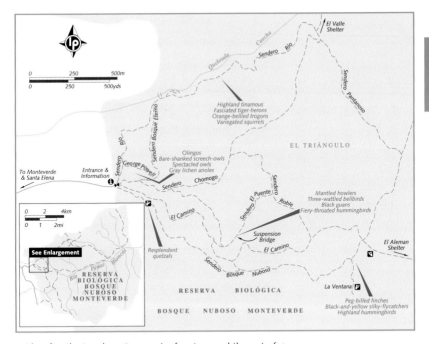

guide; after the two-hour tour you're free to spend the rest of the day on your own.

Monteverde's birds are definitely the main attraction with almost 400 species recorded from El Triángulo alone; this is the reserve's main tourist area and although it can be busy, it's very rewarding. Specials include **highland tinamous** (easiest to spot from March to August), **black guans, emerald toucanets, fiery-throated hummingbirds, orange-bellied trogons** and **three-wattled bellbirds** (try for the latter from March to July). Mixed flocks are common and typically include species such as **common bush-tanagers, spangled-cheeked tanagers, brown-billed scythebills, spotted woodcreepers, three-striped warblers** and **gray-breasted wood-wrens**. At the top of Sendero Bosque Nuboso where it heads to La Ventana lookout, wind-battered elfin forest is home to **peg-billed finches** and **black-and-yellow silky-flycatchers**.

For mammal-watchers, the cloud forest's often-limited visibility makes for difficult work, but **white-nosed coatis, mantled howlers** (especially in the valley spanned by Sendero El Puente's suspension bridge) and **Central American agoutis** are common. **Alfaro's pygmy squirrels** are fairly easy to spot and **variegated squirrels** occur in two forms here, a striking tricolored variant in grizzled gray and russet separated by a cream band (common and tame at Monteverde Lodge; see **W** www.costaricaexpedi tions.com), and an all-black morph more often seen in the reserve. RBBN Monteverde also offers excellent guided night-walks (simply turn up at the gate at 8pm and pay the fee) that occasionally turns up **kinkajous** and holds even better chances for their less common relatives, **olingos**. Senderos George Powell and Bosque Eterno produce the most olingo sightings, perhaps because this is the area where Monteverde resident and photographer Michael Fogden released a tame female he'd raised; the story goes she spawned generations of olingos a little less shy than normal because she sometimes returned to Michael's home for a visit with her offspring. More likely than tame olingos, the night-walks also reveal dozens of smaller fry including **gray lichen anoles** and **orange-kneed tarantulas**, as well as close-up views of sleeping birds and occasional nocturnal specials like **bare-shanked screech-owls** and **spectacled owls** (both most often seen near the reserve gate). Bring your own flashlight for the best views.

Contact: Tropical Science Center (☎ 645-5122; fax 645-5034; e montever@sol.racsa.co.cr)

Bosque Eterno de Los Niños

So-named because money raised by schoolchildren from around the word purchased the land, Bosque Eterno de Los Niños (the Children's Eternal Rainforest) wraps around the better-known RBBN Monteverde, providing a critical connection to the forests of the Caribbean slopes and the Arenal Conservation Area. The wildlife is essentially the same, but it's far less busy than the Cloud Forest Preserve. There is also a greater chance of picking up more species; the most accessible sector, Bajo del Tigre, sits in a transition zone between the lowlands and the forested edge of the Monteverde Plateau where **gray-headed chachalacas, spot-bellied bobwhites, orange-fronted parakeets, lesser ground-cuckoos**, **ruby-throated hummingbirds** and **rufous-capped warblers** can be spotted. Commonly seen mammals are those species conspicuous in the RBBN Monteverde, but night-walks also encounter the occasional **coyote, gray fox, striped hog-nosed skunk** and, for the very lucky, **margays**. Bajo del Tigre has a well laid-out trail system and is open to walk-in visitors. There are also two rustic stations, which make excellent bases from which to explore the reserve. Estación Poco Sol has marvelous highland hikes and San Gerardo overlooks Volcán Arenal. Both have accommodations; reservations are essential. The private owner of the reserve, the Monteverde Conservation League, accepts volunteers at the stations.

Contact: Monteverde Conservation League (☎ 645-5003; fax 645-5104; e acmmcl@sol.racsa.co.cr)

Hummingbird feeders

The Hummingbird Gallery is perhaps the best known of such feeding stations, but virtually all hotels and lodges in the region have feeders and the effect on wildlife may not be all benign. Feeders which are not regularly cleaned occasionally infect hummingbirds with a tongue-rotting fungus and they also bring about artificially high numbers of birds competing for access. Very high levels of aggression are obvious at the feeders (violet sabrewings are the worst offenders), although having said that, there's no indication the endless dogfights are causing injuries or long-term health problems. On a larger scale, but so far unmeasured, the question has to be asked: With so many hummers and other nectivores visiting the feeders, are they still acting effectively as pollinators?

Reserva Bosque Nuboso Santa Elena

Straddling the continental divide, the Santa Elena Reserve (as it's usually called) has 8mi (13km) of trails, some of which provide views of Volcán Arenal on a clear day. You can also climb an excellent observation tower which, at 36ft (11m) high, rises above the canopy and is superb for birding. Many of the most charismatic forest species are easily seen here as they move about at treetop level; **black guans**, **barred forest-falcons**, **collared forest-falcons**, **resplendent quetzals** (January to July), **three-wattled bellbirds** (January to July) and **azure-hooded jays** are among the many species commonly seen on-the-wing. You can explore the trails on your own and or else take one of the very worthwhile guided tours which leave three times daily (7:30am and 11:30am, and the terrific night-tour at 7pm). Reserva Santa Elena offers volunteer opportunities for all ages, but is particularly rewarding for students.
Contact: ☎/*fax 645-5390;* **e** *reserve@monteverdeinfo.com,* **e** *rbnctpse@racsa.co.cr*

El Jardín de Mariposas

Monteverde has around 750 butterfly species and El Jardín de Mariposas (The Butterfly Garden) is one of the best ways to learn about them. Founded by tropical biologist, Jim Wolfe, the center's guided tours take you through all stages of a butterfly's short life cycle (most live only a month) and then proceed to four greenhouses, each representing a different habitat and each with its distinctive butterfly species. **Crackers, glasswings, zebra longwings, consul leaf mimics, postmen** and **owl butterflies** are just a few of the species on display and the photo opportunities are terrific; this is perhaps your best chance at shooting **blue morphos** if you're fast – they invariably close their dazzling wings the moment they alight. The center also has an intricate **leafcutter ant** display and interpretive gardens that explain the importance of various plant species to wildlife and people. Jim accepts and trains volunteers to work in the center.
Contact: ☎/*fax 645-5512;* **e** *wolfej@sol.racsa.co.cr;* **w** *mariposa.best.vwh.net*

The Hummingbird Gallery

For guaranteed views of some of Monteverde's 26 species of hummingbird, the Hummingbird Gallery is impossible to beat. Just outside the entrance to RBBN Monteverde, the Galley has banks of hummingbird feeders that attract dozens of **green violet-ears**, **violet sabrewings**, **green-crowned brilliants**, **purple-throated mountain-gems**, **striped-tailed hummingbirds**, **coppery-headed emeralds** and **magenta-throated woodstars**, as well as very tame **bananaquits**. As dusk falls, nectar-eating bats such as **brown long-tongued bats**, **orange nectar bats** and **Handley's hairy-legged bats** visit the feeders and **olingos** sometimes raid them late at night. There is undeniable appeal in the feeders and they provide terrific opportunities for photos, but some Monteverde residents are concerned with their proliferation (see the boxed text opposite).
Contact: ☎ *645-5030; fax 645-5034;* **e** *montever@sol.racsa.co.cr* ∎

RBBN Monteverde was originally established for the golden toad, but it's probably now extinct – see the Wildlife Gallery p 213 for details.

PARQUE NACIONAL **PALO VERDE**
Wetland sanctuary

Wildlife highlights
Costa Rica's largest wetland and the country's most important site for congregations of water-associated birds. Dry season flocks of numerous ducks number in the thousands. Many species have their largest breeding populations here, including jabirus. In total, 280 species of birds, including a number restricted to the dry northwest. Easily visible mammals include white-tailed deer, collared peccaries, white-faced capuchins, white-faced coatis and two species of armadillo. Probably Costa Rica's best site for jaguarundis. The southern limit of many reptiles including Neotropical sunbeam snakes, rose-bellied spiny lizards and Central American banded geckoes.

LOCATED where two ancient basins intersect at their lowest points, Palo Verde is an enormous natural sink in Costa Rica's driest province. All the major rivers of the region drain into the park, transforming it into a flooded mosaic of lagoons and marshes in the rainy season and, more significantly for wildlife, a watery refuge in the dry; while the rest of the drought-prone region bakes, Palo Verde's water endures. Drawing in birds from the parched Guanacaste uplands and furnishing crucial winter habitat for long-distance migrants from both north and south, the dry season congregations of many species are the largest in Costa Rica. For some, Palo Verde is the only nesting site in the country. Surrounded by limestone hills, mangrove islands, floodplain savannas and a mix of dry and evergreen forests, Palo Verde's shallow, permanent lagoons act as irresistible focal points for both wildlife and wildlife-watching.

Colossal waterbird congregations
Palo Verde's birdlife is abundant and diverse year-round, but the best viewing begins around January. By then, the dry season is well under way and Costa Rica's largest breeding population of **jabirus** have begun building their massive platform nests in the dead trees around the lagoon edge; the rangers sometimes take people to see the nests, but jabirus are often visible flying over the lagoon with beaks full of sticks; the La Roca lookout and wetland tower are good. The tower is also the best place to see **black-bellied whistling ducks** and **blue-winged teal** in the tens of thousands, and smaller numbers of **muscovy ducks, fulvous whistling ducks, American wigeons, northern pintails, northern shovelers, ring-necked ducks, lesser scaups** and **masked ducks**. Look closely among the blue-winged teal flocks for the occasional **cinnamon teal**, and although they're now very rare in Costa Rica, Palo Verde holds the best chances for **white-faced whistling ducks**. If there's nothing much happening at the main lagoon, be sure to visit Laguna Varillal to the west of park HQ (the route can be unclear – ask the rangers).

A view of the Palo Verde lagoon during the dry season.

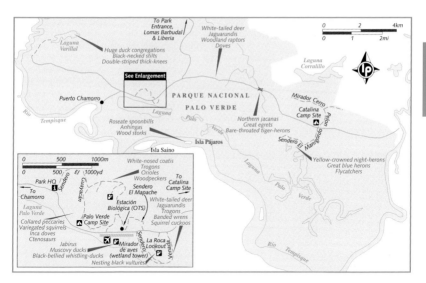

Many of the duck species congregate here before heading to the Palo Verde lagoon when Varillal dries up by February. Varillal is also excellent for **black-necked stilts** in the hundreds, **double-striped thick-knees** and **northern jacanas**. Be sure to scan the edges of the lagoons (Varillal or Palo Verde) for **spotted rails**, **yellow-breasted crakes** and **American coots**.

The lagoons also produce a regular procession of water-associated raptors. Many of them are difficult to see elsewhere in Costa Rica, especially **hook-billed kites**, **snail kites**, **crane hawks**, **black-collared hawks** and **gray hawks**. **Ospreys** are common, while **white-tailed hawks** and all four **vulture** species thermal over the flat floodplain; La Roca lookout provides an excellent vantage point to scan for **king vultures** and the rarest species here, the **lesser yellow-headed vulture**. Raptor lovers should use walk or drive (slowly) along the two main roads; many short-winged hawk species treat them as hunting expressways and it's possible to see numerous species on a single pass; **mangrove black-hawks**, **broad-winged hawks**, **roadside hawks** and **short-tailed hawks** are common, and keep an eye out for **laughing falcons** and **collared forest falcons**. The main roads are also excellent for doves and pigeons; 11 species occur here including **red-billed pigeons**, **common ground-doves**, **plain-breasted ground-doves** and **white-winged doves**. **Inca doves** are abundant and nest next to the headquarters.

From river to road

For nest-side views of many species you'll see at the lagoons, take a boat trip along the Río Tempisque (easily arranged at the park headquarters; it's the same price for up to four people, so try to get a group together). The goal and highlight of the trip is a stop at Isla Pajaros (Bird Island), a tiny mangrove clump where many species build their nests. Entirely indifferent to boat-based observers, nesting **roseate spoonbills**, **white ibises**,

Location 32mi (52km) southwest of Liberia.

Facilities Walking trails, lookout points, observation tower, boat-trips.

Accommodation Camping and basic dorms at Park HQ. It's possible also to camp at Catalina though it's abandoned and rather derelict. OTS has an excellent research station with dorms and cabanas.

Wildlife rhythms The dry season is definitely the best for visibility and for bird congregations; March and April are the driest months. On Isla Pájaros, most species nest during the dry season. The rainy season is June-November.

Contact SINAC (☎ 192 or Regional office (Bagaces); ☎ 671-1290; fax 671-1062; **e** jicaro@ns.minae.go.cr; OTS, ☎ 240-6696 or USA 919-984-5774, **e** pverde@ots.ac.cr

glossy ibises, anhingas, wood storks, Neotropic cormorants and a few heron species are on show in spectacular close-up. Clouds of black and turkey vultures wheel constantly over the island looking for dead chicks, and boa constrictors are astonishingly common. In the dry season, a trail from park HQ leads to the river bank north of the island, but most of the nesting action is on the southern side. The boat trip is by far the best way to experience Isla Pajaros and will also produce numerous herons (especially yellow-crowned night-herons), chances at pinnated and least bitterns, and numerous waders and shorebirds that perch on the mangroves waiting for low tide. Green iguanas occur along the river by the dozen and common basilisks are true to their name. At low tide, American crocodiles bask on the mud banks.

Away from the water, there is a host of additional species for which Palo Verde is renowned. Shy thicket tinamous are seen on La Venada, which is also good for three trogon species (black-headed, elegant and violaceous), streak-backed orioles, northern orioles and red-winged blackbirds. Take Sendero El Guayacán for hummingbirds; flowering saino trees along the trail bring in white-tipped sicklebills, green-breasted mangos, fork-tailed emeralds, cinnamon hummingbirds, plain-capped starthroats and ruby-throated hummingbirds. This route is also good for banded wrens, rufous-naped wrens and scrub euphonias. Other highlights include striped-headed sparrows (often scrounging around the campsite), yellow-throated euphonias, mangrove vireos and turquoise-browed motmots.

On the drive into the park, keep your eyes open for orange-fronted parakeets, yellow-naped parrots and white-fronted parrots overhead. Unfortunately, northern raccoons and ctenosaurs are often hit by cars on this stretch, but this means that king vultures sometimes make rare roadside showings; drive slowly so as not to suddenly come upon them. They're much less confiding than black and turkey vultures and take flight easily. If you miss jabirus in the park, take some of the back roads to Lomas Barbudal; they sometimes visit the more secluded rice fields there.

Fur and scales

It's not only birds that flock to the lagoon. Palo Verde's mammals are year-round residents of course, but the dwindling pools in the dry season draws them into the open. White-tailed deer and collared peccaries are the most commonly seen species. Both forage along the edges of the lagoon and drink at the smaller pools, but they're also readily encountered without trying, regardless of season: The deer constantly cross the main roads and a very tame herd of peccaries frequents the headquarters and Palo Verde campsite; tame variegated squirrels are also resident at the headquarters. Much harder to spot (but within Costa Rica, perhaps most easily seen at Palo Verde), jaguarundis forage along the lagoon edge and come to the small pools in the dry; Senderos La Venada and El Manigordo are the best, especially at dawn or dusk (Manigordo can be difficult to find; go through the derelict gate at Catalina and turn immediately southwards along on old vehicle track). Pumas are

Watching tips
Between November and March, black vultures nest in the limestone cliffs lining the trail up to La Roca look-out point; take binoculars for an intimate look at the chicks. The nearby town of Liberia is a convenient base from which to explore the parks of Guanacaste province and also experiences a staggering gathering of great-tailed grackles every afternoon. Wait at the town square at dusk for a deafening new perspective on this ubiquitous urban species.

Ask the rangers to show you Laguna Varillal for Palo Verde's best display of black-necked stilts.

also fairly common in the park and, although they might be encountered anywhere, slow night-drives along the main roads probably hold the best chances (albeit very slight); they're also good for **coyotes** and **gray foxes**. Other mammalian residents include the usual conspicuous line-up: **White-faced capuchins**, **white- nosed coatis**, **Central American agoutis** (all visible on any of the trails) and, at night around the campsite, two species of **armadillo**, the ubiquitous **nine-banded** and the less common, dry-country species, the **northern naked-tail armadillo** (they lack the nine-banded's armored tail). **Central American spider monkeys** can be seen on the forest trails (try El Guayacán and Mirador Cerro Pelon) and boat trips down the Río Tempisque often produce **mantled howlers**.

For reptile lovers, **ctenosaurs** are tame and common around the headquarters, and you might also see **rose-bellied spiny lizards** on the rocks; in Costa Rica, they occur only in Guanacaste. Indeed, a number of dry-country reptiles have the southern limit of their range here, including iridescent **Neotropical sunbeam snakes** and strikingly marked **Central American banded geckoes**. Both inhabit the leaf litter of the quieter forest trails and are mainly nocturnal; try Sendero El Mapeche and the start of Sendero El Mirador Cerro Pelon. Banded geckoes are well worth looking for; unlike true geckoes, they have movable eyelids, a difference significant enough that they are placed in their own family. **Yellow-headed geckoes** (a true gecko) are easy to see on the headquarters buildings at night. ■

Cat-tails, cows and congregations

Don't be surprised to encounter livestock fences and, in the dry season, the livestock itself. Before it became a national park, Palo Verde was cattle country and around 15,000 head grazed the marsh every dry season. When Palo Verde was protected in 1980, they were removed but, unexpectedly, the consequences for the marsh's birdlife were devastating. It turns out that cattle are the linchpin in preserving the open wetland habitat. Their grazing and trampling ensures that marsh edges remain open, creating exposed muddy areas rich in aquatic insects, small crustaceans and juvenile fish – preferred food items for a host of ducks, waders, herons and many others. When the cattle were removed, fast-growing cat-tail cloaked the once-open fringes and, by 1988, had smothered 95% of the lagoon. From a cattle-era count of 35,000 black-bellied whistling ducks and 25,000 blue-winged teal, the numbers plummeted to 3000 and 500 respectively.

Today, after some hasty underwater mowing and plowing of the cat-tails, the cattle are back. Only a few hundred are brought in between January and April, but their presence ensures the marsh remains open. The bird-counts are back to pre-1980 levels.

PARQUE NACIONAL **SANTA ROSA**

A little piece of Africa

Wildlife highlights

The largest protected stand of tropical dry forest in Costa Rica. Summer waterholes attract visible and varied wildlife, especially collared peccaries, white-faced capuchins, white-tailed deer, Central American agoutis and white-nosed coatis. Mantled howlers and Central American spider monkeys are common and Baird's tapirs are sometimes seen. Chances at jaguarundis and ocelots, as well as (very rarely) jaguars and pumas. One of Central America's most important nest-sites for olive ridley turtles. Birds are varied and number more than 300 species including some dry-forest specialties like thicket tinamous, lesser ground-cuckoos, Hoffmann's woodpeckers and olive sparrows. Reptiles include a number of species restricted to north-west Costa Rica.

WITH its acacia thorn trees, African jaragua grass and prolonged dry season, Costa Rica's Guanacaste province is more reminiscent of Africa's savanna woodlands than the Central American tropics. First impressions aside, a closer look reveals a mosaic with an unmistakably American flavor. Cacti and dry-country bromeliads mix with mahoganies, guanacaste trees and the orange-barked Indio Desnudo ('naked Indian') tree to create a habitat classified as tropical dry forest. In Costa Rica, this habitat is found only in the relatively arid northwest of the country and the largest stand of it is protected by the conservation centerpiece of the region, PN Santa Rosa.

Wildlife at the waterholes

Unlike virtually anywhere else in well-watered Costa Rica, Santa Rosa's windy, dusty dry season lasts for six months. Between mid-December and late May, the park's numerous rivers almost run dry, setting up wildlife-watching conditions akin to those of an African summer. Like there, a few fading waterholes and isolated springs provide the only source of freshwater and, while not nearly as conspicuously as in Botswana or Kenya, they attract everything from beetles to big cats.

White-faced capuchins and **white-nosed coatis** are the most common visitors and, although their drinking sessions often overlap, meetings are rarely amicable. Santa Rosa is one of the few places where capuchins habitually raid the nests of coatis for very young pups, sometimes to the degree that all the young of a season are lost. The coatis respond to the severe hunting pressure with a second breeding season later in the same year, and are the only population known to do so. Any coatis mobile enough to visit the waterhole are beyond the predatory reach of the opportunistic monkeys, but the tension between them sometimes erupts in explosive interactions at the water, superb for rare photographic opportunities. **White-tailed deer**, **collared peccaries** and **Central American agoutis** are far

Playa Naranjo is popular with summer surfers as a well as a host of wildlife.

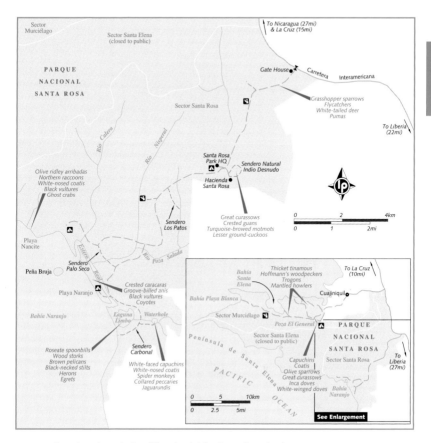

more cautious (you have to be still and quiet for these three to approach) and, although they rarely descend, **Central American spider monkeys** are common. If you've seen spider monkeys elsewhere already, take a second look; this is a unique golden race that occurs only in the north and east of Costa Rica. Numerous birds also stop by the water, mainly doves (particularly **Inca doves**, **common ground-doves** and **white-winged doves**) and **white-throated magpie-jays**, but also **white-crowned parrots**, **orange-fronted parakeets** and a Guanacaste specialty, **olive sparrows**. If the capuchins are around, birds tend to be thin on the ground; the omnivorous monkeys have been seen snatching magpie-jays from midair and grabbing incubating parrots from their nests.

The waterholes also attract far more elusive visitors, although you need to be up early for a chance. A few hours either side of sunrise is the best time for **Baird's tapirs** and, although exceptional, Santa Rosa's cats: **Jaguarundis** followed by **ocelots** are the most likely and visits by **pumas** and **jaguars** are possible. For the very keen, overnight stakeouts at the water will almost certainly yield something, although you'll need lots of moonlight (or

Location 27mi (43km) north-west of Liberia; access to the Santa Rosa park HQ and Murciélago camp site is year-round, but the roads to the coast are 4WD only and usually impassable in the rainy season (walking is permitted). Facilities Trails.
Accommodations Camp sites at park HQ, Naranjo, Estero Real (very basic) and Murciélago. Also basic dorm-style rooms at park HQ (book ahead).
Wildlife rhythms The dry season, when waterholes provide fertile wildlife-watching opportunities, lasts from December to May. Towards the end of the dry (mid-April onwards), frangipani and numerous other trees flower, attracting primates and many birds. The olive ridley laying season is July to November; the peak (September to October) is also the wettest period when some of the park roads are unpassable.
Contact SINAC (☎ 192; Santa Rosa office ☎ 666-5051; fax 666-5020;
e waldy@ns.minae.go.cr).

night-vision gear) to see it. There are waterholes or springs on Sendero Poza El General (in the Murciélago sector), Sendero Los Patos behind Playa Nancite (restricted access – see below) and, one of the best, Sendero Carbonal near Playa Naranjo (follow the signs to Ojo de Agua). Whichever you choose, station yourself unobtrusively some distance from the water to avoid disturbing thirsty animals. Inexplicably, swimming is permitted in some of the waterholes, but given wildlife's dependence on them during summer, the nearby ocean is a far less intrusive option.

Ocean armadas and beachcombers

Santa Rosa's beaches are very popular with surfers and swimmers (most visitors over the Christmas vacation are there for the water not the wildlife), but they're also used by a suite of species that need them for far more important reasons. Smallest of Costa Rica's marine turtles, **olive ridleys** nest on the beaches during the rainy season and Playa Nancite is one of only two Costa Rican sites where spectacular mass nestings occur (the other is RNFS Ostional; see Other Sites pp124–5). Female ridleys usually come ashore alone to nest, but once or twice a month during their nesting season at Nancite, thousands of females somehow synchronize their laying. Called arribadas (Spanish for 'arrivals'), the mass events last only three to 10 days, but the numbers can be staggering: On Nancite, they average around 40,000 nests and peak at an estimated 148,000. It's thought that mass nesting results in 'predator swamping' – supplying so many eggs that there are just too many for nest predators to eat – but, regardless, predators crowd the beach during the nesting season. **White-nosed coatis**, **northern raccoons** and **coyotes** are the most common (the latter two mostly at night), but even **Neotropical sunbeam snakes** (in Costa Rica, found only in Guanacaste) and **ghost crabs** pillage the nests. A small population of **American crocodiles** in the estuary behind Nancite also take adult turtles and prey on hatchlings when they emerge.

Access to Nancite is restricted so as not to disrupt the turtles; apply at the park HQ for permission to visit or watch the beach with binoculars or a spotting scope from the cliffs above. Most

Connections small and large

Santa Rosa's acacia trees and their ant guardians represent a textbook case of coevolution, in which two species travel a linked evolutionary path where each becomes increasingly dependent on the other. For the acacia, the ants provide protection from would-be browsers; indeed, they violently attack anything that touches their acacia host, including other plants, destroying epiphytes and trimming sun-stealing foliage overhead. In return, the acacias house the ants in their thorns and provide constantly flowing wells of nectar and tiny, yellow parcels of nutrition called Beltian bodies.

On a much larger level, similar connections demand that Santa Rosa cannot exist in a vacuum. To survive the dry summer, many of the reserve's species have to migrate into the cool rainforest outside the park to the east. With that in mind, Costa Rican and US conservationists have successfully linked Santa Rosa to neighboring ecosystems so that it's now part of a contiguous protected unit beginning 10mi (16km) out in the Pacific Ocean and ending in the foothills of the Caribbean lowlands. Their extraordinary success notwithstanding, more land is needed. The Guanacaste Dry Forest Conservation Fund is an extremely worthwhile way to contribute; see **w** janzen.sas.upenn.edu/caterpillars/RR/rincón_rainforest.htm.

of the laying happens at night, but early morning vigils regularly see a few stragglers, as well as **white-nosed coatis** invariably accompanied by a retinue of scavengers – **black vultures**, **turkey vultures** and **crested caracaras** mop up the eggs the coatis miss. If you want to try to see an arribada, you'll need to visit at night and then only accompanied by park staff. The cues for arribada nesting are still vague, but there is a greater chance of them happening around the first and the last quarter of the moon, and they are more common and larger during the peak rainy months (September to October).

As well as waterholes and beaches, Santa Rosa has a system of trails that is worth exploring. The best developed are those of the Santa Rosa sector; Murciélago's trails are restricted to a short path ending at Poza El General (the General's Swimming-hole) and a series of firebreaks leading to various beaches. Whether in Santa Rosa or Murciélago, all the trails have chances at most of the diurnal mammals, which visit the waterholes (as well as **mantled howlers**, which are common here), but the birdlife is the greater reward. Of course, dry-forest species are the main attraction and are best seen on the trails close to the coast; expect **thicket tinamous**, **lesser ground-cuckoos**, **Hoffmann's woodpeckers** (a local specialty), **pale-billed woodpeckers**, **scrub euphonias**, **banded wrens**, **stub-tailed spadebills**, **white-lored gnatcatchers**, **blue grosbeaks** and **elegant** and **black-headed trogons**. The acacias here (especially along Sendero Los Patos) are preferred nest-trees for **rufous-naped wrens** and **streak-backed orioles**. The birds benefit from the presence of aggressive acacia ants, which nest in the thorns and protect the tree from browsers with a double-pronged offence comprising formidable mandibles and a poisonous sting (the ants also benefit; see boxed text opposite). Inadvertently, they also deter nest-raiders; the main one here is, once again, the rapacious **white-faced capuchin**, but they avoid ant-protected trees.

Also close to the coast, two estuaries, Laguna Limbo and Estero Real, are very productive for waterbirds. **Roseate spoonbills**, **wood storks**, **brown pelicans**, **black-necked stilts**, **bare-throated tiger-herons**, **great blue herons**, **great egrets** and **snowy egrets** are common. Both estuaries are best when the tide is out (Laguna Limbo can be reached by a little path leading off Sendero Carbonal; it's easy to miss) and, as well as great birding, both have **American crocodiles**; park rangers have witnessed **jaguars** hunting the crocs in Estero Real.

Finally, spend some time inland for a slightly different mix of species. The Santa Rosa plateau (around park HQ and the Murciélago camp site) is a slightly moister area where the forest doesn't entirely dry out over summer as it does near the coast. This is better habitat is which to look for **great curassows**, **crested guans**, **spectacled owls**, **turquoise-browed motmots** and **long-tailed manakins**. Check the open pasture areas lining the entrance road to the park for **double-striped thick-knees**, **grasshopper sparrows** and various **flycatchers**. Early morning visitors driving this road may also see congregations of **white-tailed deer** on the pastures and, because of the herds, occasional glimpses of **big cats**. ∎

Watching tips

Naranjo camp site is an excellent place for reptiles. Ctenosaurs are very tame and, being so abundant here, highly territorial; the males' endless displays often result in spectacular clashes. Rose-bellied spiny lizards and Deppe's whip-tailed lizards hunt around the rock gardens and garbage bins for insects. In turn, they're pursued by numerous snakes, some of which also target the garbage area for nocturnal rodents; local specialties include road-guarders, Mexican parrot snakes, black-and-white cat-eyed snakes and Neotropical rat snakes. Apart from the ctenosaurs, in Costa Rica all are restricted to Guanacaste province.

PARQUE NACIONAL **TAPANTÍ**
Window on the Talamancas

> **Wildlife highlights**
> More than 300 bird species, including resplendent quetzals, three-wattled bellbirds, mixed tanager flocks and diverse hummingbirds. Common mammals include Alfaro's pygmy squirrels, pacas, Central American agoutis, mantled howlers, white-faced capuchins and tayras. Perhaps the best chance (albeit very slight) in Costa Rica for oncillas. Baird's tapirs, red brockets, pumas and ocelots are common, but mostly hard to see. Nightwalks can be productive for at least four species of opossum.

> **Watching tip**
> Check the picnic sites after dark for some nocturnal scroungers, including northern raccoons, common opossums and occasionally tayras. Walking carefully along the Río Grande de Orosí at night sometimes produces water opossums, Central American woolly opossums and gray four-eyed opossums.

RUNNING from San José's southern suburbs to the Panamanian border, the Cordillera de Talamanca is Costa Rica's longest and highest mountain range. Except for a small slice west of the Interamericana, its entire length is safeguarded by a mantle of interlinked protected areas collectively called the Reserva de la Biosfera de La Amistad (La Amistad Biosphere Reserve). Straddling the continental divide and, at points, extending into the lowlands to within a few miles of both Pacific and Caribbean coasts, La Amistad protects the country's most biologically diverse region. It's also largely undeveloped and difficult to explore, but there are two tourist-friendly options; one is PN Chirripó (see pp92–3), the other is the even more accessible PN Tapantí. Reachable on a day-trip from San José, Tapantí is a window on the wildest region in Costa Rica and, with more than 23ft (7m) of rain per year, one of the wettest.

Strictly speaking, PN Tapantí is correctly called PN Tapantí-Macizo de la Muerte; the Macizo de la Muerte sector was added in April 2000, linking Tapantí to Chirripó's northern boundary. The Tapantí sector is still the only one open to the public, but its short road and trail system is as productive as anywhere in the park. Visitors occasionally complain that the trails at Tapantí do not take in much of the reserve, but so long as you go when it's quiet (weekends and vacations can be very busy), you have as much chance here of encountering wildlife as anywhere in the Talamancas; indeed because of its popularity, some species are very tame indeed. Take the Sendero Oropendola for very relaxed **Central American agoutis, white-faced capuchins** and **white-nosed coatis**. **Alfaro's pygmy squirrels** are easily observed, usually chiseling away at bark to feed on the sap; often a shower of epiphyte-covered bark from above is the first giveaway. Sendero Oropendola is also very good for **tayras**; perhaps because of the many picnic sites on the trail (crowded and noisy on vacations), they're used to people here and sometimes permit prolonged views.

For more retiring species, the Sendero Natural Arboles Caídos is better. On its own, Tapantí would be too small to support shy species and those requiring large home ranges, but its unbroken connection to adjoining conservation areas means

Central American agoutis are abundant and tame around Tapantí's many picnic sites.

that **Baird's tapirs**, **mantled howlers** and **red brockets** are common. Tapantí also has all six of Costa Rica's cat species, though they're no less elusive here than elsewhere. A **puma** with cubs was sighted fairly regularly on the entrance road and Sendero Natural Arboles Caídos during 2002; most sightings were very early in the morning (which is also productive for **ocelots**). More unusually, Tapantí has reasonable chances for Costa Rica's rarest cat, the **oncilla**. Similar to a margay (see p162), but slightly smaller, darker and with a slimmer tail, the oncilla in Central America is only known from the La Amistad region. Silent night-walks with a flashlight are the only way you might see one; oncillas probably prefer higher areas, so try the upper reaches of the road and Sendero Natural

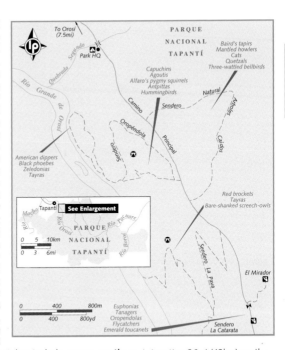

Arboles Caídos. Other night-sights include **pacas**, **northern raccoons** (especially along the Río Grande de Orosí) and, usually spotted high in the trees and only with considerable luck, **cacomistles**.

For most visitors, mammal sightings will be the exception, but everyone can count on prolific birdlife. All the trails are productive, although the road edge along Camino Principal is probably better; a gate blocks the road to vehicles at El Mirador, but proceeding on foot is permitted and, because most visitors stay around Sendero Oropéndola's picnic sites, it's very quiet and rewarding. Among the 300-odd species on record here, the flashiest include **purple-crowned fairies**, **white-bellied mountain gems**, **black-bellied hummingbirds**, **green-fronted lancebills**, **striped-tailed hummingbirds**, **collared trogons** and **emerald toucanets**. **Resplendent quetzals** and **three-wattled bellbirds** are seen on the upper reaches of the road, and colonies of **chestnut-headed oropendolas** nest along the road's edge. Mixed flocks of **tanagers** and **flycatchers** are common along the roadside and include **blue-hooded euphonias**, **blue-and-gold tanagers**, **hepatic tanagers**, **white-winged tanagers**, **olive-sided flycatchers** (especially September to October) and resident **tufted** and **black-capped flycatchers**. Take to the trails for more furtive species including **bare-shanked screech-owls** (with regular predawn calls), **ochre-breasted antpittas**, **buffy tufted-cheeks**, **barred becards** and **brown-billed scythebills**. The edges of the Río Grande de Orosí produce a few specials such as **American dippers**, **black phoebes** and, in the riverside bracken and bamboo, **zeledonias** and **silvery-fronted tapaculos**. ■

Location 26mi (42km) southeast of San José. Buses go to Orosí then walk or taxi the remaining 7.5mi (12km).
Facilities Walking trails and lookouts.
Accommodations Camping and a rustic house sleeping 15 (book ahead) at park HQ. Numerous options in Orosí.
Wildlife rhythms Weather here is consistently rainy year-round, but early mornings are nearly always clear and excellent for wildlife activity. Tapantí is very busy on weekends and vacations; mammal sightings, particularly of shy species, are more likely during the week.
Contact SINAC (☎ 192; regional office (San Isidro General) ☎ 771-3155; 771-4836, fax 771-3297;
e cmcg@ns.minae.go.cr).

PARQUE NACIONAL **TORTUGUERO**

Nature's Venice

Wildlife highlights

Without a doubt, one of Costa Rica's top wildlife destinations. Mammals are particularly conspicuous and relaxed, especially mantled howlers, Central American spider monkeys, white-faced capuchins, both sloths and Neotropical river otters. Baird's tapirs, West Indian manatees and jaguars are elusive, but excellent sightings occur sporadically. More than 300 bird species, resident and migratory; especially rich in herons, kingfishers, waders and migrants. Great green macaws are a highlight. One of the most important nesting sites in Central America for green turtles and also used by leatherbacks; both species easily seen on guided walks. Other herps such as spectacled caimans, green iguanas, striped and green basilisks and poison dart-frogs are abundant.

TRAVERSED by a snarl of rivers, lagoons and canals and drenched by yearly rainfall that regularly exceeds 16.5ft (5m), it's hardly surprising that Tortuguero's wildlife-watching takes place largely by boat. And while many visitors assume that only aquatic species and water-loving birds will be on show, the channels meander through high-canopy rainforest where arboreal wildlife is prolific and terrifically visible. Like a window on rainforest life, the wide channels reveal those species that seek out forest edges in order to forage, watch for predators or rivals, or simply to sunbathe early in the morning; at the other extreme, the narrow backwaters are home to shy skulkers and species which rely on cover for their survival. Coupled with nocturnal beach walks along one of the most important sea turtle nesting beaches in Central America, it's a combination for some superb sightings.

Well-watered wildlife

To get the best from Tortuguero, be on the water early, or – regardless of time of day – go out following rain. Showers are a regular feature of the Tortuguero experience (bring a raincoat), but contrary to expectation, they can enhance the viewing enormously. As soon as the downpour clears, mammals, birds and reptiles hustle into the open to sunbathe and dry out; it's most conspicuous on the rainforest edges lining the wide main canals like Lagunas Agua Fría and Tortuguero. As well as **mantled howlers, Central American spider monkeys** and **white-faced capuchins**, sun worshippers include both species of **sloth**, **bare-throated tiger-herons** (very abundant here), **anhingas**, **Neotropic cormorants**, **sungrebes**, **ospreys**, **green iguanas** and **basilisks** (**green** and **striped**). Rain or shine, the main waterways produce a constant stream of additional waterbirds; 14 members of the heron family are resident (though the shyer species are better seen on the more secluded channels – see below), plus **glossy** and **green ibises**, **roseate**

Tortuguero's wide waterways offer exceptional chances for boat-based wildlife viewing.

spoonbills and **wood storks**. **Muscovy ducks** are seen fairly often and, in winter, **blue-winged teal** and **northern shovelers**. Usually overhead, nine species of **parrot** can be spotted. Most sought-after, the **great green macaw** is best seen during December to April when massive almendro trees are fruiting; if the discarded woody seeds have an edge cleanly bitten off, it's a sign of macaws. The smaller **orange-chinned, crimson-fronted** and **olive-throated parakeets** are fairly reliable alongside ubiquitous **mealy** and **red-lored parrots**.

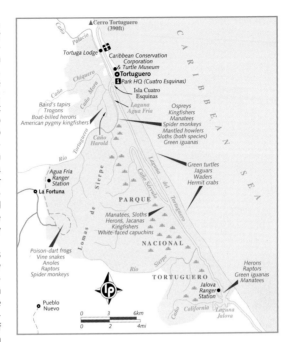

Many migratory species from North America follow the Caribbean coast and Tortuguero's wide channels can become busy flyways at the right time. From early September, 200-strong flocks of **eastern kingbirds** mix with constant streams of **barn swallows** and **purple martins** and, during October, up to 30 **peregrine falcons** can be spotted in a single day. Tortuguero's bird list tops 300 and to enjoy a comprehensive cross section of it, the Caribbean Conservation Corporation (CCC) runs two mist-nesting programs each year – one between March and June, and the other between August and November. Volunteers participate for a fee and will handle hundreds of birds of between 50 to 100 species (see the CCC's contact details below).

For retiring species, leave the main waterways and explore the quiet backwaters. Tortuguero is superb for **kingfishers** (all six Costa Rican species are virtually guaranteed) most of which are visible anywhere, but the rare **green-and-rufous** and **American pygmy** are better seen where it's quiet; try Caños Harold and Servulo where other regulars include **boat-billed herons, black-throated trogons, slaty-tailed trogons, fasciated antshrikes, double-toothed kites, white-fronted nunbirds** and, down low in cover and hard to spot, **bay wrens**. Your best chances are here for **agami herons, rufescent tiger-herons, least bitterns** and **sunbitterns**, though none is common.

Birds aside, **Baird's tapirs** are occasionally spotted in the narrow channels and normally shy **Neotropical river otters** are particularly conspicuous. Tortuguero's otters are reasonably habituated to boats, and visitors often enjoy sightings of pairs playing together for hours; keep a reasonable distance and they're likely to ignore you. Scarce until the day warms up, but then very common, **spectacled caimans** tolerate even the closest approach; the photo opportunities are terrific. Less

Location 52mi (84km) north of Limón, access by boat or small plane.

Facilities Trails, small display at park HQ, turtle museum at CCC. Park entry is US$6/day (pay at park HQ), but $10 buys a permit valid for up to four days.

Accommodations Many lodges and guesthouses in and around Tortuguero village. Camping is permitted at park HQ, ranger stations and at some guesthouses.

Wildlife rhythms Best times for turtles are: Leatherbacks (March to June); green turtles (June to November – peak is August and September); hawksbills (best in July). Migratory birds arrive almost year-round (July to May), but peak periods are spring (March to May) and fall (August to November). The short dry season runs from January to April and there is a further dry period around September to October.

Contact SINAC (☎ 710-7542; fax 710-7673; e cmcg@ns.minae.go.cr). Caribbean Conservation Corporation (USA ☎ 1-800-678-7853; fax 352-375-2449; e ccc@cccturtle.org; w www.cccturtle.org).

relaxed, **brown wood turtles**, **black wood turtles** and **tropical sliders** bask on exposed logs and are easy to spot, but drop quickly below the surface if approached too hastily.

Tortuguero is possibly Costa Rica's finest site for **West Indian manatees**, but they are difficult to see. The best chances – albeit slim – for observing them are around 'blowing holes' or sopladeros (deep hollows in the riverbed where manatees congregate, perhaps to play or to wait for high tide so they can swim upriver to feed). There are sopladeros where Caño Servulo joins the Laguna del Tortuguero, around Isla Cuatro Esquinas and at Laguna Jalova. However, by far the most manatee sightings occur in Caño Harold and the adjacent stretch of the Río Tortuguero (known as Laguna Agua Fría), and in Caño Servulo.

The boating options at Tortuguero are many. The area's many hotels and lodges mostly use power boats. The wildlife here is inured to the constant presence of boats and seems largely indifferent to the outboards, but a far more rewarding option is to canoe or kayak; it's more peaceful, it permits a closer approach to many birds and, for photographers, you're not having to wrestle with the vibrations of the engine. Canoe hire is available at many villagers and hotels; check at the park HQ or the information kiosk at the center of town.

Place of the turtle

Tortuguero means 'turtle-catcher' (harking back to earlier years when turtle harvesting was common) and the black sand beach here is the largest nesting site in the Atlantic for **green turtles**. Every year, from June to November, between 5000 and 50,000 female greens come ashore after dark to lay their eggs. The Caribbean Conservation Corporation has studied them since 1954 and it was essentially founder Archie Carr's doing that Tortuguero became a national park. To see the turtles, you have to join a night-walk along the beach with a CCC-trained guide; check in at the research station or information kiosk in the center of town ahead of leaving times (8pm and 10pm) to secure a place. For a more hands-on experience, you can join their research participant program that tags and measures turtles and monitors their nests (contact CCC, see Contact on this page). Greens are the most common species, but small

Barra del Colorado beleaguered

Adjacent to Tortuguero and much larger (at least on paper), RNSF Barra del Colorado is also far less visited. Partly, that's because it's more remote, but being a wildlife refuge (rather than national park), it also permits game fishing – long Barra's focus rather than wildlife-watching.

Even so, the wildlife here is essentially the same as Tortuguero's and viewing it is becoming more accessible; most of the refuge's fishing lodges now also offer wildlife tours and there are a couple that concentrate on them. Hopefully it isn't too late. Although the well-watered areas close to the coast are largely intact, huge tracts of the rainforest in the west of Barra del Colorado have fallen to illegal logging and settlement. It's thought to be partly the reason why jaguar sightings are increasing in Tortuguero: The cats seek refuge there as they lose habitat in adjacent areas. However, Tortuguero can only support so many jaguars and eventually the population will stabilize, probably close to the level it has always been. Try to arrange a visit to Barra; the more wildlifers who go there, the greater the chance it will survive.

numbers of **hawksbills** also nest here and, very occasionally, **loggerheads**. If you visit earlier in the year, giant **leatherbacks** are guaranteed between March and June.

Although the chances are slight, turtle-watchers also encounter **jaguars**. The big cats swim the Laguna del Tortuguero to patrol the beach for nesting turtles; in the 2001 nesting season, 102 turtles were killed by jaguars, including one of the giant leatherbacks. Jaguars have always preyed upon turtles here, but the average is usually less than 10 per season. The reason for the huge increase is unknown, but may stem from habitat clearing on the park's boundaries, driving more cats into the reserve. The effects on the turtle population remain to be seen, but are probably negligible given the number of turtles here. Jaguars are seen at both night and day (overcast, rainy days are best) and early morning river trips occasionally experience the sighting of a lifetime, catching them as they swim across the lagoon after a night's beach-combing.

For walkers, the beach tours are the best option, but there are a couple of trails elsewhere in the reserve. Both the park HQ (Cuatro Esquinas) and the Jalova ranger station have short trails and, far less accessible, a challenging and poorly defined trail runs from the Agua Fría ranger station into the Sierpe Hills on the little-visited western side of the park. The trails are usually swampy and none is as productive for wildlife as boating, but they can be rewarding for smaller life. **Brown** and **green vine snakes**, **slender anoles** and **strawberry poison dart-frogs** are abundant on all (also easily seen at Tortuga Lodge), and the more retiring **green-and-black poison dart-frog** can be found on the Sierpe Hills Trail with a little searching; they're especially active early in the morning after rain.

The trail at park HQ (called the Tortuguero Nature Trail) ends up on the beach, which is good for waders especially during the winter migration (September to March); common species include four species of **plover**, **willets**, **sanderlings** and **spotted sandpipers**. Rarer visitors include both **yellowlegs** (**greater** and **lesser**), **least** and **western sandpipers**, and **American oyster-catchers**. ■

Above: A good field guide is invaluable for identifying Tortuguero's endless procession of bird species.
Below: Because they have been protected for so long, the spectacled caimans here are unusually tolerant of boats.

Watching tips

Just outside the park, Tortuga Lodge (Costa Rica Expeditions) offer a good chance at some species you might miss. There is a nice trail system that often produces Baird's tapirs, strawberry poison-dart frogs (assured) and the bright yellow form of the eyelash pit viper (locally called 'oropel'). Just behind the lodge is a little lagoon with a resident American crocodile and a pair of Neotropical river otters (the otters were mating during winter 2002).

VOLCANO PARKS
Life on the earth's edge

POISED on the eastern edge of the Pacific Rim of Fire, Costa Rica's foundations are in constant volcanic flux. The country sits directly above the junction of three tectonic plates inexorably grinding against one another and giving rise to earth-moving on a colossal scale. The floor of the Pacific Ocean is relentlessly dragged beneath the margins of the North American and Caribbean plates and then spewed back up as super-heated liquid rock through cracks in the earth's crust. Over millions of years, this rock recycling has given rise to Costa Rica's central mountainous backbone, now slightly more than 2mi (3.2km) above sea level at its highest point. Strewn with at least 112 volcanic formations, these *cordilleras* (mountain ranges) are largely dormant today but seven of Costa Rica's volcanoes are still active. All of them fall within protected areas, or – in the case of the most impressive ones – are the focus of their own national parks. Worthwhile to visit just to see the earth angry, a number of the volcano parks also make rewarding wildlife-watching destinations. This section gives a summary of the best ones.

Parque Nacional Rincón de la Vieja

With an accessible active crater, hot mud points, thermal springs and numerous fumaroles (gas vents), Rincón de la Vieja is one of the most volcanically diverse sites. It also has a good trail system, excellent for taking in the wildlife. Almost 260 bird species occur, including easily-seen **great curassows**, four **toucan** species (with good chances at **yellow-eared toucanets** and abundant **keel-billed toucans**), **turquoise-browed motmots**, **plain-brown** and **olivaceous woodcreepers** and **black-cheeked woodpeckers**. **White-faced capuchins**, **Central American agoutis** and **white-nosed coatis** are very common and tame, and both **mantled howlers** and **tayras** are fairly easy to spot. **Central American coral snakes** and their mimics, harmless **false coral snakes**, are unusually easy to see, and tame **ctenosaurs** linger at the camp site and picnic tables for hand-

Great curassows are fairly easy to spot at both PN Rincón de la Vieja and PN Arenal.

outs. The open savanna areas on the way to the La Cangreja waterfall are good for **green spiny lizards** snatching insects from the rocks. Four species of flamboyant **morpho** butterflies are everywhere.

16mi (25km) north-east of Liberia

Parque Nacional Arenal

This is Costa Rica's most active volcano and, although Arenal hasn't blown its top since 1968, minor eruptions occur constantly; the best views are from the north and west, and nighttime vigils reveal the red glow of lava at the top. It's forbidden to climb to the crater, but trails take in old lava flows and pass through wildlife-rich forest. At 1657m, Arenal is the lowest of the active volcanoes and has more diverse wildlife than high-altitude sites like Poás. **Mantled howlers** and **white-faced capuchins** are common and **variegated squirrels** frequent lodges and camp sites. Birdlife is very rich and includes specialties like **lattice-tailed trogons**, **rufous** and **broad-billed motmots**, **bare-necked umbrellabirds**, **purple-throated fruitcrows**; among many hummers are **blue-chested hummingbirds**, **striped tailed hummingbirds**, **green-fronted lancebills** and **bronze-tailed plumeleteers**.

Looking down on a crater lake at 11,257ft (3432m) Volcán Irazú.

The gravel road to the park entrance (first turn south after crossing the Lake Arenal wall) is excellent for **great curassows** (early in the morning is best), as well as very tame **white-nosed coatis**. Sadly it's very popular to pull over and feed the coatis which now wait on the roads for handouts; predictably, some end up killed by cars.

150km north-west of San José

Parque Nacional Volcán Poás

Costa Rica's most visited national park, Poás owes its popularity to its accessibility. A road to the top stops just short of the huge, main crater and it's extremely busy on weekends and holidays. Except for **red-tailed hawks** and **highland hummingbirds**, wildlife is fairly scarce at the top, but there are some short trails which are more productive. The Laguna de Botos trail runs through cloud forest stunted by the acidic air and freezing temperatures, ending at an extinct water-filled crater. The benches here make good vantage points to watch for **green violet-ears**, **volcano hummingbirds**, **magnificent hummingbirds** and **fiery-throated hummingbirds**, all relentlessly chasing **slaty flowerpiercers** that dare visit the same flowers. **Sooty** and **clay-colored robins** and both **silky-flycatchers** (**black-and-yellow** and **long-tailed**) are common. The longer Escalonia Trail and the entrance road produce more elusive species including **black guans**, **resplendent quetzals** (especially February to April), **bare-shanked screech-owls**, **buffy-crowned wood partridges**, **spotted wood quails**, and **ochraceous** and **timberline wrens**. **Forest rabbits** and **coyotes** are common – the latter are sometimes seen crossing the entrance road early in the morning. This is the country's best site for **montane squirrels**, so much so that it's often called the Poás squirrel in Costa Rica.

22mi (35km) north-west of San José

☎ *192 or Park Office 482-2424, fax 482-2165,*

e *accvc@ns.minae.go.cr* ■

SEABIRD ISLANDS
Evolution at work

COSTA Rica's Pacific coastline is dotted with little chunks of rock which, like islands everywhere, have their own very distinctive fauna. Except for Isla del Cocos, most are a short boat trip away, but all are isolated or small enough that mainland predators never colonized them. For nesting birds, that makes islands a rare predator-free refuge and, indeed, the main wildlife attractions here are huge colonies of seabirds and coastal species. Islands are also the home of unique populations of familiar mainland species which, when isolated sufficiently, become different enough to be classified as new subspecies. If the isolation is prolonged and complete, entire new species emerge. Island endemics are rare in Costa Rica, but there are a few species which you'll only see by leaving the mainland.

PN Isla del Cocos

Occasionally called Costa Rica's Galápagos, this is the county's only oceanic territory and the only island with endemic vertebrates. Most sought-after are three birds, the **Cocos cuckoo**, **Cocos flycatcher** and **Cocos finch**. All are seen on the forest trail up to Mount Iglesias though the cuckoo is furtive and hard to spot; also try the riverside trails at Chatham Bay and Wafer Bay. The finch occurs everywhere on the island and is impossible to miss. Endlessly active, they ignore approaches to within 6ft (2m). Reptilian endemics, **Pacific dwarf geckoes** and **Townsend's anoles**, are more elusive; the anole occurs on the forested trails, but the gecko is nocturnal and, as overnight stays on the island are prohibited, you're extremely unlikely to be seen.

Cocos is also the only spot in Costa Rica you're likely to see **great frigatebirds** (as well as occasional **magnificent frigatebirds**), **red-footed boobies**, **white terns** (known here as Espíritu Santo – Holy Ghost – because of their habit of hovering curiously above people's heads) and both Costa Rican **noddies** – **black** and **brown**. The last three are mostly absent from around

Isla del Caño is a seldom-visited island some 12mi (19km) off Península de Osa.

September to February. Among the 88 additional species on record are several pelagic species: **Dark-rumped petrels**, two **shearwaters** and four **storm-petrels**. **Peregrine falcons** can be spotted from September to March The only terrestrial mammals are introduced rodents, cats, goats, pigs and white-tailed deer; except perhaps for the deer, all are causing extensive damage to the native wildlife and are the focus of various control operations. Cocos is accessible only by boat (36 hours from the mainland) largely by expensive diving tours.

RNFS Isla Bolaños

Just north of PN Santa Rosa, Isla Bolaños is a tiny island with no trails, but birdwatching by boat is rewarding and it's possible to walk the beaches at low tide (with a permit from SINAC). If you opt for the latter, take particular care not to disturb nesting **American oystercatchers** between March and May; most nests are on the island's eastern tip. Other highlights include nesting **brown pelicans** on the north side of the island (between January to May) and Costa Rica's largest colony of **magnificent frigates** on the southern cliffs. **Black vultures** linger around the colonies for dead chicks, and **white-throated magpie jays** are very common. Non-birds are scarce, but **ctenosaurs** are abundant.

Small, isolated islands are often the sole breeding refuges for seabirds.

RBs Guayabo, Negritos and Los Pajaros

This cluster of four islands (Negritos is actually two) sits in the Nicoya Gulf and, although they're not especially close to one another, they're biologically similar and managed as a single unit. They are also primarily for the protection of wildlife rather than tourism so there's no camping, and landfall is only possible on Guayabo (hiking on the beach only and permits essential); otherwise, viewing is by boat. Guayabo boasts Costa Rica's largest breeding colony of **brown pelicans** and is the most reliable place in the country to enjoy occasional **blue-footed boobies**. A small population of **peregrines** winters here and **magnificent frigates** are easily seen (they nest on a tiny un-named island just west of Guayabo). **Yellow-naped parrots** and **brown boobies** nest on the Negritos Islands; boat-based viewing can make the former (but not the latter), difficult to spot. The Nicoya Gulf is also known for its visits from scarce **reddish egrets** in winter and from pelagic species: **Wedge-tailed shearwaters** (January to March), **sooty shearwaters** (May to October) **Audubon's shearwaters** (year-round but uncommon), **least storm-petrels** (December to June) and **black storm-petrels** (October to April).

RB Isla del Caño

Just off the coastal border of PN Corcovado, tiny Isla del Caño has only a fraction of the mainland's diversity, but it's little visited (except by divers and snorkelers) and makes a worthwhile break for visitors looking for solitude. Wildlife is fairly sparse, but **brown boobies** and **ospreys** both breed here and are easily seen. Camping is possible (permits essential) and nightwalks have excellent chances at two mammals rarely seen on the mainland; **pacas**, which were reintroduced to the island, and **gray four-eyed opossums** . **Boa constrictors** are **Fleischmann's glass frogs** are also readily seen by spotlighting. ∎

OTHER SITES – COSTA RICA

PN Barra Honda

The main appeal of this small national park is its maze of caves. There are 42 here, most of them still unexplored and all, except the Terciopelo cave, requiring some degree of technical climbing ability. One of them, Pozo Hediondo, is used by several species of bat, including common long-tongued bats, gray short-tailed bats, woolly false vampires and the real thing, the common vampire. Above ground, there are a couple of trails where it's easy to spot mantled howlers, white-faced monkeys and variegated squirrels, as well as dry-forest bird species such as white-faced magpie jays, Hoffmann's woodpeckers and lesser ground cuckoos. Permits need to be arranged in advance for any caving except in Terciopelo.

14mi (22km) east of Nicoya
SINAC ☎ 192 or Regional Office, ☎ 682-5267; fax 685-5667; e jicaro@ns.minae.go.cr

RNA Cabo Blanco

Protecting the southernmost tip of the Nicoya Peninsula, Cabo Blanco has only a couple of trails open to non-researchers, but they pass through the peninsula's largest protected tract of evergreen forest where wildlife is varied and fairly easy to spot. Three primates, as well as variegated squirrels, white-tailed deer and red brockets, are common and jaguarundis are seen sporadically. Birding is rewarding, offering good chances at great curassows and seabirds are abundant: Brown pelicans,

magnificent frigates and brown boobies (this is Costa Rica's largest colony) roost on the cliffs either side of the two beaches and on Isla Cabo Blanco, a small island 1mi offshore. There are no organized trips to the island, but they can sometimes be arranged with the rangers.

7mi (11km) south of Montezuma

PN Cahuita

Popular among swimmers and sun-worshippers from the nearby relaxed village of the same name, Cahuita was created to protect Costa Rica's largest coral reef. Accumulative damage from a 1991 earthquake, El Niño and run-off of topsoil and pesticide has taken its toll, but at least 120 reef fish species can still be seen, as well as nice examples of elkhorn and smooth brain coral. The reef is accessible to snorkeling. Common land attractions include white-faced capuchins, mantled howlers, both sloth species, green iguanas and varied birds, especially water-associated species including green ibis, rufescent tiger-herons and colonies of boat-billed herons. The raccoons here are the less common crab-eating species; they forage around the camp site at night.

Adjacent to Cahuita village.
SINAC ☎ 192 or Regional Office ☎ 755-0302;
e ajenkins@ns.minae.go.cr

RNVS Gandoca-Manzanillo

Abutting the Panamanian border, Gandoca-Manzanillo protects the least altered mangrove forest on the Caribbean coast and, along with Cahuita, is the only place in Costa Rica with a living coral reef. Four species of marine turtles nest on Playa Gandoca, including endangered leatherbacks between March and July (peak; April to May). A local conservation organization, ANAI, runs an excellent leatherback conservation

project that accepts volunteers (w www.anaicr.org). Swamp forest and rainforest protects a varied mammal fauna (most are difficult to see) and the birdlist numbers 358 species. The Laguna Gandoca used to have small numbers of West Indian manatees, but no-one is sure if they still occur.

45mi (72km) south-east of Puerto Limón
SINAC ☎ 192 or fax 754-2133;
e ajenkins@ns.minae.go.cr

PN Guanacaste

Contiguous with PN Santa Rosa (except for the Interamericana), PN Guanacaste connects the dry tropical forest of the lowlands to the cloud forest of the Cordillera de Guanacaste highlands. This is critical for 'altitudinal migrants', species which take refuge from Santa Rosa's dry summer in Guanacaste. Among them, parrots and hummingbirds join Caribbean slope species, such as rainbow-billed toucans, yellow-eared toucanets, collared aracaris and golden-hooded tanagers. The mammal fauna here is slightly more diverse than PN Santa Rosa (pp 110-3), but the most visible species are essentially the same. With three research stations, Guanacaste is more the domain of biologists than tourists, but visitors can explore on day trips and, room permitting, stay in the dorm-style accommodation. It's important to book in advance through the Santa Rosa office.

37mi (59km) north of Liberia (park HQ)
SINAC ☎ 192; Santa Rosa office ☎ 666-5051; fax 666-5020;
e waldy@ns.minae.go.cr

PI La Amistad

Costa Rica's largest single protected area by far, La Amistad is connected to PN Chirripó in the west and an equally-sized protected chunk of Panama in the east (hence 'International Park'). This is the wildest and most biologically diverse region of the country, but most of the park is undeveloped and very difficult to reach. Most visitors stay in the Las Tablas area, where there are three ranger stations (Progresso is the most accessible) and a few lodges nearby. La Amistad's species count is extremely high, with large populations of Costa Rica's most endangered mammals (including all six cat species), 400 birds and 263 species of reptiles and amphibians. For the dauntless, La Amistad offers considerable rewards, but you'll need to be self-sufficient and very competent in back-country hiking. A local guide and a compass or GPS is essential.

Progresso is 105mi (168km) south-east of San Isidro de General
SINAC ☎ 192 or Regional Office (San Isidro de General) ☎ 771-3155/771-4836; fax 771-3297;
e cmcg@ns.minae.go.cr

PN Las Baulas de Guanacaste

Usually abbreviated to Las Baulas, this park is one of the most important nesting sites for the world's largest and most endangered marine turtle, the leatherback (*la baula* in Spanish). On nights between October and March, female leatherbacks lay their eggs at three beaches here, together with small numbers of olive ridleys (June to December), hawksbills (April to November) and Pacific green turtles (June to September). Turtle-watching is only permitted with a guide or ranger and flash photography is forbidden – measures designed to minimize disruption. Northern raccoons are sometimes seen on the night tours and their relatives, white-nosed coatis, roam the beach during the day. Two large mangrove forests are home to American crocodiles and spectacled caimans, as well as numerous birds, including roseate spoonbills, anhingas and wood storks. In the last decade, the numbers of nesting leatherbacks have plummeted by as much as 90%. An Earthwatch-supported research project investigating the decline accepts paying volunteers (**w** www.leatherback.org/labaulas.html)
32mi (51km) south-west of Liberia

RB Lomas Barbudal

Adjacent to PN Palo Verde, this quiet reserve is little-visited but has many of the same attractions as its more popular neighbor. It lacks Palo Verde's large wetlands and their waterbird congregations, but otherwise the birding is excellent, especially for dry-forest species. Collared peccaries, mantled howlers and white-nosed coatis are easily seen and the white-faced capuchins here are extremely used to people; they've been studied since 1990 in a project which accepts volunteers (**w** www.sscnet.ucla.edu/anthro/faculty/jmanson/assistants.htm)
13mi south-west of Liberia
SINAC ☎ 192 or Regional Office (Bagaces) ☎ 671-1290/671-1455; fax 671-1462.

RNFS Ostional

Topping even Santa Rosa's Nancite beach, Ostional is Costa Rica's most important nesting site for the olive ridley (known locally as *lora*). Like Nancite, mass nestings known as *arribadas* can be enormous, with as many as 500,000 turtles (but usually fewer) laying en masse. Ostional villagers are permitted to harvest turtle eggs for the first 36 hours of an arribada– the only legal harvest in the region – after which they

monitor the beaches for poachers. Turtle tours run by locals further enhances their stake in the species and deliver the best chances in Central America of seeing an arribada. The nest season is from July to November with the peak period around September-October; arribadas are more likely to occur around the first and the last quarter of the moon.
31mi (50km) south-west of Nicoya
SINAC ☎ 192 or Regional Office (Bagaces) ☎ 671-1290/671-1455; fax 671-1062.

Photo far left: Brown pelicans.
Center left: West Indian manatee.
Center right: Basilisk lizard.
Above: Roseate spoonbill.

PANAMA
The bridge between two continents

Highlights

- A female harpy eagle screaming at intruders from her nest 100ft up in a *coiba* tree at Punta Patiño, Darién Province
- Watching a male resplendent quetzal feeding on miniature avocados in misty PN Volcán Barú
- The nonstop action of a canopy flock at Pipeline Rd, PN Soberanía – guaranteed to turn any birdwatcher's head
- Squadrons of parrots – giant macaws, colorful amazons and swift-flying parakeets – crisscrossing the sky at Cana, Darién Province
- Snorkeling over the coral reefs in balmy Bocas del Toro while frigatebirds drift lazily overhead
- Listening to forest-falcons and howler monkeys as night falls over the Canopy Tower, PN Soberanía
- Sitting by an army-ant swarm on Cerro Pirre, Darién Province, watching and waiting for a chestnut-vented ground-cuckoo to reveal itself

Remote parts of Panama, such as Darién Province, still offer a chance to get away from crowds and travel the traditional way.

PANAMA is literally a bridge – a narrow isthmus barely 100mi (160km) wide that spans the gap between the two great landmasses of North and South America. Its geological history is complicated, but in general terms it was across this isthmus that the rich biodiversities of the two continents collided, mixed and speciated. The isthmus probably rose and fell several times over millions of years, cleaving an ocean in two and allowing successive invasions of plants and animals to occur in both directions. Panama's highest mountain, 11,408ft (3478m) Volcán Barú, stands as testimony to this dynamic past; today this extinct giant towers over the western end of the land bridge, which from here sweeps east for approximately 350mi (565km) to where the vast lowland rainforests of Darién abut north-west South America.

Relative to its size, the country's biodiversity is staggering. Among ecotourists, Panama is known primarily as a birding destination, and the country boasts the richest avifauna in Central America – 940 species have been recorded, including 11 endemics, some 66 species shared only with Costa Rica and many found elsewhere only in South America; In the whole of Central America, only Panama has a healthy population of harpy eagles; and the resplendent quetzal, Central America's number one bird, can be comparatively easy to see here. Among the 218 mammal species are several endemics and many, such as Geoffroy's tamarins and capybaras, common only to South America; a casual visitor could probably see 20 mammal species without too much effort. The biological inventory is still incomplete, but other vertebrate tallies include some 226 species of reptile and 164 of amphibian. Several coral-fringed archipelagos boast wildlife that has been isolated long enough to evolve into new species, and the distinct marine faunas of the Caribbean Sea and Pacific Ocean are close enough to enjoy on the same day.

An excellent system of national parks and other reserves protects substantial stands of rainforest, coral reefs and uninhabited islands; further habitat and wildlife corridors are owned by Ancon (Asociación Nacional para la Conservación de la Naturaleza), Panama's main private conservation organization.

Despite a tropical climate outside the hurricane belt, easily accessible biological riches and some excellent wildlife guides and facilities, the country still attracts far fewer ecotourists than neighboring Costa Rica. But that's probably why in Panama they claim that one birdwatcher could see 20 quetzals in a day, but that in Costa Rica 20 birders will see only one quetzal. ∎

SUGGESTED ITINERARIES

One week The proximity of superb stands of lowland forest to Panama City mean even a few days will be long enough to get an introduction to the country's amazing wildlife. If you have a few hours of daylight to spare on arrival, head to Parque Natural Metropolitano on the outskirts of the CBD. Also aim to spend at least one morning at PN Soberanía's Pipeline Rd and other sites close to Panama City, and another on a relaxing cruise up the Canal to Isla Barro Colorado for great views of howler monkeys and other mammals. Your other great priority should be to fly down to Cana in PN Darién, one of the world's great birding destinations, where you should spend a minimum of 3 nights and make the ascent of Cerro Pirre for the various endemics. Treat yourself to a night at the Canopy Tower in PN Soberanía as a finale.

Two weeks Follow the one-week itinerary then travel to PN Volcán Barú (2 nights) to look for birds endemic to Panama and Costa Rica, as well as legendary species such as resplendent quetzals and turquoise cotingas. Head to the northwest coast, birding en route in the Caribbean lowlands, and chill out in Bocas del Toro (2 nights) with some seabirds, waders and a bit of snorkeling.

Alternatively, spend a whole week in Darién, with at least 4 nights at Cana and Cerro Pirre, then fly across to Punta Patiño to look for harpy eagles and other specialties on the coast. Use the remaining week to thoroughly work Pipeline Rd at PN Soberanía and other sites near Panama City (3 or 4 nights), then head up to Nusagandi for the remainder of your stay, filling in any downtime at Parque Natural Metropolitano.

One month A month gives you time to pick the eyes out of Panama – a 'best of' trip. Spend a week in Darién, doing the Cana/Cerro Pirre/Punta Patiño circuit; a week exploring Panama City environs, including Nusagandi; and a week traveling from Volcán Barú through the Caribbean lowlands to Bocas del Toro. With advance planning you could hook up with a week-long trip to seldom-visited Isla de Coiba, which offers scarlet macaws and endemic species, or spend the last week lingering in a favorite spot, doing the cruise to Isla Barro Colorado … exploring, snorkeling and relaxing in Bocas del Toro …

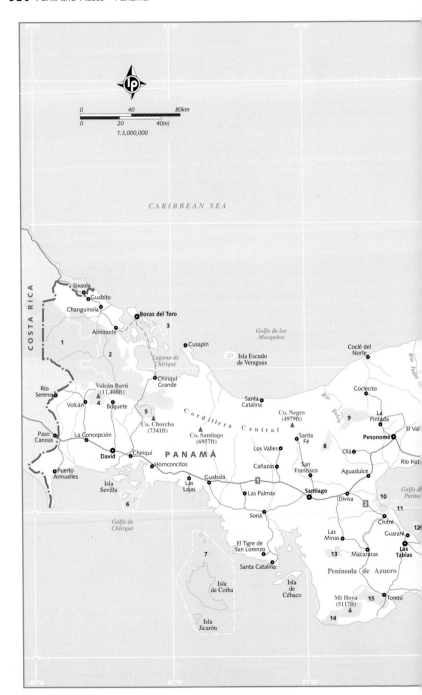

1 Parque Internacional La Amistad
2 Bosque Protector de Palo Seco
3 Parque Nacional Marino Isla Bastimentos
4 Parque Nacional Volcán Barú
5 Reserva Forestal Fortuna
6 Parque Nacional Marino Golfo de Chiriquí
7 Parque Nacional Isla de Coiba
8 Reserva Forestal La Laguna de La Yeguada
9 Parque Nacional Omar Torrijos Herrera
10 Refugio de Vida Silvestre Cenegón del Mangle
11 Parque Nacional Sarigua
12 Refugio de Vida Silvestre Peñón de la Honda
13 Reserva Forestal El Montuoso
14 Parque Nacional Cerro Hoya
15 Reserva Forestal La Tronosa
16 Refugio de Vida Silvestre Isla Iguana

17 Parque Nacional y Reserva Biológica Altos de Campana
18 Parque Nacional Interoceánico de las Américas
19 Monumento Natural Isla Barro Colorado
20 Parque Nacional Soberanía
21 Área Recreativa Lago Gatún
22 Parque Nacional Portobelo
23 Parque Nacional Chagres
24 Summit Botanical Gardens & Zoo
25 Parque Nacional Camino de Cruces
26 Reserva de Producción de Agua Tapagrá
27 Parque Natural Metropolitano
28 Refugio de Vida Silvestre Islas Taboga y Urabá
29 Reserva Natural Punta Patiño
30 Reserva Forestal Canglón
31 Bosque Protector del Darién
32 Parque Nacional Darién

CENTRAL PANAMA

Biodiversity at the doorstep

Forests flanking the famous Panama Canal, and indeed the Canal itself, support an astonishing range of species within easy reach of Panama City.

Wildlife highlights
Internationally famous birding close to Panama City plus the opportunity to see some common rainforest mammals. Parque Natural Metropolitano in downtown Panama City boasts 227 bird species, including the skulking rosy thrush-tanager; birds at world-famous Pipeline Rd in PN Soberanía too numerous to list but the record stands at 360 species in 24 hours. Huge shorebird concentrations on mudflats adjacent to Panama City in season and easily seen specialties at Juan Díaz mangroves near the city's edge. Common mammals include Geoffroy's tamarin, especially at Parque Natural Metropolitano; white-faced capuchins, mantled howlers, agoutis, coatis and both sloths in PN Soberanía; and capybaras can be seen along the Canal itself.

IT is a delicious irony that Panama's famous canal – the source of much of the country's wealth – would quickly silt up without the flanking rainforests that form its watershed. In recognition of this vital fact, much of the lowland forest connecting the Pacific Ocean with the Caribbean Sea along the canal is now protected by PNs Soberanía and Camino de Cruces. Local and international birdwatchers flock to sites such as Pipeline Rd in this valuable wildlife corridor; and the southern end of PN Camino de Cruces is contiguous with Parque Natural Metropolitano, a mere 10 minutes' drive from the city center. Thus while based in Panama City (or if just passing through), a visitor has access to excellent rainforest and a superb sample of Panama's staggering biodiversity.

Mangroves and rainforest in the big city

Parque Natural Metropolitano is ideally situated for an early morning walk or a half-day excursion, and one of the best wildlife trails is Camino Mono Titi, which takes you (steeply) uphill through the forest to the summit of 490ft (150m) Cerro Cedar. **Central American agoutis** are common and 'mono titi' is the local name for **Geoffroy's tamarin** – the park supports a population of these small monkeys and this is one of the best trails to see them. Look for **lance-tailed manakins** along this trail, and mid-canopy flocks should contain a variety of **tanagers**, **flycatchers** and **woodcreepers**. There can be good birding at the summit where the canopy is at eye level: At sunrise forest species sunning themselves or prospecting for an early morning feed can include **toucans**, **squirrel cuckoos**, various **tanagers**, **yellow-backed orioles** and **violaceous trogons**; and locally common **hummingbirds** flit among flower-ing bushes. On the descent turn off at Sendero la Cieneguita, a narrower, less-frequented track hemmed in by the forest where you may be rewarded with an elusive gem – the **rosy thrush-tanager**. This is also a good trail for finding

Geoffroy's tamarins. Other sought-after birds recorded in the park include **pheasant cuckoos** and a Panamanian endemic, the **yellow-green tyrannulet**.

Magnificent frigatebirds float effortlessly overhead wherever you are in Panama City. **Brown pelicans**, too, are common, and **Neotropic cormorants** and **snowy** and **cattle egrets** pass over in formation at dawn and dusk. Wader and waterbird buffs shouldn't miss the mudflats at Panama Viejo, one of the most import-ant sites in Panama for migratory shorebirds. Work the foreshore near Casas Reales, where a vast expanse of mud exposed at low tide attracts thousands of waders in season. Vagrant **gulls** and **terns** (including the fabulous **Inca tern**) have turned up from both North and South America to loaf among the **laughing gulls** and **royal terns**; and large numbers of **whimbrels**, **willets** and **short-billed dowitchers** are often punctuated by various **peeps** (small waders), **marbled godwits**, **black-bellied** (gray) **plovers**, **red knots** and **surfbirds**. Larger wading birds include **white ibises**, **wood storks** and a variety of **herons** and **egrets**, such as **great** and **little blue herons**, and **snowy** and **great egrets**.

Juan Díaz mangroves is an area adjoining the southeastern corner of the city (best visited with a guide) whose bird riches belie the rather unappealing nature of the site. Part of the area is used as a garbage dump, but as many as 72 bird species have been seen in a morning's birding here. Shallow marshes attract **black-bellied whistling-ducks**, **wattled jacanas**, **red-breasted blackbirds** and **pied water-tyrants** (here at the northernmost- end of their range); and **fork-tailed flycatchers** and an occasional **pearl kite** sits on overhead wires. Two **hummingbirds** – **scaly-breasted** and **sapphire-throated** – are easily seen here and this is a good site for the mangrove-frequenting **straight-billed woodcreeper**.

The canopy at eye level

Pipeline Rd (Sendero Oleoducto), an access road that traverses PN Soberanía, is one of the best rainforest birding sites in Central America (if not the world): it was born in 1996 that members of the Panama Audubon Society set a Christmas Bird Count record of 360 species in 24 hours! Gates keep out all but official vehicles so you can walk along the road for as much of its 17.5mi (28km) length as you want, through primary and secondary forest offering almost nonstop birding on an easy gradient. This is an ideal site for beginners to get to know Panama's lowland forest birds. Pipeline Rd's bird list spans nearly every Central American family and you will almost certainly see various **hummingbirds**, **parrots**, **antbirds**, **manakins**, **icterids**, **woodcreepers** and **tanagers**. The **slaty-tailed trogon** is PN Soberanía's

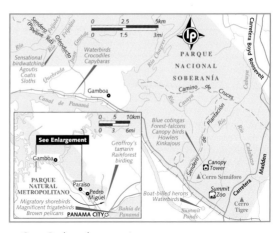

Location Parque Natural Metropolitano 1mi (1.5km) north of the city center. PN Soberanía 20mi (32km) from Panama City. BCI 25mi (40km) north-west of Panama City.

Facilities Walking trails, information center and museum at Parque Natural Metropolitano. Walking trails in PN Soberanía.

Accommodations Canopy Tower (☎ 264-5720, **e** stay@canopytower.com, **w** www.canopytower.com) at PN Soberanía. Wide range of accommodation available in Panama City.

Wildlife rhythms Raptor migration is at its peak in October and March; shorebirds are most abundant at Panama Viejo from October to March, but some, especially first-year birds, are usually present year-round.

Contact Panama Audubon Society (☎224-9371, 224-4740, **e** audupan@pananet.com, **w** www.pananet.com/audubon/home.html).
Ancon Expeditions (☎ 269-9414, 269-9415, fax 264-3713, **e** info@anconexpeditions.com, **w** www.anconexpeditions.com).

official bird, and four other **trogon** species might also be encountered: **Black-throated, black-tailed, violaceous** and **white-tailed**; **motmots** include **blue-crowned, rufous** and **broad-billed**; and **purple-throated fruitcrows** are relatively common. A first-timer is virtually assured of an amazing tally and with such a high diversity even experienced birders often see new species; Pipeline Rd's proximity to Panama City also means it's easy to come back to winkle out sought-after birds, such as **sunbitterns**, when you have a spare morning or afternoon. Pipeline Rd can also offer good spotlighting – nocturnal birds recorded here have included eight **owl** species (notably **black-and-white** and **crested**, but commonly **mottled**), both **common** and **great potoos**, a variety of nightjars and, incredibly, a solitary oilbird (a rare straggler from Colombia).

At Semaphore Hill (Cerro Semáforo), also in PN Soberanía, a former US Air Force radar installation has been refitted as the Canopy Tower, a small hotel used almost exclusively by visiting birdwatchers. From the hotel's rooftop observation deck guests have the luxury of watching canopy flocks at eye level and can scan across the surrounding valleys for birds on the move. Star attractions are the **blue cotinga**, which is seen regularly in the early morning, and elusive **forest-falcons** that here are heard almost daily. The rising sun stirs flocks of **amazons**, and birds perched on exposed branches to catch some early rays may include **scaled pigeons, masked tityras**, and sometimes large, mixed groups of **rainbow-billed** and **chestnut-mandibled toucans. Raptors** start to thermal as the day warms up (the tower makes an ideal site to watch their annual migrations); and nearby *Cecropia* trees attract various **tanagers** and canopy-dwellers such as **green shrike-vireos** that can otherwise be hard to see from the ground. Adjacent to the Canopy Tower's access road where it turns off the Gamboa Rd, Sendero de Plantación is open to the public and also offers excellent birding.

Several mammal species should be seen by exploring the Pipeline Rd and Sendero de Plantación by day, and especially by night. **Mantled howlers** abound in the forest, and **Geoffroy's tamarins** and **white-faced capuchins** are relatively common; you may smell or even see **collared peccaries**, but you'll almost certainly see **Central American agoutis** and **white-nosed coatis**. Both **sloths** are common, **northern tamanduas** are seen regularly and

Bringing back the harpy

Panama's national bird, the harpy eagle, was once found in lowland rainforest throughout Central America. But these large, bold eagles are often the targets of hunters and harpies were extirpated from the Canal Zone during the 20th century. The Peregrine Fund, an international organization dedicated to the conservation of the world's raptors, has created a small captive breeding nucleus of harpy eagles unable to return to the wild (eg, because of injury) at the Neotropical Raptor Center, near Panama City. Ultimately the Peregrine Fund aims to reinstate these birds throughout their former range, but it's a long road: A female released in 1998 was retrapped and brought back into human care after she repeatedly strayed outside protected areas in the Canal Zone. A male harpy eagle, hatched in 1997 and released into PN Soberanía in 1998, was not so fortunate and was shot by a hunter in 2000. Recognizing that the cooperation of local people is essential in preserving this species, the Peregrine Fund is now also devoting resources to wildlife education in villages surrounding officially protected areas. For more information on Panama's harpy eagles and the Peregrine Fund visit its Web site at **w** www.peregrinefund.org

tayras occasionally; and prized nocturnal sightings have included **western night monkeys, ocelots, jaguarundis** and **olingos**.

Open water and edge habitat along the Canal itself attracts waterbirds that wouldn't necessarily be seen in the adjoining national parks, and lily-choked backwaters and other features are also worth exploring. If you're on a boat trip through the Canal (eg, en route to BCI – see below – or an organized cruise) scan the eastern shore for basking **American crocodiles** and, in the early morning or late afternoon, **capybaras** (the Canal marks the westernmost limit of this South American animal's range). Gamboa Ponds is also a great site for **capybaras** at night, and during the day for **rufescent tiger-herons, white-throated crakes, purple gallinules**, kingfishers, **ospreys** and **great egrets**, as well as **American crocs** and **turtles**. Summit Ponds is an excellent site for **boat-billed herons**, and other water-frequenting species could include **American pygmy** and **Amazon kingfishers**, and a variety of **herons** and **egrets**.

Barro Colorado Island (BCI)

Formed when Lake Gatún was flooded during the construction of the Panama Canal, this forested island has been a research center for the Smithsonian Tropical Research Institute (STRI) since 1923 and is one of the best places in Panama to see diurnal mammals. You stand an excellent chance of seeing **mantled howlers** (sometimes at very close quarters) plus **white-faced capuchins** and **Central American spider monkeys**; and other easily-seen species along the well-marked trails include **agoutis, coatis, red brockets** – BCI has a large population – and **red-tailed squirrels**. BCI's bat fauna is particularly rich and **greater white-lined bats** roost under the eaves of some buildings. An abundance of prey supports a healthy population of cats, including **ocelots** and **pumas** – the latter have been recorded by remote cameras – and **jaguar** tracks are occasionally found. At present visitors can see BCI only as part of a day trip organised through STRI (☎ 212-8026, **e** visitstri@tivoli.si.edu), but bona fide researchers who stay overnight have a good chance of seeing **pacas, collared peccaries** and **nine-banded armadillos**. ∎

Lily-choked Gamboa Ponds at the mouth of Río Chagres is a great spot for capybaras; here the world's largest rodent is at the westernmost part of its range.

PARQUE NACIONAL **DARIÉN**

Riches of Panama's last frontier

Wildlife highlights

Cana is one of the world's Top Ten birding destinations, with a list of 400-plus species including 60 found nowhere else in the country. Daily sightings include up to four macaws and numerous other parrots; and dusky-backed jacamars, red-throated caracaras, rufous-vented ground-cuckoos and black-tipped cotingas are among other sought-after specialties. Cerro Pirre has a suite of endemic birds and is the only site in Central American for several species, such as saffron-headed parrots and golden-headed quetzals. Common primates throughout the area include Geoffroy's tamarins, white-faced capuchins, mantled howlers and brown-headed spider monkeys. White-lipped peccaries and gray foxes are seen regularly and rare mammals sighted have included pumas, bush dogs and Baird's tapirs.

PANAMA'S largest wilderness features vast swathes of primary forest, the country's largest stands of mangroves and species-rich secondary forest where historic settlements have been obliterated by the jungle. PN Darién is Panama's largest national park and a World Biosphere Reserve, but much of the region is inaccessible – and will hopefully remain that way, for in areas where roads have penetrated, environmental destruction has quickly followed. The region is rich in gold and other resources, but it is the wildlife riches that people now come to see: Here at the easternmost point of the land-bridge the amazing biodiversity of South America has spilled into Central America and the park is contiguous with PN Los Katíos, a largely pristine tract of forest in Colombia's Chocó Province (also rich in wildlife). The effort of getting to Darién is amply repaid: Cana, the most accessible site, is now well-established on the world birding circuit and presents the opportunity to see an astonishing range of Panama's birds and some hard-to-see mammals. The shoulders of 5200ft (1605m) Cerro Pirre rise above Cana, and it's worth the climb up Pirre to see a number of birds endemic to these mountains. RN Punta Patiño forms a corridor to PN Darién and features giant mangroves and one of the world's most-wanted birds, the harpy eagle.

Everybody's experience is different, but Cana is 'birds central' for the Darién. You'll probably start to identify birds even before you land at the airstrip – **king vultures** soar among the ubiquitous **turkey** and **black vultures**, and **macaws** are easily seen on the approach over the treetops. Indeed, parrots bombard the senses as soon as you alight: Flights of **mealy** and **red-lored amazons**, and **brown-hooded** and **blue-headed parrots** can be seen all day, but especially at morning and evening; and small flocks of fast-flying **orange-chinned parakeets**, and four species of **macaws** (**chestnut-fronted**, **blue-and-yellow**, **great green** and **red-and-green**) crisscross the valley in their daily search for food trees. **Blue-and-yellow macaws** are usually seen in pairs

In less than a century Cana's forest has reclaimed a town, mining equipment and a railway, and is now one of the world's premier birding destinations.

and are distinctive even when early morning mist envelopes the valley. Outstanding among the raptors are **white hawks** and one of Darién's prizes – **crested eagles**.

Cana's airstrip is flanked by forest edge and is an ideal place to scope out **dusky-backed jacamars, red-throated caracaras, rainbow-billed** and **chestnut-mandibled toucans, collared aracaris** and **crested guans** – all seen regularly on tall trees. Flocks of **swifts (band-rumped, white-collared** and **gray-rumped)** hawk and wheel, particularly at dusk, when they are often accompanied by **southern rough-winged swallows** (the **white-thighed swallow**, a forest dweller, has also been seen here). **Swallow tanagers** frequent the taller trees.

Flowering bushes and hummingbird feeders around Cana Lodge attract birds all day. A variety of hummers includes **rufous-tailed** and **blue-chested hummingbirds, white-necked jacobins** and **green thorntails. Tanagers – golden-hooded, crimson-backed** and scads of **flame-rumps** – flit back and forth; and other visitors include **yellow-billed caciques, white-headed wrens** and various **tyrants. Barred puffbirds** perch in trees overlooking the clearing and a **bat falcon** often scans from tall trees. Look from the balcony at the dining area for **black-tipped cotingas, collared aracaris**, more **macaws** and **Chocó toucans**, which have recently been identified at Cana. It's a long shot, but a **puma** was once seen by day crossing the lodge clearing!

Pauraques are easily spotlit around the lodge after dark, but keep your eyes (and ears) open for **rufous nighthawks**. Both **common** and **great potoos** are sometimes seen here – try the Boca de Cupe Trail – and other nocturnal possibilities include **mottled owls** and **Central American pygmy-owls**. By spotlighting before daylight you'll also have a good chance of seeing **gray foxes** around the buildings or on the airstrip – watch for **snakes** wherever you walk and for large **marine toads** snapping up insects attracted to the lodge's lights.

On the trail of ants and antbirds

Aim to be up as soon as the **mantled howler monkeys** start calling before dawn – the best chance of seeing them is along one of the excellent trails that start around the lodge, where you should also see **Geoffroy's tamarins, white-faced capuchins** and **brown-headed spider monkeys** (which around Cana are all-black). All the trails are worth exploring and range from the 100yd–Sendero a la Locomotora to a 25mi (40km) trail that runs all the way to the town of Boca de Cupe.

An old steam engine, a relic of Cana's mining days, sits rusting in the jungle at the end of Sendero a la Locomotora. Thousands of leafcutter ants now use the railway tracks as a highway – if you haven't looked at leafcutters closely, this is an ideal place: There's a huge nest straddling the tracks and nearby you can watch a production line of ants dumping waste on a massive fungal slag heap (see Other Invertebrates, pp214–15).

Great jacamars (see the boxed text, p136) are often seen near the start of the Sendero las Minas and you shouldn't have to venture far to see more goodies, including **crimson-crested woodpeckers, slate-colored grosbeaks, dusky-faced tanagers** and **orange-billed sparrows**. Several offshoots from the main

Location Cana is 140mi (225km) southeast of Panama City by air (charter flights only); or 25mi (40km) by foot from Boca de Cupe. Punta Patiño is accessible only by air to La Palma (scheduled flights) then boat (by arrangement only). **Facilities** Well-marked walking trails around Cana and up Cerro Pirre. Walking trails near Punta Patiño Lodge. **Accommodations** Lodges at Cana and Punta Patiño; tented camp on Cerro Pirre. **Wildlife rhythms** Great green macaws are seen most commonly during the rainy season at Cana. Humpback whales are most often seen in the waters near Punt Patiño in October to February. Harpy eagles nest February to April. **Contact** Ancon Expeditions (☎ 269-9414, 269-9415; fax 264-3713; **e** info@anconexpeditions.com; **w** www.anconexpeditions.com).

The spectacled antpitta is just one of many antbird species that could be encountered at Cana.

trail are also worth exploring and crossing a stream you'll reach some more mining relics, including a liana-draped smokestack that's starting to look like a tree. The Boca de Cupe Trail is another excellent birding trail and relatively open secondary forest near the start allows great viewing of specialties, such as **gray-cheeked nunlets**; another sought-after bird, the **viridian dacnis**, has been seen along this trail in low numbers.

Army-ant swarms could occur on any trail, and apart from obligate ant-followers like **bicolored** and **ocellated antbirds**, Cana boasts numerous scarce and sought-after species in this specialized group: among them are **immaculate, bare-crowned** and **dull-mantled antbirds, black-crowned antpittas** and **rufous-breasted ant-thrushes**. And Darién's forests offer one of the best chances anywhere of seeing the elusive **rufous-vented ground-cuckoo** – most sightings have been with large ant swarms on the Cerro Pirre and Boca de Cupe Trails.

The last Andean outpost

Cerro Pirre is allegedly the very peak from which the Spaniard Balboa first saw the Pacific, but it also has high ecological importance as the only footprint the Andes mountains makes on Central America. Those who make the arduous 5.5mi (9km) hike up will be rewarded with a number of endemic birds and further chances to see mammals. Birds are the stars on the Pirre Trail, but you should see **brown-headed spider monkeys, mantled howlers** and **white-faced capuchins** on the way without too much trouble. **White-lipped peccaries** are common on Pirre (although you'll probably smell rather than see them), and two species of **pygmy squirrels** – Alfaro's and western – are also present, although they are tough to spot and hard to identify. Keep an eye out for **jaguar** prints and scratch marks along the way; **Baird's tapir** has been encountered and, in keeping with the region's special status, Central America's rarest large mammal – the **bush dog** – has also been seen on the trail.

After you've recovered from the climb, even an afternoon's birding should be rewarded with some of Pirre's endemic birds (keen birders should concentrate on looking for these species). Two endemic hummers – **rufous-cheeked (Pirre) hummingbird** and **greenish puffleg** – can be seen around Pirre Camp; **Pirre bush-tanagers, chestnut-capped brush-finches** and **varied solitaires** are common at times; and foraging tamely among the

The bird that saved a valley

Gold was mined at Cana as early as the 16th century and at one time some 20,000 people scratched out a living here. During the last attempt at mining, early in the 20th century, a railway was carved out of the jungle and heavy machinery shipped in from Boca de Cupe. Eventually this mine also closed: The buildings have long since rotted away, bats now inhabit the mineshafts, and the furnaces, smokestacks and railway lie rusting in the undergrowth. As the forest slowly reclaimed the valley its wildlife recovered and the lease was up for sale when Ancon looked at buying the site. But under the terms of the title the owners were obliged to keep mining at Cana. Ancon lobbied hard to get the terms changed so Cana would be preserved for posterity, and eventually convinced President Ernesto Pérez Balladares to visit and see for himself what was at stake. Balladares was the first Panamanian president to officially visit PN Darién, and while walking Las Minas Trail the first bird he saw was a great jacamar; this magnificent iridescent member of the jacamar family was enough to convince him that Cana should be a reserve, not a mine.

tents are **slaty-backed nightingale-thrushes**. A bench nearby overlooks another peak, Setetule, and makes a convenient spot from which to look for **tanager** flocks moving through and **raptors** drifting down the valley; **white-headed wrens** roost near the lookout. The half-day walk to Pirre's summit, 1000ft (300m) higher than Pirre Camp, is highly recommended (and far less strenuous than the climb to Pirre Camp). The trail passes through epiphyte-festooned trees that get gradually smaller as you climb, allowing eye-level views of bromeliads. Along the way you'll have a chance at endemics, such as **green-naped tanagers**, **sooty-headed wrens**, **Pirre warblers** and beautiful **treerunners**. Check flowering ericaceas (epiphytic, tubular flowers growing in sprays) for two Colombian specialties, the **tooth-billed hummingbird** and **green-fronted lancebill**. Real prizes have included the **golden-headed quetzal** (Pirre is the only site in Central America for this Andean specialty) and **saffron-headed parrots** (another hard-to-see species restricted to neighboring Colombia and Venezuela).

The birds on Cerro Pirre are noticeably different from Cana, and include several endemic species as well as more widespread montane birds, such as the chestnut-capped brush-finch.

Luck plays an important role in what you see on the trail, but an early descent to Cana could be rewarded with **great curassows** and **great tinamous** on the path, and sightings of gems, such as **crimson-bellied woodpeckers**, **ornate hawk-eagles**, **tody motmots** and **blue cotingas**; **spectacled owls** are sometimes seen by day around the halfway mark.

Home of the harpy eagle

RN Punta Patiño is a huge reserve owned by Ancon that protects extensive lowland forest and mangroves. During the boat trip to Punta Patiño Lodge you'll almost certainly see **brown pelicans**, **magnificent frigatebirds**, **laughing gulls** and **Neotropic cormorants**, but watch for cetaceans: **Bottlenose dolphins** and **humpback whales** frequent these waters. Other birds include **terns** (**royal**, **sandwich** and **gull-billed**), **American oystercatchers** and **waders** on the beach near the lodge.

A swampy flat near the lodge supports up to 60 **capybaras** – you should have no trouble seeing these massive rodents after dark with a flashlight. A few **crocs** are also present, though hard to see, and the capybaras attract **jaguars** from time to time – in this remote, undisturbed area you probably have as good a chance of seeing *el tigre* as anywhere. You'll almost certainly see **gray foxes** around the lodge, even during the day, but especially at night; and **tayras** are seen with reasonable frequency in a patch of dry forest nearby.

But the greatest attraction at Punta Patiño is the magnificent **harpy eagle** – Darién supports a high density of these powerful predators, and several pairs are known to nest in the reserve. To reach the eagles you must travel by boat up the Mogué River, where towering uncut mangroves support **Amazon kingfishers**, **white ibises**, **great** and **little blue herons**, and waders such as **willets**, **whimbrels** and **spotted sandpipers**. Late afternoon or early morning are good times to look for **crab-eating raccoons** venturing down to the water's edge. To get to the eagles involves a visit to the Embera village of Mogué; **black oropendolas** are a specialty bird of the secondary forest near the village. ■

Watching tips
The weather on Cerro Pirre can become wet and misty at short notice so allow yourself some time to work the montane forest – aim to spend at least two nights at Pirre Camp and give yourself time to bird on the way back down to Cana. If you come across an ant swarm, wait quietly for birds to appear – many antbirds are wary, but they will eventually get used to your presence and by putting in some time you stand a better chance of seeing specialties.

PARQUE NACIONAL **VOLCÁN BARÚ**

On the trail of the quetzal

Wildlife highlights
Mist-shrouded forests of mighty Volcán Barú support resplendent quetzals, many birds found only in Panama and neighboring Costa Rica plus turquoise cotingas and other key species. PN Volcán Barú offers the chance at some 250 bird species plus montane squirrel (the most likely mammal sighting) and great walking through cloud forest; Fincas Hartmann and Lerida are two ecofriendly coffee plantations that entice birders with regular sightings of quetzals.

Location 270mi (440km) west of Panama City.
Facilities Marked walking trails.
Accommodations Los Quetzales (lodge) tel (507) 771-2291, **e** stay@losquetzales.com, **w** www.losquetzales.com; basic campground in PN Volcán Barú; good variety in Boquete.
Wildlife rhythms Quetzals are most easily seen between January and August.
Contact ANAM tel 775-3163

Watching tips
If you're desperate to add the homely volcano junco to your list, it's easier to see it in Costa Rica's PN Chirripó.

PANAMA'S highest mountain, 11,408ft (3478m) Volcán Barú, towers above the Chiriquí Highlands – a hotspot for many of the 61 endemic birds Panama shares only with Costa Rica. Barú is now extinct, but its convulsions created fertile soils that support bird-friendly coffee plantations and its rugged shoulders are cloaked in prime habitat for the much-sought resplendent quetzal.

Sendero los Quetzales is a walking trail that traverses PN Volcán Barú between Cerro Punta and Boquete through cloud forest and high, mixed deciduous forest. Open areas and secondary growth near Los Quetzales Lodge support **spotted wood-quails** (easier heard than seen) and **yellow-bellied siskins**; watch for **fire-throated, magnificent (admirable)** and **volcano hummingbirds**; **violet sabrewings** visit feeders at the lodge itself. Look at the tops of trees – though they are often mist-enshrouded – for **long-tailed silky-flycatchers**. Their sibling species, **black-and-yellow silky-flycatchers**, are also common, and mixed flocks could contain **slaty flowerpiercers, spangle-cheeked tanagers, mountain robins, prong-billed barbets, ruddy treerunners** and **yellow-thighed finches**. **Black-cheeked warblers, slate-throated redstarts** and **sooty-capped bush-tanagers** are common; and watch ahead for **black-billed nightingale-thrushes** running along the trail (especially near where the Sendero crosses Río Caldera). You might also pick out the call of the **wrenthrush** above the roar of Río Caldera, but this skulker is hard to see in the undergrowth. The lowest point in the national park is 5900ft (1800m), so this is prime habitat for **montane squirrels** – they could be seen anywhere along the higher reaches of the trail. Likewise, a **resplendent quetzal** could be spotted nearly anywhere, but these shy birds are best sought early in the breeding season when males are growing their spectacular trains and starting to call for mates. Walk quietly and keep talk to a minimum when looking for quetzals.

Barú's summit, most easily reached by road from Boquete, is the only spot in Panama where you can see **volcano juncos**, and two more Panama–Costa Rica endemics that can be seen at treeline are **large-footed finches** and **timberline wrens**. Two coffee plantations high on Barú's slopes, Fincas Hartmann and Lerida, grow ecofriendly coffee and preserve remnant patches of good birding forest (they also actively encourage birdwatchers). Bird-friendly coffee-growing practices include allowing emergent trees to shade the beans, providing sanctuary for sedentary and migratory species alike. **Resplendent quetzals** can be seen at both fincas (although the usual rules of quetzal-watching apply), and **turquoise cotingas** are seen regularly around the hacienda at Finca Lerida. Finca Hartmann preserves a patch of forest above 4500ft (1370m) with some excellent birding that can include tantalizing attractions, such as **silver-throated tanagers, sulphur-winged parakeets, turquoise cotingas** and **red-headed barbets**. ∎

OTHER SITES – PANAMA

Bocas del Toro
This Caribbean archipelago offers a number of treats for wildlifers who can tear themselves away from the laidback lifestyle. Magnificent frigatebirds, brown pelicans, brown boobies, common noddies, and royal, sandwich and gull-billed terns are all seen regularly on the boat crossing from Almirante. Mangrove and gray-chested swallows loaf on

waterside decks; and mudflats exposed at low tide in Bahía Sand Fly attract shorebirds and Würdemann's heron, a color morph of the great blue heron. There's good snorkeling in the lee of PN Isla Bastimento, and tawny-crowned tanagers, bay wrens, and the Bocas races of the golden-collared manakin (thought by some to be a distinct species) and strawberry poison-dart frog can be seen along the trail to the island's surf beach. Local boat operators (check with Ancon Expeditions ☎ 269-9414, e info@ancon expeditions.com) can take you to look at nesting red-billed tropicbirds and brown boobies at Swan Caye (Isla de los Pájaros), or to Changuinola Channel, a banana canal that's worth exploring for waterbirds,

northern jacanas, olive-fronted parakeets and Montezuma oropendolas.
12mi (20km) north-east of Almirante

PN Isla de Coiba
This little-visited Pacific Island is Panama's largest and has been isolated from the mainland long enough for unique wildlife to evolve. Uninhabited apart from a penal colony (whose success is partly owed to the presence of large numbers of fer-de-lances on land and tiger sharks offshore), Coiba offers excellent diving and snorkeling to well-equipped vessels, and the chance to spot humpback whales, orcas (killer whales), and spotted and common dolphins. PN Isla de Coiba protects the whole island (including large stands of primary forest) and adjoining waters. Mammals to watch for include the Coiba Island howler (considered by many to be a distinct species) and the endemic Coiba Island agouti. Although many of Coiba's 147 recorded bird species are shared with the mainland, this is the only place in Panama where scarlet macaws can be reliably seen and world birders should head

here for the endemic Coiba spinetail (although some researchers regard it as a race of the rusty-backed spinetail of South America). Access to Coiba is difficult, but Ancon Expeditions (☎ 269-9414, e info@ancon expeditions.com) can organise guided tours and dive operators that visit the island include MV Coral Star (w www.coralstar.com)
200mi (320km) south-west of Panama City

Nusagandi
The Pemasky (Project for the Study and Management of Wilderness Areas of Kuna Yala) Nature Park is an ecotourism project owned and operated by the Kuna Indians as a buffer between the Kuna Yala Indian Reserve and the deforestation creeping north from the Interamericana. This preserve offers some of the best birding in eastern Panama and the chance of seeing some rare specialties, including speckled antshrikes, broad-billed sapayoas, black-headed ant-thrushes and black-crowned antpittas. Accommodation is at the Kuna-operated Nusagandi Nature Lodge (contact Ancon Expeditions ☎ 269-9414, e info@ancon expeditions.com) and the Kuna also offer guided walks on the Kuna Medicinal Forest Trail.
45mi (72km) north-east of Panama City ■

Mangroves fringe the lee of Bocas del Toro's main islands and myriad small islands form a network of channels.

WILDLIFE GALLERY

Recognizing, understanding and finding Central America's key wildlife

INTRODUCTION

BRIDGING North and South America, with habitats ranging from dry, lowland savannas to permanently moist cloud forests, Central America is an exuberant mixing zone for the wildlife of two different hemispheres. Including the flora, well over half a million species occur here, all in an area smaller than Texas.

Central America's terrestrial mammal tally is around 330 and may yet climb even higher. The New World is one of the few regions on earth where mammals new to science are still being uncovered, most of them bats and rodents. In fact, these two groups collectively constitute over 75% of the mammal fauna here, a statistic which may not excite everyone, but it includes some of the most impressive, unusual and observable species: dog-sized rodents, prehensile-tailed porcupines and bats that make tents, fish on the wing and subsist on blood.

Indeed, except for a few versatile colonists from North America like coyotes and white-tailed deer, the great bulk of mammals here are New World specialties. Together with Australasia, the Neotropics harbor the last of the marsupials; two other early experiments in mammalian evolution, sloths and anteaters, are found only in the New World. There are eight species of primate which

do not occur further north than southern Mexico and, more widely spread, 24 carnivores including six species of cat. Like anywhere, Central America's mammals are not as diverse or conspicuous as its birds, but for wildlifers who are prepared to work a little, there are some terrific sightings to be had.

The region has long been established on the world birding circuit and birders all over the world usually put Central America (especially Costa Rica and Panama) high on their 'must-visit' list. WIth over 900 species so far recorded – many of them endemic to the region – visitors are guaranteed to see a great variety in even a short trip, while those prepared to winkle them out will be rewarded with gems such as the bizarre cotingas, huge macaws, colorful manakins and the pièce de résistance, the resplendent quetzal. And among the many new birds, North American birders in particular will see several familiar species – typically migrants – in an unfamiliar setting. The following pages provide a basic introduction to Neotropical birds and show more than 100 of the most-commonly seen species, plus a few rarities.

Although invariably sidelined by mammal and bird sightings, there is a legion of less popular wildlife which is literally all around you. Collectively, reptiles, amphibians and invertebrates are held in ludicrously low esteem by people, but of course, each has its ecological part to play. Indeed, in many cases, theirs is more wide-reaching role than that of the charismatic mega-vertebrates; they pollinate flowers, disperse seeds, provide food for lots of other things and eat the ones we call pests on a scale that easily outstrips big game. They are also, generally speaking, far easier to see. With only a slight shift of focus, all those quiet moments when there are no mammals or birds around are easily filled by the things we mostly ignore or avoid.

We've featured a few of the species most likely to be spotted, but there are thousands more. Indeed, in the case of invertebrates, there are probably thousands of species in the Neotropics awaiting discovery. We hope the Wildlife Gallery gives you an insight into this group of creatures which, mostly with little justification, are often hated or feared. ■

OPOSSUMS

The eyes have it

Apart from Australasia, Latin America is the last refuge of the ancient group of mammals called marsupials. Thirteen species are found in Central America (one, the Virginia opossum, has very successfully colonized North America) and all are opossums. Like all marsupials, opossums lack a placenta and cannot nourish the embryos internally beyond a couple of weeks, so they give birth to highly 'premature' babies after a very brief gestation. At birth, the tiny young migrate to the pouch where they attach to a teat to complete their development.

Alston's mouse opossum is the region's largest species of mouse opossum.

Except for the Virginia and common opossums, all Central American species are small and easily confused with rodents. The easiest way to tell them apart is by eyeshine: Opossums usually show both eyes whereas most rodents only show one at a time. Most species are arboreal and omnivorous, feeding on small animals, fruit and nectar, although the aquatic water opossum (or yapok) eats fish, frogs and crustaceans. All opossums are nocturnal and seen only by spotlighting; check trees and, for water opossums, wade quietly in streams. ■

*The **gray four-eyed opossum** gets its name from the white 'eyebrow' markings.*

> **Hotspots**
> **Community Baboon Sanctuary** Water opossums possible.
> **RBBN Monteverde** Chance of Alston's mouse opossum.

NINE-BANDED ARMADILLO

Armored high jumper

While it's best known from the southern United States, the nine-banded armadillo is most abundant in the tropics (after sloths, it is thought to be the most common mammal of undisturbed rainforest). Encased in leathery plates studded with bone 'scutes', armadillos rummage nosily in leaf litter for prey – a single feed can comprise some 40,000 ants or termites. They also take fruit, fungi, small vertebrates or carrion, but their weak jaws and tiny peg-like teeth restrict them to the softest choices.

Recognition Yellow-gray; 'kidney-shaped' with 7–10 midbody bands. 6.5–15.5lb (3–7kg).
Habitat Forest, savanna and dry scrub.
Behavior Solitary, nocturnal.
Breeding Probably year-round in Central America.
Feeding Omnivorous: Invertebrates, fruit, carrion.
Voice None known; snuffles.

Armadillos are often found on night-walks simply by listening. They're very noisy on the move, which is unexpected because their armor is not a fail-safe defense: large cats, ocelots and even domestic dogs can bite through it and, unlike some South American species, they're unable to roll into an impregnable ball. Their advantage comes in retreat. Protected by their armor, armadillos crash blindly into dense undergrowth where predators are reluctant or simply unable to follow. With a head start established they make for a burrow, but if capture is imminent, they perform surprise vertical leaps up to 3.5ft (1m) high. Presumably, the unusual tactic is intended to startle a predator long enough to make an escape. ■

> **Hotspots**
> **PN Palo Verde, PN Rincón de la Vieja**

NORTHERN TAMANDUA

The ripper

Armed with scythe-like claws on massive front feet, the tamandua (or lesser anteater) is built for ripping open ant and termite nests. They feed almost exclusively on these communal insects, but many species wield potent chemical defenses that force the anteater to rip, eat and run. Feeding bouts rarely last longer than five minutes because by then the number of chemical-laden soldiers scrambling to the nest's defense have become too high for even a tamandua. Away from the nests, termite feeding sites and tunnel-like commuting 'trails' are usually dominated by tasty workers rather than soldiers, so tamanduas can spend twice as long mopping up. Even though tamanduas are kept constantly on the move by their prey's resistance, brief bouts at the nest and longer ones away from them probably work in the long-term favor of the anteater: Rather than destroying entire nests, they 'crop' from many, doing relatively little damage to each and unintentionally ensuring a renewable supply. That's important because tamanduas remember nest sites and return to them by consistently following the same routes. Very good guides know tamandua trails, otherwise, listen for the sound of ripping wood or termite 'carton' (wood-chip paste cemented with fecal glue); it invariably means a tamandua feeding. ■

Recognition Cream with black 'vest' and prehensile tail. 8.5–20lb (4–9kg).
Habitat Most forest types.
Behavior Solitary; nocturnal or diurnal; often visits ground.
Breeding Single young born after 150-day gestation.
Feeding Ants, termites and occasionally bees.
Voice Usually silent.

Hotspots
Isla Barro Colorado, PN Manuel Antonio

SILKY ANTEATER

The banana-tree angel

Smallest of Central America's anteaters, the silky anteater's name translates from Spanish as the banana-tree angel. Silky or pygmy anteaters spend the day curled up in clumps of lianas (where they're virtually impossible to find) and only emerge at night. Spotlighting holds the best chance to see them, but you'll need to search along small vines and branches – silky anteaters spend most of their life on stems about the width of a pencil. The tight-rope act protects them from all but the most lightweight predators and also gives them access to ant nests which few other ant-hunters can reach.

Silky anteaters eat up to 5000 ants a night, moving continuously to balance their energetic demands with the need to avoid soldier ants rushing to their nest's defense. They cover up to 1000 times their own body length each night; that's about 600ft (180m), but the effort requires almost the same amount of energy they recoup from their ant diet. It means they walk a constant physiological fine line, as well as a physical one, so to conserve the precious surplus, silky anteaters lower their metabolic rate and body temperature during the day. They also don't budge from their nests, so if you know where one went to sleep wait there at sunset for it to appear. ■

Recognition Squirrel-sized, golden fur; long, prehensile tail. 8oz (275g).
Habitat Rainforest, secondary forest and mangroves.
Behavior Nocturnal, arboreal and solitary.
Breeding Single young; two breeding seasons a year in good conditions.
Feeding Mainly ants, occasionally other insects.
Voice Soft whistling in alarm.

Hotspots
PN Corcovado, Isla Barro Colorado

TWO- & THREE-TOED SLOTHS

Recognition Three-toed sloth (main picture): Three elongated claws on each foot; short, stubby tail and raccoon-like face mask; 5–12lb (2.5–5.5kg).
Two-toed sloth (above): Two claws on the *front* feet (back feet have three each); no tail and no mask; 9–18lb (4–8kg).
Habitat Evergreen and secondary forests, also pastures with scattered trees. Two-toed more common in highlands; three-toed more common in lowlands.
Behavior Both highly arboreal; activity tends to depend on temperature – especially for three-toed, which is more diurnal. Two-toed mainly nocturnal, crawls and crosses forest gaps on the ground.
Breeding One young born after 6-month gestation; carried on mother's chest for about 6 months.
Feeding Mainly leaves; two-toed also takes fruit, and possibly lichens and moss.
Voice Both mainly silent. Three-toed sloth: Whistles; males scream when fighting. Two-toed sloth: Hisses in threat, bleats in distress.

Hotspots
PN Tortuguero (both), PN Manuel Antonio (three-toed), RBBN Monteverde (both, especially two-toed)

Live slow, die old

Found only in Neotropical forests, sloths are the ancient remnants of a unique group of mammals that arose when South America was an isolated island – one of many groups to do so, but one of the few to survive to modern times. Curled up high above the rainforest floor, Central America's two sloth species can be hard to distinguish: toes, tails and faces are the deciders (see 'Recognition' in sidebar). Male three-toed sloths also have a distinctive black and yellow patch on their back which looks rather like the false 'eyes' many butterflies have for startling predators. It's unlikely that the sloth's main enemies – jaguars and large eagles – pay it much heed though, and it probably has more to do with males recognizing and avoiding one another; they fight with surprisingly savage vigor in defense of their patch, a trait yet to be observed in the drably colored two-toed sloth.

True to their name, sloths spend about 70% of every 24 hours asleep or inactive, but most of that time is devoted to digestion. They subsist on an nutrient-meager diet consisting almost entirely of hard-to-digest leaves, so they have to process huge volumes. Their convoluted gut can store about a third of their body mass but, to reduce their weight so they can remain aloft, they've sacrificed muscle mass – part of the reason they're so sluggish. A very slow metabolism reduces their daily energetic demands and their body temperature fluctuates, reptile-like, according to the ambient temperature. On cool mornings, they head to the treetops to warm up, a habit which makes them vulnerable to harpy eagles. Another habit, climbing down to defecate and urinate on the forest floor, exposes them to attack from terrestrial predators. They limit the risk by storing all excrement for a once-a-week session, but why they come down at all is a mystery. One theory proposes that it serves to fertilize their food trees to encourage new, easily digestible growth, but it's never been tested (and would probably be just as effective from onhigh anyway). So long as they're not sunbathing or voiding, sloths are rarely caught and are thought to live until they're 30. ∎

GEOFFROY'S TAMARIN

Panama's miniature monkey

Smaller than a large squirrel and uttering birdlike twitters and whistles, it's hard to believe Geoffroy's tamarin is a not-so-removed relative of humans. Tamarins and marmosets are primates, just as we are, albeit ones which have followed a different evolutionary path from ourselves for at least 35 million years. There are around 30 species, all restricted to the Neotropics and more are probably awaiting discovery: nine new marmosets have been discovered in Brazil's rainforests since 1990. The most northern-living of the family, Geoffroy's tamarin is the only species in Central America and, with a distribution that lies almost entirely within Panama (they may still occur in northern Colombia, but recent sightings are lacking), is also called the Panamanian tamarin.

Similar to squirrel monkeys, Geoffroy's tamarins do well in forest that is recovering from disturbances like fire or treefall. Called secondary forest, it's a habitat rich in tamarin prey such as cicadas and large grasshoppers, as well as nectar and sap. Secondary forest is common throughout Central America because of habitat clearing by people, and tamarins probably benefited up until recently from shifting agriculture (clearing the forest and then abandoning it after a few years or even a single season). Today, like squirrel monkeys, tamarins rarely benefit from human-generated secondary forest because they are captured for the pet trade and occasionally hunted.

Tamarins live in small groups with a social system that's unique for primates. Typically, only one female in the group breeds, but all adults care for the youngsters. Indeed, if you see an adult carrying young babies, it will probably be the father and he passes them back to the mother only for suckling and occasional grooming. Twins are the norm for tamarin births and, as they grow, other group members share the carrying duties with dad. Cooperative care is thought to free up the alpha female to have another set of twins, which is advantageous for speedy occupation of secondary patches as they appear in the forest. Tamarins are difficult to spot unless they're used to people, but listen for two to four ascending long whistles, often the first clue that a group is nearby. ∎

Recognition Tiny. Mottled black and brown fur with white chest, limbs and belly. Bare, dark-gray face with white crest. 14–21oz (400–600g).

Habitat Primarily lowland humid forest, especially secondary patches and edges of clearings. Avoids very open areas.

Behavior Diurnal and arboreal. Gregarious; groups number up to 40, but normally 2–9. Groups are territorial and usually patrol the boundaries first thing in the morning (7–9am). Retire to treetop nests or vine tangles around 10m above ground an hour or so before sunset.

Breeding Twins (sometimes 1) offspring born between March and June. Gestation 140–180 days.

Feeding Fruit, insects, gum, buds and flowers. Occasionally take small vertebrate prey such as lizards, frogs and nestling birds, as well as snails and arachnids.

Voice At least 10 different calls. Most are birdlike whistles and chirps. Strident trills in alarm. Also long rasps given in aggressive encounters.

Hotspots
Parque Natural Metropolitano, PN Darién, Isla **Barro Colorado**

CENTRAL AMERICAN SQUIRREL MONKEY

Recognition Small, slender monkey. Orange-brown color with darker shoulders, hind legs and tail. Black skull-cap and muzzle, white face, throat and chest. Nonprehensile tail. 1–2.5lb (400g–1kg).
Habitat Secondary humid forest on the Pacific slope of Costa Rica and Panama.
Behavior Highly gregarious, living in troops of 15–70. Diurnal and highly arboreal, travelling and foraging almost entirely in trees. Comes to ground for brief spurts and crosses open areas very reluctantly.
Breeding Highly seasonal, between February to April (dry season). One young born after 7-month gestation.
Feeding Mainly leaf-eating insects, eg, grasshoppers, katydids and caterpillars; also small fruits and flowers. Suffers considerable food stress in the wet season when these items are rare and may travel extensively to forage.
Voice Many calls including trills, twitters and chucks. Also protest squeals and peeps when separated.

An endangered primate

In South America squirrel monkeys are abundant and wide-spread, and seen so often that visitors tend to ignore them soon after arrival. But known here as the titi or mono titi, this is an entirely different species that occurs only in the Pacific lowlands of Costa Rica and Panama. More alarmingly, it is the most endangered primate in Central America; from an esti-mated 200,000 in 1983, there are only about 3500 left. Apart from the ubiquitous threats of habitat clearing and hunting, squirrel monkeys are captured for pets, but they also suffer from being a conservation 'blind-spot'. Historically, the species has often been regarded as an import from South America. Because the next nearest population lies over 500km south, biologists thought that they'd arrived with Amerind-ian traders and, accordingly, granted them little in the way of modern conservation attention. In fact, a suite of sophisticat-ed molecular and genetic analyses has demonstrated that they are a unique species and probably have been so for at least 500,000 years.

If that doesn't convince you, their social system is com-pletely different from South American squirrel monkeys. There are no strong dominance hierarchies and aggression, and males do not 'lord over' females in their troop. Females cooperate to spot danger and collectively repel attacks on young monkeys from raptors and chestnut-mandibled toucans (which have been observed gliding into monkey troops at PN Corcovado and using their massive bill to scoop newborns off their mother's back). Perhaps as a result of such predation pressure, all the females in a troop synchronize their births to fall within a week-long period.

Also called the red-backed squirrel monkey, the titi prefers disturbed forest that is regrowing (secondary forest); regrowth usually supports more of their main prey, which declines as the forest matures, causing the monkeys to move on. Sec-ondary forest is in-creasing due to habitat clearing, but titis rarely benefit because of the presence of people. ■

Hotspots
PN Corcovado, PN Manuel Antonio

WHITE-FACED CAPUCHIN

Handy, highbrow hunters

Recognizable as the organ-grinder's monkey of choice, capuchins were exported in the thousands during the 19th and early 20th centuries to 'dance' on European and American street corners. Thankfully long out of fashion, the practice probably caused some local declines in capuchin numbers, but they are still a common and easily observed species in Costa Rican and Panamanian parks. If you watch them long enough, you might see one of the reasons they were so favored by the organ-grinders – their dexterity. Capuchins are master manipulators of objects. Like many primates, they break off branches to hurl in the general direction of ground-based danger (including unwary human observers), but unlike most primates (except the great apes), they have also learned to hold on to such weapons and use them as clubs; in PN Manuel Antonio, biologists observed a fer-de-lance bashed repeatedly using the technique. Capuchins also smash nuts open with rocks, probe insect burrows with twigs and rub themselves with at least three different plants known for their insecticidal and medicinal properties. It's difficult to say whether such tool-use carries the same sort of connection with intelligence as is supposed in human evolution. They do have unexpectedly large brains for their size, although they are far less sophisticated tool-users than chimps and many of their efforts seem accidental rather than calculated.

Even so, like many large-brained mammals, capuchins are versatile and opportunistic foragers: When faced with dry-season shortages of their staple diet, they become active predators. They regularly snatch up small reptiles and plunder bird nests for eggs or chicks. More dramatically, they pluck incubating white-crowned parrots from their nest-holes and raid coati nests to kill the pups. Even highly agile adult squirrels are sometimes caught, usually by 'relay-chasing' (troop members cooperate to take over the pursuit when a squirrel looks like escaping). Adult males do most of the hunting, but all individuals may join in the chase and share the kill if it's a large one. Hunting happens year-round, but it's most easily observed in northwest Costa Rica during the dry season. ∎

Recognition Smallish monkey, mostly blackish-brown with creamy-white head, chest and shoulders. Pink face. Prehensile tail. 4–9.5lb (2–4.5kg).
Habitat Fairly wide tolerance; inhabits most sorts of forest, mangroves and occasionally savanna. Easily seen in dry forest; makes daily visits to waterholes in dry season.
Behavior Highly gregarious in groups up to 30, usually with 1 adult male plus many females and youngsters. Diurnal with activity peaks during early morning and late afternoon. Arboreal, but spends a lot of time foraging and playing on the ground.
Breeding One offspring (rarely twins) born after 5–6 month gestation. Most births occur in the dry season (December to early April).
Feeding Fruit, flowers, insects, larvae and small vertebrates up to the size of coati pups. Also raids crops, especially corn.
Voice Many; adults growl in threat and 'trill' to coordinate troop movements; also 'huhs', chatters, screams and whimpers.

Hotspots
PN Santa Rosa, PN Palo Verde, RB Lomas Barbudal, PN Manuel Antonio

YUCATÁN BLACK & MANTLED HOWLERS

Recognition Large, dark, stocky monkey with long prehensile tail. Mantled howler has light saddle except in parts of Panama (where Yucatán black howler does not occur). Males have heavy beards. Mantled: 8–17lb (3.5–7.5kg). Yucatán black: 11–18lb (5–8kg).
Habitat Most forests types, preferring humid forest and riverine strips in dry forest.
Behavior Diurnal and mainly arboreal. Gregarious. Yucatán black howler groups usually have a single male and a few females plus youngsters; mantled howlers have 1–3 males and 5–10 females with youngsters.
Breeding One offspring born after 6-month gestation. Mantled youngsters are silver-gray and attain their adult coloration by about 3 months.
Feeding Mostly young leaves and fruit especially of fig and breadnut trees. Also some older leaves and flowers.
Voice Booming roar (the female's roars are shorter and higher-pitched than the males). Also soft alarm woofs and contact grunts.

Hotspots
PN Santa Rosa and **PN Palo Verde** (mantled); **Community Baboon Sanctuary** and **Cockscomb Basin WS** (Yucatán black)

Bough-riding boomers

If you're out walking around dawn or dusk and hear a thundering roaring chorus that has you convinced you're about to become jaguar food, chances are the racket is coming from howler monkeys. Howlers greet sunrise and sunset with deafening, booming calls that resonate through the forest for miles and hearing them is virtually a given in the right places. Used by all howler species, the calls are thought to help space out different family groups. Individual families are loyal to the same patch and where there are lots of howlers, like in Belize's Community Baboon Sanctuary, they're aggressively territorial; where densities are low, they're less proprietary about turf, and home ranges overlap. Even so, this doesn't make the residents any less vocal; calling lets other howlers know which shared areas are being used and avoids any unexpected meetings. All the adults in a group call and they also call when disturbed or excited; the calls of other howlers (or even played recordings of them), thunder, rain, planes overhead or people below can stimulate a bellowing torrent.

Central America's two species of howlers are essentially the same beast, ecologically speaking. The mantled howler (above) occurs throughout the region except in Belize and is mainly black with a distinctive blondish-brown saddle; it's the more gregarious species with groups comprising about 12 to 25 members. The Yucatán or Mexican black howler (below) is entirely black, occurs only in Belize, northern Guatemala and the Yucatán, and forms smaller groups of between two and six. Both species are primarily folivores (leaf eaters), and are the only monkeys in the region with a leaf-dominated diet. Abundant and always available, leaves are a reliable resource, but they're crammed with toxic tannins and have a low energy quota; as a result, except for howlers and sloths, few mammals concentrate on them. Howlers choose young leaves, which have less tannin, and eat lots of fruit. Oddly, howlers are called congos in Costa Rica and baboons in Belize though neither has any African connection at all. ■

CENTRAL AMERICAN SPIDER MONKEY

Sweet-toothed swingers

Named presumably because of their bristly, lanky limbs, spider monkeys otherwise have little in common with their arachnid namesakes. Supremely adapted for life in the trees, spider monkeys very rarely descend to ground and ordinarily remain in the middle to upper levels of the canopy. In young forest, that might be as low as 10m above ground, but they prefer older, taller trees and you'll generally have to search much higher for sightings. Inside protected areas, spider monkeys are quite confiding, but when disturbed, they make a hasty, acrobatic exit, either running on all fours along large boughs or by brachiating (swinging hand over hand). Assisted by their completely prehensile tail, spider monkeys can brachiate as fast as people can run on the ground, bridging gaps in their canopy escape route with prodigious leaps. It's an impressive, if fleeting, display. Relaxed spider monkeys offer far better views; in particular, watch that sinuous tail. Never still, it constantly seeks out a hold and can support the full weight of the owner. Critical to the spider monkey's treetop lifestyle, the tail is also crucial to young monkeys gaining their independence: a year-old Santa Rosa male which lost his tail resorted to suckling, playing alone and being carried by his mother.

With a sensitive sweet tooth (they can discriminate lower concentrations of sugar than any other primate so far tested) spider monkeys are very selective feeders and their diet is dominated by the ripest fruit available. They forage in small groups usually numbering less than eight and are often seen in pairs and trios, but this gives little indication of the troop size – which may be as high as 40.

Subunits of the troop maintain contact with loud, whinnying calls and are aware of other group members that they can't see. After the day's foraging, the group usually assembles at a sleeping site high in emergent trees. In Panama, their range overlaps with that of the brown-headed spider monkey; the two sometimes hybridize, suggests they are actually races of the same species. ∎

Recognition Very long, slender limbs and prehensile tail. Highly variable (but localized) color, ranging from blackish-brown, golden-brown to blonde-gray. Underparts usually paler. Face has pinkish, unpigmented mask (usually black in brown-headed species). 11–20lb (5–9kg).

Habitat Prefers undisturbed evergreen forests. Also in riverine forest, dense dry forests and mangroves.

Behavior Diurnal and gregarious. Troops may have numerous adult males and females (with youngsters), but smaller troops tend to have only a single adult male. Troop splits up to forage in small groups but aggregates at night-time. Rests at hottest time of the day sprawled on high boughs.

Breeding One offspring born after 225-day gestation. Youngsters are born black and gradually attain their adult coloration.

Feeding Mostly ripe fruit; also young leaves and occasionally flowers and rotting bark.

Voice Whinnying contact calls, yapping barks and screams. Growls when uncertain of danger.

Hotspots
PN Santa Rosa, PN Guanacaste, PN Corcovado

BATS

The nightshift

With at least 136 known species, bats comprise almost half of Central America's mammal species and, as the only mammals capable of powered flight, resemble birds in their ecological 'roles'. But whereas most birds are diurnal, all the region's bats are nocturnal and perform many of the same roles that birds do, only at night. Like birds, many species eat insects. All bats have good vision, but the further refinement of echolocation lets them pinpoint nocturnal prey by firing off bursts of ultrasonic vocalizations. The reflected signal allows the bat to instantly discern insect from obstacle and attack – or evade – in total darkness. Despite the sophistication of the system, aerial insectivory is actually the bat 'ancestral condition'. In other words, it arose very early in bat evolution (bats probably evolved from small terrestrial insectivores) and is still the most common niche for bats worldwide.

Honduran white bats roost in leaf tents in groups numbering as many as 12.

Faced with the diversity of rainforest resources, Central American bats have diversified to fill a gamut of niches that rival birds. At least 25 species are fruit specialists, 11 feed on nectar and pollen, two are strict meat-eaters and one – the greater fishing bat – gaffs fish from the surface using elongated claws that look like grappling hooks. Many are omnivorous and three species eat nothing but blood. With such a range of lifestyles, bats are important players in rainforest ecology and, like their feathered counterparts, are key 'industry species' that pollinate plants and disperse their seeds.

*A specialist frugivore, **Seba's short-tailed bat** eats up to 35 fruits per night.*

Unless you accompany a bat specialist on a mist-netting trip, most bat encounters will be a whisper of wings from impossible-to-identify passers-by. Large caves invariably house at least one species, sometimes with attendant boa constrictors snatching them as they exit for the night; don't explore bat caves without an expert as bat guano can harbor dangerous diseases. There are some 15 species of tent-making bats in Central America, which snip the supporting veins and midribs of large leaves (especially heliconias, palms and bananas) to create distinctive day-time shelters; carefully look inside for views of some marvelous species including the tiny Honduran white bat. The spectacular greater fishing bat is often attracted to lights near docks where small fish congregate to feed on insects. ∎

Underwood's long-tongued bat is best seen at middle elevations on the Caribbean slope.

> **Hotspots**
> **PN Santa Rosa** Caves have common vampires, leaf-nosed bats and short-tailed bats. **Lamanai Outpost Lodge** Good for greater fishing bats, insect gleaners and proboscis bats. **La Selva** Numerous tent-makers, including Honduran white bats.

COMMON VAMPIRE BAT

Blood bankers

Most notorious of bats, vampires are the only mammals in the world that are true sanguivores (blood feeders). There are actually three species of vampires in Central America: Two are rare specialists on bird blood that crawl along the underside of branches and make surgically precise incisions in a sleeping bird's legs or feet to feed. Living in large, ammonia-reeking cave colonies up to 2000-strong, the common vampire is the bat most likely to bite your neck. It feeds almost exclusively on the blood of large mammals, but before you pack the garlic charms and wooden stakes, people are rare targets. Vampires prefer large ungulates such as tapirs, deer and peccaries, locating quarry with their excellent vision and smell; they have echolocation, but it's poorly developed compared with insectivorous bats. Vampires usually land on the ground near a potential feed then run and leap onto the leg with an agility unmatched among bats. They thus keep up with mobile meals-on-the-hoof, scurry spider-like to a feeding site (usually legs, shoulder or neck) and evade flailing hooves. Enlarged incisor teeth with scalpel-sharp edges scoop out a shallow feeding trough (a largely painless experience for the host) and anticoagulants in the bat's saliva prevent clotting until they've lapped, not sucked, their fill (see photo inset).

Back in the roost, vampires regurgitate blood to colony members which had an unsuccessful night's foraging. Bats can bloat themselves with more than they actually need and, as large mammals can be hard to find, it pays to help other bats – relatives are probably favored – that might return the favor in the future. The spread of livestock in has, without doubt, helped the vampire proliferate and some populations now target little else. However, as a vector of rabies they cause considerable losses to livestock, and human persecution includes blowing up and burning roosts – indiscriminate methods which also have an impact on harmless bats. ■

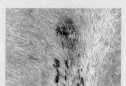

Recognition Midsized bat, gray-brown with pale underparts. Fairly large, triangular ears. Length 2.5–3.5in (7–9cm), wingspan 13.5–15.5in (35–40cm).

Habitat Roosts in caves, disused mines, hollow trees, abandoned buildings and under bridges. Forages in diverse habitats including forests, pastures and open areas where there is prey.

Behavior Roosts communally, usually in colonies with less than 50 members. Females form enduring associations, grooming and regurgitating blood for one another. Single adult males fight one another for access to each female group.

Breeding Breeds year-round, probable rainy season peak. One (rarely twins) young born after 7-month gestation. Suckled for as long as 10 months supplemented with regurgitated blood from 3 months. Young accompany their mother on foraging trips from 4 months.

Feeding Eats only the blood of large vertebrates. Mainly mammals, especially livestock in settled areas; sometimes poultry and people.

Voice Six different calls, mostly associated with aggression during feeding. Soft contact calls between females and young.

Hotspots
PN Santa Rosa, PN Corcovado, Barra Honda

TREE SQUIRRELS

Picnic pals

Diurnal, common and tame around lodges and picnic areas, tree squirrels are a virtually guaranteed tick on your mammal list. The trick is knowing which is which: There are nine species in the region and all are arboreal, but most come to ground to fetch seeds and fallen fruit or to cross open areas. The montane squirrel and the red-tailed squirrel are seen on the ground more than most, the latter especially at park camp sites. The two pygmy squirrels, Alfaro's and western, also come to ground, but they move with such speed it's difficult to catch more than a fleeting impression of them.

The variegated squirrel has so many color varieties that up to 14 subspecies are recognized.

One of the best ways to view squirrels is at their nests. Tree cavities are used as night quarters and by females with young. Red-tailed and variegated squirrels can have up to three litters a year and during the peak of fruit availability, all adult females are pregnant or raising litters. Nests can be conspicuous if you know where to look; good guides will probably know of some. Set yourself up before sunrise to see them emerge and, on cool mornings, sunbaking. ■

Red-tailed squirrels roam the grounds of San Jose's Parque Zoologico Simon Bolivar.

> **Hotspots**
> **Monteverde** Variegated, Deppe's and Alfaro's pygmy squirrels common. **Isla Barro Colorado** Red-tailed easily seen.

MEXICAN PORCUPINE

Treetop pincushions

The Mexican porcupine is more closely related to agoutis and pacas than to Old World porcupines and its bristly defenses are a nice example of convergent evolution (in which unrelated – or, in this case, distantly related – species evolve similar characteristics). Unlike the largely terrestrial 'true' porcupines, Mexican porcupines are built for a life above ground. Flexible grasping 'fingers' and a wholly prehensile tail allow them to forage in the flimsiest parts of the canopy and they're normally spotted high in the crowns of trees. That makes viewing best in the dry, low-canopy forests of Costa Rica's northwest, although they can also be seen by looking inside large hollow trees where they den during the day; look for piles of their distinctively flat, oval droppings at the base of hollows.

Recognition Blackish with yellowish spines. Pink bulbous nose. 3–13.5lb (1.5–6kg).
Habitat Most forest types.
Behavior Nocturnal, solitary.
Breeding One young; probably seasonal.
Feeding Leaves, fruit, buds, seeds and twigs.
Voice Usually silent. Breeding pairs may yowl and scream.

Also known as hairy porcupines, Mexican porcupines have thick, soft fur which mostly conceals their quills. Contrary to local mythology, they can't shoot the quills at aggressors, but the quills are barbed and detach easily. Most predators leave them alone, although experienced margays sometimes take them, as do large cats when porcupines come to ground to cross open areas. Another species, Rothschild's porcupine, occurs in Panama and can be told apart by its overall spiny, rather than furry, appearance. ■

> **Hotspots**
> **PN Santa Rosa, RBBN Monteverde**

CENTRAL AMERICAN AGOUTI

Scatter-hoarding speedsters

Probably the most commonly encountered mammal in protected lowland and mid-altitude forests, agoutis belong to the same tribe of uniquely Neotropical rodents that includes guinea pigs, capybaras and pacas. The latter are their closest relatives (and confusingly, have the scientific name *Agouti paca*, though they're not agoutis) and, like pacas, agoutis are prized for their tasty flesh. But whereas pacas freeze or make for water to evade predators, agoutis rely on high-speed escapes through the underbrush. They are impressively swift over difficult terrain, but their loyalty to their tiny territories often means their undoing. Agoutis are very reluctant to abandon their patches and run in large circles when pursued, hemmed in by invisible territorial boundaries. Further aggravating their vulnerability, they bark continuous shrill alarm calls as they run. Normally, they stop after about 50m and quietly hide, but for human hunters in the know, the barking only serves to advertise their escape route. Agoutis are also important prey items for ocelots, jaguarundis and tayras and, in the dry season, male coatis become significant predators on young ones when fruit and insects are at a low ebb.

Because they rely on speed, agoutis don't store fat like the more robust paca; instead, they cache food for dry-season shortages. When seeds and fruit are abundant, agoutis bury them for later use, but to avoid creating convenient one-stop eateries for larger species like peccaries, they disperse their hoard throughout their territory. Biologists call this scatter-hoarding and since agoutis invariably forget or simply abandon some of the caches, they probably act as critical seed dispersers for many forest tree species. Agoutis are usually seen alone, but form mated pairs, most likely to collectively defend their scatter-hoards from other agoutis. The female alone is responsible for raising her offspring, but the male takes the lead in food-cache defense when the babies are young and so ensures the female has the resources and time to raise their progeny. She hides the youngsters in a burrow or crevice too small for predators (or herself) to access and they emerge to suckle when she visits. ∎

Recognition Large rodent. Variable coloration but normally rusty-brown with grizzled rump. Rounded back and long dark, skinny legs. Tiny, naked tail difficult to see. 6.5–9lb (3–4kg).
Habitat Most forest types, less so in highlands. Also secondary growth, plantations and gardens.
Behavior Diurnal but occasionally active at night, especially where hunted by people. Monogamous pairs share a 2–3 hectare territory until one dies. Pairs tolerate other agoutis in the territory when food is abundant, otherwise they chase intruders. Usually seen alone.
Breeding 1-2 young born after 120-day gestation. Young are precocial (born fully-furred with eyes open).
Feeding Seeds and fruit. Seedlings, leaves, flowers and fungi when food-stressed.
Voice Grunts followed by yapping bark in alarm. Growl, grunt and rumble in fights and scream in distress. Young 'creak-squeak' when separated.

Hotspots
La Selva, Isla Barro Colorado, PN Santa Rosa, PN Corcovado

CAPYBARA

Recognition Very large; yellow-brown, small tail. 55 –110lb (25–50kg).
Habitat Swamps, lake and river edges.
Behavior Mainly nocturnal, crepuscular where protected.
Breeding Up to 8 young after a 150-day gestation.
Feeding Aquatic vegetation and riverine/floodplain grass.
Voice Alarm cough.

Hotspots
PN Darién (Punta Patiño), **Panama Canal**

Guinea pig Goliath

Weighing as much as a rottweiler, the capybara is by far the world's largest rodent. It belongs to the same rodent superfamily as guinea pigs and, like guinea pigs, capybaras are gregarious: They live in groups numbering up to 25, usually with numerous adults of both sexes. But whereas the females live in relative harmony, the males vigorously contest a dominance hierarchy – one male is supreme boss with each male below him organized in a chain of decreasing status. Top males get most of the matings and stay in the center of the group where the females collect to minimize the risk of predation; subordinate males are exiled to the periphery where they have to remain vigilant for jaguars. Their role as sentries might be why the dominant male doesn't expel them entirely. Male aggression is usually fairly low-key, but fights can be savage when females are in heat; both peak during the wet season.

Capybaras are strong swimmers and when danger threatens they take the plunge. Females cluster around the youngsters to protect against crocodile attacks, although adults are also sometimes taken. Capybaras occur widely throughout South America, but their distribution in Central America only extends into Panama as far as the Canal Zone; look around the Canal's large lakes and islands. ∎

PACA

Recognition Stocky. Reddish brown with rows of white stripes and spots.
Habitat Forest, gardens and vegetation near water.
Behavior Strictly nocturnal, spending day in a burrow.
Breeding Single young.
Feeding Fruit, seeds, flowers and seedlings.
Voice Very loud growls with tooth-grinding.

Hotspots
Cockscomb Basin WS, La Selva, Río Bravo

Speaker cheeks

Weighing up to 28.7lb (13kg) and apparently delicious, pacas rank high on local hunters' wish lists. They also tend not to run far when chased, relying instead on a brief, explosive dash for cover and then freezing. Remaining completely motionless for as long as 45 minutes, the paca is easy to find (for hunters and wildlifers alike), but if water is nearby it's a different story. Pacas submerge like little hippos and simply disappear; presumably, they surface when the danger has passed or is somewhere out of sight. In any case, coupled with their strictly nocturnal behavior, this behavior has helped pacas survive where hunting might otherwise have wiped them out. They occupy forested strips along rivers when all surrounding cover has been cleared and small forested patches (even in city suburbs). In protected areas they can be abundant.

Pacas are usually seen alone, but actually form monogamous pairs which are well equipped to defend their small territories. Massively inflated cheek bones amplify an astonishingly loud growl that warns off intruders, and their rump is heavily thickened beneath extremely fragile skin, which tears easily so that an aggressor struggles to land a damaging bite. Such defenses are less effective against ocelots and large cats which easily overpower them. ∎

GRAY FOX

The climbing fox

The gray fox is the region's only fox species and, at around the size of a housecat, is unlikely to be confused with its collie-sized cousin, the coyote. Its similarity to cats doesn't stop at size: Uniquely among the dog family, it has sharp, highly curved claws and flexible wrists which can rotate inwards. They equip the gray fox with a catlike capacity for climbing and although they're most often encountered on the ground, foxes are just as comfortable in trees. Apart from sunning themselves on high canopy branches and sometimes denning in trunk hollows (gray fox pups can climb unaided from four weeks old), they effortlessly dart up the nearest tree when confronted with danger; if there are no trees, they just as easily scale vertical rock faces and even telephone poles.

Their climbing ability notwithstanding, gray foxes spend most of their time on the ground searching for fallen fruit and soil-dwelling arthropods. Terrestrial dens in burrows, rock piles and hollow logs are generally more utilized than arboreal ones. The gray fox's multilevel lifestyle is not a recent development. In fact, they live much as the earliest members of the dog family did 35 million years ago. The gray fox is not quite that ancient, but at around six to nine million years, it's the oldest surviving canine on the planet. ■

Recognition Grizzled gray, cream underparts, rusty neck and legs. 2.5–3.5ft (0.7–1.1m).
Habitat Forests, woodlands.
Behavior Nocturnal or diurnal. Solitary.
Breeding Bears 2–12 pups after 58–65 day gestation.
Feeding Fruit, arthropods, small vertebrates, carrion.
Voice Usually silent.

Hotspots
Cockscomb Basin WS, PN Darién (Punta Patiño)

COYOTE

Adaptable invader

Perhaps the only large mammal in the region to have benefited from human-wrought changes to the environment, the coyote is actually increasing its range. Highly adaptable, they benefit from forest clearance because pastures are rich in rodents; coyotes are large enough to kill deer but small enough to survive on mice. Additionally, roads provide an endless source of carrion (they're commonly seen scavenging roadkills in northwestern Costa Rica) and they have little competition from large carnivores, which do not adapt so easily and disappear. Claims of coyotes invading from Mexico since the 1960s are exaggerated, but there is little doubt they have moved southwards in historical times.

A highly flexible social life is one reason they thrive. Coyotes are usually monogamous, with pairs staying together for as long as four years, but when sufficient food is available they form small wolflike packs (grown pups help to raise newborns). In difficult times, coyotes abandon group living and each goes its separate way, including the mated pair. Probably the most persecuted carnivore in the world (North American farmers and hunters kill around 400,000 a year), the coyote is a superb survivor which few people take the time to appreciate. ■

Recognition Lanky, with grizzled gray-brown fur. 4.5–6.5ft (1.5–2m).
Habitat Most.
Behavior Diurnal or nocturnal, solitary or in groups.
Breeding Bears 2–12 pups after 58–65 day gestation.
Feeding Omnivorous: live and dead animals, garbage.
Voice Wailing howls, often in chorus.

Hotspots
PN Santa Rosa, PN Guanacaste, Río Bravo

TAYRA

Recognition Large, long-legged weasel. Long, bushy tail. Dark brown to black, usually with white throat patch and sometimes a lighter head; distinctly blonde-headed race occurs in Guatemala, Belize and Mexico. 3–5 ft (1–1.5m). 6.5–13.5lb (3–6kg).

Habitat Fairly wide tolerance, usually in well-forested areas. Also fruit and cacao plantations.

Behavior Usually diurnal or crepuscular. Dens at night in hollow logs, tree holes, rock piles or burrows. Mostly solitary, but sometimes in groups (probably females with dependent young).

Breeding Bears 1–3 young after 63–70 day gestation. Probably aseasonal.

Feeding Fruit, small rodents and medium-sized vertebrates such as agoutis, iguanas and rabbits. Rarely small primates such as squirrel monkeys and tamarins.

Voice Grunts, growls, hisses. Clicking contact call. Sharp snort or bark given in alarm.

Tree otters

Because they are largely diurnal, there's a chance of bumping into a tayra on a forest trail, although if you do it will probably head for the trees. With their flat-footed, erratic bouncing gait, tayras give the impression of being earthbound, but in fact they are sinuously arboreal and move like large squirrels in the branches. A tayra surprised on the ground will scale a nearby trunk in a second and, more often than not, momentarily pause a few yards up to bark a strident warning at the intruder before disappearing into branches as high as 65ft (20m) up. In closed-canopy forest, they jump monkey-like between adjacent trees before coming back down to ground a safe distance away and then vanishing into the undergrowth. If you witness a tayra's arboreal ability, you'll understand why they're also sometimes known as tree otters.

Tayras hunt in the trees or on the ground. Like all the mustelids, they are highly opportunistic and anything smaller than them is fair game. Constantly inquisitive, they assiduously quarter the terrain – be it earth or tree – exploring burrows, holes and crevices. A large percentage of their diet is invertebrates – probably because they're encountered so often rather than being a preference; unlike their relative the grison, tayras don't spend much time nosily riffling through leaf litter to find insects. They seem to prefer larger prey and devote their energies to locating reptiles, rodents and medium-sized mammals in their refuges. They also eat a great deal of fruit, either fallen to the ground or plucked from the branches – seeds from various fruits are found in up to 70% of their scats. They often leave scat piles near their night-time dens; look for seed-and-fur laden deposits near large burrows and rock crevices or beneath tree hollows. ■

Hotspots
PN Santa Rosa, **La Selva**, **PN Darién** (Punta Patiño), **PN Tapantí**

NEOTROPICAL RIVER OTTER

Water dogs

The only otter in Central America, this species is very similar to its better-studied relative familiar to wildlifers in the USA, the North American river otter. Like all otters, they rely on unpolluted, undisturbed bodies of water, but they are quite tolerant of human activity so long as the water is clear and riverbank vegetation is thick. Known also as freshwater otters, they're also occasionally spotted in coastal mangroves, but they need freshwater to wash salt from their fur; extensive river systems with constantly flowing stretches (they usually avoid sluggish, silted water) are best.

Recognition Brown, lighter on belly; 11-30lb (5-14kg).
Habitat Mostly undisturbed habitats, always near water.
Behavior Usually active by day, especially early morning and late afternoon. Becomes nocturnal where persecuted. Mostly solitary.
Breeding Litter size 1-5, usually 2-3. Breeds year-round, peaking in spring.
Feeding Fish, mollusks and crustaceans; occasionally small mammals, birds, reptiles and insects.
Voice Grunts, purrs, whistles and chirps. Hah! when uncertain; screams in distress.

River otters are usually solitary, but adult pairs sometimes indulge in prolonged play sessions – which are a delight to watch if you're lucky enough to one. Females with emerged pups (older than 10 weeks) are similarly playful, but mothers are extremely vigilant and disappear at the slightest disturbance. They den in burrows called holts – either natural cavities in riverbanks or shelters which the otters excavate themselves. Females have also been observed using cave systems some distance from the main river to raise their young. Holts can be fairly easy to spot and are a good sign to keep your eyes open for otters, but you won't find them by walking; take a canoe or boat trip. Often the giveaway is otter 'spraint', pungent droppings which function as territorial markers. Spraint is typically deposited on raised, dry sites close to water: check on logs, exposed tree roots, rocks, sand bars and even the pillars supporting bridges. Fish scales and fragments of crayfish exoskeleton make them unmistakable.

Neotropical river otters are called water dogs in Belize and the Spanish equivalent *perro de agua* in the rest of Central America. Otters *are* distantly related to dogs, but they are actually members of the weasel family and, like many members of the group, are very curious. So long as they're not persecuted, they sometimes approach boats to check out the occupants with a characteristic hah! call.

Hotspots
Tortuguero NP, Caño Negro WR, Crooked Tree WS, La Selva

KINKAJOU & OLINGO

Recognition Both are golden to dark brown with a yellow-cream belly. Kinkajou larger 4.5–10lb (2–4.5kg) with a long, prehensile tail; olingo 2.5–4.5lb (1.1-2kg) with slightly bushy, banded tail.
Habitat Kinkajou found in most forest types; olingo mainly in undisturbed forest.
Behavior Kinkajou: Mostly nocturnal and forages alone. Dens in tree hollows.
Olingo: Nocturnal, arboreal and solitary. More agile than kinkajou – runs swiftly along branches and leaps monkey-like between trees. Dens in hollows or clefts.
Breeding Kinkajou: single young (occasionally twins), usually in the dry season. Olingo: poorly known, but usually has single young.
Feeding Mainly fruit, flowers, nectar and seeds; occasionally beetles, leaves and buds.
Voice Kinkajou: Whistles, grunts, chirps, hisses and screams. High-pitched bark ('wik') repeated in alarm. Olingo similar, also a 2-note alarm-bark.

Hotspots
Community Baboon Sanctuary, Cockscomb Basin WS (kinkajou); **RBBN Monteverde, PN Arenal** (olingo).

Honey bears and berry bandits

Kinkajous and olingos are closely-related members of the raccoon family and the two are easily confused. Their carnivorous pedigree notwithstanding, kinkajous prefer a diet of fruit, flowers and seeds, and have the arboreal adaptations that go with it. They are the only Neotropical carnivore with a prehensile tail (inset) and, like an extra limb, it can support an adult's entire weight. In unison with super-flexible ankles and a spine which twists through 180°, it allows them to hang upside down, to descend trunks head-first and to forage at the very tips of small branches. Olingos (below) are smaller and more slender, but the easiest way to tell them apart is by the tail. Olingos' tails aren't prehensile so they won't be grasping branches (virtually a constant in kinkajous and if not, the tail tip is characteristically curled up).

Often called honey bears because of their rounded cub-like face and fondness for nectar, kinkajous are usually characterized as loners, but they actually form small, tightly-knit social groups with complex relationships. Males are the more sociable sex, probably because they can better defend territories by pairing up. Both males mate with the group's single female, but one usually dominates and he also has precedence to any females encountered outside the group. Regardless, except for occasional congregations in fruiting trees, kinkajous usually forage alone and most social interaction takes place in their shared day-time dens.

Kinkajous are very common and easily spotted on night-walks. Olingos are best viewed when absorbed with a cluster of fruits, but be sure to look closely; in fruiting trees, lone olingos occasionally feed alongside the kinkajou's small social groups. In fact, dietary overlap between the two species is profound and, despite their apparently amicable encounters, olingos may come off second-best in the long run. The larger kinkajou reaches high densities wherever it occurs, which may exclude olingos from doing likewise. And, unlike kinkajous, olingos do not adapt well to human activity and are now considered threatened in the region – staking out hummingbird feeders at night in and around protected areas can sometimes deliver a sighting. ■

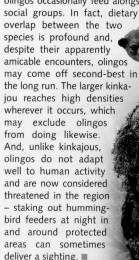

WHITE-NOSED COATI

United she stands, divided he rules

Easily the most visible carnivore in Central America, the most mysterious thing about these sociable members of the raccoon family is their name. Most often, they are simply 'coati', but you might also hear talk of the 'coatimundi', an apparently distinct species that is strictly solitary. In fact, the names refer to the same species, but they accurately reflect the coati's dichotomous social life. Coati females and their young live in extended bands numbering as many as 65, but once males pass their second year, they leave the group and live essentially as loners. They join the band only for breeding, which – unusually for Neotropical carnivores – seems to be a seasonal event; in Panama, where it has been well studied, it happens in January and February. Typically, only one male is accepted into the group (although females may also mate with 'floaters' hanging around) and females collectively repel males outside the breeding season.

The coati's social system is unique among carnivores and is probably related to competition for food. They eat mostly fruit and insects, both of which tend to occur in 'patches' rather than being evenly spread. Male coatis reduce competition for these patches by leaving the band and feeding on their own, but lone females are unable to do likewise because the significantly larger males easily dominate them. So females stay in bands which, by force of numbers, can drive away males from food patches. Interestingly, the breeding season occurs at the end of the wet season when there is plenty of ripe fruit available. Presumably, the timing reduces the competitive tension in the group to a minimum, but even so, males only remain in the group for about a month.

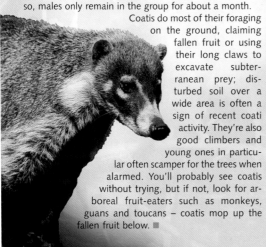

Coatis do most of their foraging on the ground, claiming fallen fruit or using their long claws to excavate subterranean prey; disturbed soil over a wide area is often a sign of recent coati activity. They're also good climbers and young ones in particular often scamper for the trees when alarmed. You'll probably see coatis without trying, but if not, look for arboreal fruit-eaters such as monkeys, guans and toucans – coatis mop up the fallen fruit below. ∎

Recognition Dark to rusty-brown color, usually with lighter grizzled shoulders. Long, mobile snout. White markings on face, muzzle and throat. Very long tail, lightly banded and usually held distinctively upright. Length 3–4.5ft (1–1.5m). 6–14.5lb (2.5–6.5kg).
Habitat Fairly wide tolerance, but usually in well-forested areas. Also fruit and cacao plantations.
Behavior Diurnal and highly sociable. Female groups number up to 65 (but usually 6–30); males solitary except for breeding season and occasional brief visits to bands.
Breeding 1–6 young born April to May (Panama) after 77-day gestation. Females leave the band to give birth in a nest, usually built in a tree. They return to the band when the young are about 5–6 weeks old.
Feeding Mainly fruit and invertebrates. Also eggs and small reptiles. Rarely vertebrates up to tamarin size.
Voice Band members are very vocal using soft grunts, barks and whines. A sharp bark is given when alarmed.

Hotspots
Isla Barro Colorado, PN Santa Rosa, PN Arenal, PN Rincón de la Vieja

JAGUARUNDI

Recognition Slender; uniform red, gray-brown or black. 3–5ft (1–1.5m).
Habitat Forest, savanna; avoids deep rainforest.
Behavior Usually solitary; diurnal or crepuscular.
Breeding 1–4 kittens after 60–75 day gestation.
Feeding Rodents, small birds, lizards and invertebrates.
Voice Whistles, chirps.

Hotspots
Cockscomb Basin WS, PN Palo Verde

A cat called wander

In spite of the name, this unusual cat looks nothing like a jaguar. In fact, with its lean, low-slung body and elongated head, it looks more like a member of the weasel family; indeed, jaguarundis are sometimes called otter-cats and are easily mistaken for tayras. The giveaway is a characteristically feline tail (long and slender compared with the tayra's heavy, bushy one) – a useful clue, given that most jaguarundi sightings are glimpses of the rear end vanishing into cover.

Despite this, jaguarundis are the most often-seen cats in the region, their largely diurnal and terrestrial habits contributing to regular sightings. Typically on the move a couple of hours before dawn, they stay active till around midday and, after a siesta, head out again in the late afternoon until sunset or even well after dark. Most of their time is spent foraging for small ground-dwellers, and they seem to cover an enormous area: Radio-collared males in Belize occupied home ranges from 88 to 100 sq km – up to 3½ times the size of jaguar territories in the same area. Given that mammal home ranges usually correlate with body size (larger animals have to occupy larger areas to satisfy their resource needs), this pattern is baffling. Little-studied despite their relative visibility, much about these enigmatic cats awaits discovery. ∎

MARGAY

Recognition Richly spotted, house-cat sized. 5.5–11lb (2.5–5kg).
Habitat Dense, moist forest; riverine forest in dry habitat.
Behavior Nocturnal, solitary and highly arboreal.
Breeding 1 kitten born after 76–84 day gestation.
Feeding Small mammals, birds, reptiles, insects, eggs.
Voice Largely silent

Hotspots
Río Bravo, La Selva, Cockscomb Basin WS

Up on the canopy catwalk

Like the feline equivalent of a monkey, the margay is one of the cat family's most arboreal members. Uniquely among cats, they have an ankle that swivels 180 degrees, enabling them to dash down tree trunks headfirst, scramble along horizontal branches upside down and dangle from branches by a single hind paw. That amazing ankle, elongated claws and a long tail acting as a counterbalance make the margay a superb tree-dwelling hunter: Although they commute between trees on the forest floor and take the occasional ground-dweller like agoutis, most of their prey lives high in the canopy. Climbing rats, mouse opossums and squirrels form the bulk of their diet, and they have also been recorded killing capuchins and Mexican porcupines. Most hunting takes place in the early morning (between 1 and 5am) and by sunrise they'll be bedded down in a comfortable tree fork up to 33ft (10m) above the ground.

Margays resemble two other Neotropical cats, the ocelot (whose much larger size gives it away) and the oncilla. Oncillas are rare and are very unlikely to be seen. Don't be confused by local nomenclature; oncillas are also called tiger cats, but if you hear this term in English-speaking Belize, it means margay. ∎

OCELOT

Most-spotted of the spotted

At a glance, the ocelot is very similar to the margay, but size is usually a speedy way to distinguish them: Ocelots are much larger, weighing up to three times more – so if it's bigger than a house-cat it has to be an ocelot. For anyone fortunate to have a close-up look, more elaborate markings tend to be another ocelot hallmark (but be cautious – variation in both species overlaps somewhat). Ocelot spots are typically stretched out as oval rosettes, often running together in long parallel rows of blotches with smaller, simple spots inside them. The face is also more heavily marked with elongated spots and stripes, especially along each cheek and on the forehead. Spots aside, the ocelot's tail looks 'unfinished' – it's shorter than the hind legs and doesn't touch the ground. If you do glimpse a spotted cat, but not well enough to decide, the chances are it's an ocelot. While none of the Neotropical cats is easy to see, the ocelot is the most-spotted, spotted species in Central America.

With a range that includes every country south of the USA (including a tiny population in southern Texas) except Chile, it's also the most widely distributed spotted species. Like margays, ocelots are mainly nocturnal, but unlike their smaller relatives, they're largely ground-lovers, readily following game-trails and human-made walking paths (which are good places to look for their tracks). Being larger than margays, they're quite able to tackle much heftier quarry including sloths, brocket deer and young peccaries, but their diet is generally dominated by small mammals, ground-dwelling reptiles and birds. Like all cats, superb vision and hearing locates most targets, although they also devote considerable time to sniffing along pathways, and one researcher suggests they follow scent trails left by prey. Being territorial, calling cards left by other ocelots also provoke intense interest. Regardless of the source, ocelots absorbed in an interesting odor can sometimes be approached, but the slightest noise will break the spell. ■

Recognition Medium-sized cat with oval blotches. Melanistic individuals occur, but not recorded from Central America. 18–26.5lb (8–12kg).

Habitat Wide tolerance including savannas, wetlands, dry woodland and rainforest. Usually remains close to cover and only ventures into open habitat at night. Lives close to human settlement as long as there is dense cover available.

Behavior Solitary, territorial and mainly nocturnal or crepuscular; may also be active on overcast days.

Breeding Probably year-round. Bears 1–3 kittens after 79–85 day gestation.

Feeding Mostly small mammals, lizards, snakes and birds. Capable of taking prey weighing up to 20kg. Covers large carcasses with leaf litter and returns to them for repeat feeds.

Voice Rarely heard in the wild; captives yowl and caterwaul when breeding.

Hotspots
La Selva, **Cockscomb Basin WS**, **Río Bravo**

PUMA

Recognition Large, uniformly colored cat, in various shades of yellow-brown, reddish or gray-brown. Long, tubular tail, often with a dark tip. Cubs spotted until about 4 months. 77.5–159lb (35–72kg).
Habitat Extremely wide tolerance; all kinds of forest, savannas, grasslands and wetlands. Occasionally mangroves.
Behavior Solitary and territorial. Marks and defends ranges from same-sexed individuals. Terrestrial, but climbs well. Usually nocturnal or crepuscular, sometimes diurnal in protected areas.
Breeding Year-round (possibly seasonal in far north America). Bears 1–6 cubs (average 2–3) after 88–96 day gestation.
Feeding Mainly small rodents, agoutis, pacas, porcupines and deer; less so birds and reptiles. Also livestock and dogs.
Voice Many including growls, purrs and low contact grunts. Females chirp to cubs which respond with birdlike whistles. Also a piercing scream, probably for locating mates. Unable to roar.

American lion

Early Spanish explorers encountering the only large, uniformly colored cat in the Americas thought they were looking at small lionesses and called them *león, león de montaña* and *león americano*. The names endure, but apart from the tawny fur of some individuals (color varies considerably), pumas are not especially lionlike. In fact, their Mexican name, *leopardo*, gives a better idea of the animal; in many ways, the puma is the ecological equivalent of the Old World leopard, a solitary and highly adaptable generalist. Like leopards, pumas have a huge distribution with a high tolerance for diverse habitats, and catholic food habits to match. Pumas range from the Canadian Yukon to the southern tip of Chile, a north-south spread unequaled among American land mammals. They occupy virtually every habitat type, but in Central America occur mainly in rainforests and woodlands. In reserves they're also spotted in grasslands and swamps, but avoid open areas where there are people, and only venture into pastures and agricultural areas if there is cover nearby.

A key part of the puma's success formula is a readiness to eat just about anything, ranging from insects to tapirs. However, Central American pumas kill mostly small to medium-sized mammals, probably because they far outnumber big game and perhaps also to avoid competition with jaguars. Pumas may persist where large prey has been wiped out (unlike jaguars) and, where forests have been cleared for grazing, they exploit population flushes of small, open-country rodents such as cotton rats which weigh less than 3.5oz (100g). Even if cotton rats were the only option in altered habitat, pumas could probably survive there, but the presence of livestock invariably leads to conflict. Throughout their range, pumas are heavily persecuted for stock-killing (real and imagined) and they respond with exceptional shyness. Even in protected areas, they are extremely elusive; look for puma signs such as scrapes on pathways and small mounds of leaves topped with scats and urine. ∎

Hotspots
PN Santa Rosa, PN Guanacaste, PN Darién

JAGUAR

Skull crusher

The jaguar is the largest cat in the Americas and the third-largest in the world, but unfortunately size does not convert into visibility. Easily topping the most-wanted list for mammal-watchers in Central America, the jaguar also ranks as one of the most elusive. The main reason is a simple matter of rarity. By virtue of their supreme position in the feeding hierarchy, top predators are naturally less common than their prey, so simple chance means you're more likely to bump into a peccary or coati than a jaguar. It also means that jaguars require large areas to support enough prey to survive; annually, an individual jaguar needs the equivalent of 53 white-tailed deer, 18 peccaries, 40 coatis, 25 armadillos and 55 ctenosaurs. While many areas seem large enough to support such numbers, they're of little use if they only have enough prey for one or two jaguars. Owing to clearing for cattle ranches, and overhunting of jaguar prey, suitable habitat for viable populations in Central America now occurs in only a handful of protected areas.

Under such protection, jaguars are quite versatile predators and prey ranges from small rodents to tapirs. They are the only big cat which regularly kills by biting though the top of the victim's skull (other large cats usually suffocate their prey), their massive head and robust canines uniquely suited to the task. They use the same technique to crack the heavy shells of large river turtles and in Costa Rica's PNs Corcovado and Tortuguero jaguars patrol the beaches for nesting sea turtles. Boa constrictors and spectacled caimans are also fair game and, in some areas, reptiles are the main source of food after large mammals. Perhaps reflecting their preference for aquatic prey, jaguars are rarely far from water: They are excellent swimmers that readily take to rivers and swamps, and are most often spotted resting on sunny riverbanks. For the best chance of seeing *el tigre*, abandon the walking paths and take an early morning river cruise or canoe ride. ∎

Recognition Unmistakable. Large, robust leopardlike cat. Marked with large rosettes, usually with smaller spots inside. Melanistic individuals not common in Central America. 80–200lb (36–90kg) in the region.
Habitat Closely associated with dense cover and permanent water sources. Most common in humid forests.
Behavior Solitary and territorial; male territories about twice as large as females' and overlap multiple female ranges. Terrestrial, but climbs and swims well. Widely considered nocturnal, but often diurnally active with crepuscular activity peaks in undisturbed areas.
Breeding Probably year-round, but possible birth-peaks in the rainy season. 1–4 cubs born after 91–111 day gestation.
Feeding More than 85 prey species recorded: Mainly peccaries, armadillos, pacas, tamanduas, brocket deer, sloths and iguanas. Prey heavily on livestock In some areas (mainly Brazil and Venezuela).
Voice Loud, coughing *uh-uh-uh* roar, probably a territorial call. Also close contact grunts, growls and hisses.

Hotspots
Cockscomb Basin WS, PN Corcovado, PN Tortuguero, Chan Chich

WEST INDIAN MANATEE

Recognition Rotund, spindle-shaped body with paired front flippers and paddle-shaped tail. No dorsal fin. Gray to brown with sparse, short hairs. 440–1325lb (200–600kg).

Habitat Atlantic coast, lagoons and estuaries; occasionally 1–2mi (2–3km) out to sea, but mostly inshore. Often found quite far upriver from ocean.

Behavior Methodically and constantly feeds with short rest bouts interspersed according to no set pattern. Usually solitary, but may be seen in small groups. Pairs are usually a female and calf which may stay together for up to 2 years.

Breeding Single calf born after a 400-day gestation. Calf suckles underwater.

Feeding Aquatic vegetation (freshwater and marine), especially sea grasses, water lettuce and water hyacinth.

Voice Mainly silent; occasional squeaks, chirps and grunts, especially between females and calves.

Hotspots

PN Tortuguero (especially Caño Servulo and Agua Fría), **Swallow Caye**, **Southern Lagoon**

Sea elephants

Belonging to a unique group of sea mammals comprising only four species worldwide, manatees are thought to be an ancient offshoot of the same evolutionary branch that gave rise to elephants. However, with at least 55 million years separating the two, their kinship is only apparent in a few fairly obscure anatomical similarities and a broadly similar diet. Like elephants, manatees are herbivores and require huge amounts of vegetation each day. Grazing on a variety of aquatic plants, a large adult can process as much as 110lb (50kg) every 24 hours, producing a prodigious amount of waste in the process; fresh floating droppings (similar to a horse's) and almost continuous, bubbling streams of flatulence are useful ways to find them. Manatees are reputed to have excellent hearing, but they're most sensitive to fairly high frequency sounds such as their squeaking vocalizations. It means that quiet approaches are often rewarded with good viewing, although sadly it also makes them vulnerable to collisions with motorboats (which emit low frequencies). Illegal hunting is also a significant problem. For all their bulk, manatees are extremely placid and, apart from 15.5 mph (25km/h) bursts of speed over short distances, they have no defenses. Humans are their only recorded predators (though presumably large sharks could take them in open water) and they can be killed simply by being held under water until they drown.

Fortunately, the effort required to be a good manatee hunter seems to be losing appeal among younger locals who are more interested in the tourism allure of manatees. The best places to look for them are quiet river stretches with little boat traffic (take a canoe) that have 'blowing holes' or *sopladeros* (deep depressions in the riverbed where manatees are thought to congregate in small social groups to play or to wait for high tide so they can swim upriver to feed). In PN Tortuguero there are numerous sopladeros in and near the lagoon (see PN Tortuguero in the Parks and Places chapter). Belize's Southern Lagoon protects the largest manatee population in the region and can provide good viewing (visibility permitting). ■

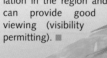

BAIRD'S TAPIR

River rhinos

Known also as the Central American tapir or by its Spanish name *danta*, Baird's tapir is Central America's largest land mammal. Despite their bulk (adult males weigh up to 660lb /300kg) they are also one of the most retiring, and sightings occur with about the same frequency as those of their penultimate predator, the jaguar. Humans (the ultimate predator) are the main reason that tapirs are so rarely seen: Being so large makes them a sought-after source of protein and their habit of commuting between feeding patches and waterholes on very distinctive 'tapir trails' makes them extremely vulnerable to hunting. They are now restricted to the least accessible wilderness areas and, even where they're not hunted, tapirs give people a wide berth. The best ways to spot them are on river trips (they're powerful swimmers) or waterhole watches, especially at night. Tapirs have poor eyesight, but acute hearing and smell; so stay downwind and remain silent.

The tapir's closest relatives are rhinos and horses, although with their elephantine snout you could be forgiven for thinking they are cousins to the elephant. Indeed, they grasp leaves, twigs and fruits with their 'trunk' and, like elephants, occasionally stand on their hind legs to reach treats such as molasses-flavored guacimo fruits; small saplings are simply bulldozed over. Foraging is a solitary affair, but all the individuals in an area probably know one another and pairs or trios occasionally gather in loose social congresses at favorite spots such waterholes and mud wallows. Sightings of two animals are usually of a female and calf; youngsters stay with mom for as long as a year, possibly to benefit from her protection until they reach a size that deters predators. This means that tapirs give birth only about every 18 months, further increasing the species' vulnerability to hunting. Unlike more prolific species which can breed every year, tapir populations are slow to recover. Even so, they will return to areas once hunting has stopped, a process taking place right now in the mountains surrounding RBBN Monteverde. ■

Recognition Very large and solid. Blackish-brown skin with sparse black hair, cream on cheeks and neck. Young dark reddish-brown with white spots and stripes. 400–660lb (180–300kg).

Habitat Dense forests, both evergreen and dry, generally close to water. Also swamp (especially palm swamp) and riverine habitat. Often rests in mud wallows or shallow water.

Behavior Diurnal (usually with crepuscular activity peaks) or nocturnal; strictly the latter where hunted. Solitary, but usually amicable during meetings.

Breeding Single young born after 13-month gestation. Probably aseasonal. Youngster hidden for first 10 days then travels with mother.

Feeding Mainly browses leaves, twigs, fruits and seeds. Also flowers and occasionally grazes on grass at forest edges.

Voice Vocal communicators using long-distance whistles to find/avoid other tapirs. Also grunts, murmurs and a low alarm-snort.

Hotspots
PN Corcovado, PN Santa Rosa, RBBN Monteverde

COLLARED PECCARY

Recognition Grizzled gray with cream collar. 27–64lb (12–29kg).
Habitat Especially dry forest.
Behavior Both nocturnal and diurnal.
Breeding 1–4 (usually 2) young in rainy season.
Feeding Mainly fruits, seeds, roots and invertebrates.
Voice Barks, grunts 'woof' when alarmed.

> **Hotspots**
> PN Santa Rosa, La Selva, PN Corcovado

Jaguar foe or fodder?

With a ferocious reputation for shredding jaguars, the collared peccary probably sits somewhere near the lethal fer-de-lance on most wildlife watchers' wish-lists. Travelling in sounders numbering up to 50 and sporting interlocking blade-like canines, there's no doubt they can be formidable when pressed, but like virtually all creatures peccaries prefer retreat over attack. Unwitting walkers sometimes stumble into their midst from downwind; peccaries have excellent hearing and smell, but poor eyesight, so try to avoid surprising them. As for jaguar-killing, where peccaries are abundant they are typically the big cat's number one quarry and comprise as much as 50% of their diet. In theory, a large peccary herd could kill an inexperienced cat, but jaguars (and pumas) definitely have the odds in their favor. Presumably, if a cat does get into trouble, it heads for a tree – peccaries can't climb.

Collared peccary sounders are peaceful units with regular social behavior. They usually feed together amicably and females suckle one another's youngsters. Mutual rubbing of a large scent gland on the back probably cements the bonds and gives the herd a familiar group smell. Their moldy cheese odor also signifies territory: rocks, trees, mud wallows and waterholes may reek of it. ∎

WHITE-LIPPED PECCARY

Recognition Blackish-brown; white chin, cheek and throat. 58–88lb (26–40kg).
Habitat Evergreen forest.
Behavior Nocturnal or diurnal.
Breeding 1–3 young born year-round.
Feeding Mainly fruit, seeds, roots, bulbs and leaves.
Voice Doglike alarm-bark; threatening tooth-chatter.

> **Hotspots**
> PN Corcovado, PN Darién (Cerro Pirre)

White-lipped wanderer

Although larger and forming sounders up to 300-strong, the white-lipped peccary is actually less conspicuous than the collared peccary. The main problem is its vulnerability to over-hunting and habitat loss. The same forces affect collared peccaries of course, but collared peccary herds in protected areas are fairly safe because they remain in smallish home ranges year-round. White-lipped peccaries travel enormous distances, walking single-file along forest paths and invariably wandering into the reach of people. They are now endangered in Central America and are restricted to extensive tracts of evergreen forest which can accommodate their wanderlust.

So why the nomadism? It's probably related to food. White-lipped peccaries are primarily fruit-eaters, with powerful jaws to tackle the rock-hard fruits of palms (they can be heard cracking palm nuts 50 yards away). But fruits occur in unpredictable patches that peccaries must travel to find; in the fruiting slump of the dry season, they may disappear from their wet season range entirely. It's unclear if they cycle seasonally between the same areas (which would make them migratory), but unlike other peccaries, they appear not to mark their surroundings with scent; their mobility renders territorial claims meaningless, so they mark one another. ∎

WHITE-TAILED DEER

Rambunctious rutter

The same species that occurs in the millions across the USA, the white-tailed deer in Central America is both smaller and less conspicuous than its northern counterpart. North American populations have benefited from the human-caused extinction of their predators, but Central American white-tails have themselves suffered from excessive hunting and loss of their dry woodland habitat. Ironically, they actually benefit from the loss of denser habitats like rainforests and adapt well to disturbed patches if some cover is left. Being able to both graze and browse, white-tails thrive in mosaics of woodland with scattered grassy fragments – areas which provide some of the best deer-viewing. They emerge from thick cover at dawn and dusk to feed in the open, and during the rut between July and November, these areas become arenas for testosterone-drenched males establishing their dominance.

White-tailed deer are usually seen on their own (does are accompanied by their spotted fawns in the dry season) or in small groups. Only the males carry antlers, which are shed each year and are less than half the size of those on North American males. Look for low shrubs stripped of their bark from males disrobing their antlers of velvet between February and May. ∎

Recognition Usually gray-brown (reddish in Panama). 55–95lb (25–43kg).
Habitat Mostly dry forests.
Behavior Nocturnal or diurnal (usually crepuscular).
Breeding Single (rarely 2) fawns born February to May.
Feeding Twigs, leaves and fallen acorns and fruit.
Voice High-pitched whistling alarm-snort.

Hotspots
PN Santa Rosa, PN Palo Verde, Río Bravo

RED BROCKET DEER

Forest rocket

Smaller, stockier and redder than the white-tailed deer, the red brocket is also more reclusive. A denizen of dense evergreen vegetation, it has a swag of characteristics befitting a forest dweller: Unlike the upright, long-legged white-tail, red brockets have short legs, a hunched profile and small, unbranched antlers – all to permit speedy passage though thick forest when danger threatens. For the same reason, they also run with head held low, like a diver plunging into water; if you glimpse a bolting deer but aren't sure of ID, the white-tail usually runs with its head held high.

Crashing escapes notwithstanding, red brockets try to avoid danger by first staying put. Their main predators, the cats, usually locate prey in dense cover by first hearing it and then following up with vision that's hyper-sensitive to movement. Red brockets avoid their attention by freezing when they sense danger and fleeing only if the threat comes to investigate. The ruse sometimes permits excellent viewing, but if you approach too closely or linger too long, they'll bolt; the best tactic is to keep walking past slowly. If pursued, red brockets may take to water. Even the fawns are accomplished swimmers, immersing themselves entirely and surfacing under concealing overhangs of riverbank vegetation. ∎

Recognition Small, rust-colored; fawns have white spots. 27–71lb (12–32kg).
Habitat Evergreen forests.
Behavior Nocturnal or diurnal.
Breeding Single (rarely 2) young born year-round.
Feeding Fruits, fungi, flowers and leaves.
Voice Usually silent; bleats in distress.

Hotspots
Isla Barro Colorado, PN Corcovado

TINAMOUS

*Long, musical whistles at dawn are a hallmark of the common (but elusive) **great tinamou**.*

Indian alarm clocks

To evolutionary biologists, tinamous represent a link to a time when the southern continents were joined as the supercontinent Gondwana: They are the closest living relatives of the ratites (giant flightless birds such as the ostrich and emu) and evolved before Gondwana split 135 million years ago into modern-day South America, Africa and Australasia. Rheas are the only surviving Neotropical ratites, but tinamous rapidly diversified and 45 or so species are known today. Six species occur in Central America, although these chicken-sized birds are rather drab skulkers of undergrowth and are most commonly encountered at the edges of rank grass and along forest trails (especially in the early morning). Males incubate the eggs (a ratite trait) and all tinamous can fly for short distances (unlike ratites), although running is their most common mode of escape. Cryptic in behavior and modest in coloration, tinamous nonetheless have beautiful, quavering calls that are most often heard at dawn and dusk; the great tinamou's whistle tells the Chocó Indians when to rise and when to start the cooking fire at dusk. ■

*The **highland tinamou** is a wide-ranging species, but usually only found above 4000ft (1200m).*

> **Hotspots**
> **PN Corcovado** Great tinamous abundant and easily seen. **PN Chirripó** Highland tinamou. **PN Santa Rosa** Thicket tinamous.

CRACIDS

Birds of the dawn

The guans, and closely related chachalacas and curassows, are known collectively as cracids, and belong to the large order of so-called gamebirds. Most cracids are both pheasant-sized and shaped (although curassows are considerably larger), and all are fruit-eating forest birds that are equally at home on the ground or in trees. Guans are mainly black or dark brown with colored facial or throat patches that are thought to help pair-bonding in their dense forest habitat; the drab coloration of chachalacas suits their preference for open woodland; and the sole curassow in the region, the great curassow (see photo on p120), is a mainly ground-feeding rainforest bird. All cracids fly well (although they will usually run from danger before taking flight) and are often seen feeding high in the canopy, where they run along large branches with ease, craning their necks to pick fruits from sprays. Among the six species in the region, the black guan is endemic to Costa Rica and Panama. Cracids are often very vocal before daybreak, and the crested guan was revered as the Maya bird of the dawn. However, many species are declining under severe hunting pressure. ■

*Illegal hunting has reduced the numbers of **crested guans** near human settlements.*

*The **black guan** is endemic to the montane forests of Panama and Costa Rica.*

> **Hotspots**
> **Cockscomb Basin WS** Crested guans. **Monteverde** Cloud forest species, such as black guans and gray-headed chachalacas.

OCELLATED TURKEY

Iridescent heavyweight

Standing more than 3ft (1m) high and weighing in at 10lb (4.5kg) or more, an ocellated turkey tom is a large bird indeed. Endemic to the Yucatán Peninsula, it is one of only two turkey species – the other being the familiar wild turkey of the American backwoods from which originated the barnyard bird of Thanksgiving fame. Ocellated turkeys can easily be seen strutting about rather tamely at several ecolodges in Belize, yet basic facts about the bird's ecology and even its calls are as yet unrecorded. The Maya kept domestic turkeys, but these were the other turkey species, which is also found in northern Mexico and was introduced to Europeans. The ocellated turkey doesn't appear to be a threatened species, although like all so-called game birds it is almost certainly affected by hunting, and there are no reliable estimates of its total population and abundance.

Much about ocellated turkey biology is inferred from the well-studied wild turkey. Like their northern relative, ocellated turkeys are sociable birds that live in flocks of up to 20 birds. They spend much of the day on the ground and roost in trees at night; turkeys fly strongly (although the bulkier males typically run away from danger) rising with powerful wing strokes then gliding for sometimes great distances. Males gobble to attract hens, and posture with tail cocked and fanned, wings drooped and bright blue head pressed flat against the back to further demonstrate their prowess: The burnished copper look of a wild turkey tom is impressive, but the male ocellated takes turkey iridescence and adornments to the limit ('ocellated' refers to the blue, eyelike spots on the tail and tail coverts). Females nest away from the flock, keeping their offspring separate for several weeks before mingling with other broods. Like other game birds, young turkeys can walk and forage almost as soon as they hatch; hatching is synchronized so the family can move together for protection and shelter. If left alone, numbers can build up quickly and even repopulate an area – as demonstrated by the dramatic comeback of the wild turkey in recent decades. ■

Recognition Adults unmistakable: Overall metallic blue-black, breast feathers fringed orange, with extraordinary iridescence on wings and back; naked head and neck bright blue with orange wattles. Males 36–40in (90–102cm).

Habitat Deciduous woodland, dense forest and adjoining grassy clearings (the latter especially in fall).

Behavior Typically runs uphill to escape predators. Dust-bathes. Swallows grit to grind nuts and seeds in gizzard.

Breeding Lays 8–15 eggs in scrape on ground in April; hatch early June. Only hens incubate and tend poults.

Feeding Omnivorous; mainly seeds, leaves, fruits and insects, all taken from the ground; also eats corn when available. Hatchlings eat insects.

Voice Males gobble – *wump-wump-wump pom-pom-pom-deedle-gunk* – to attract females.

> **Hotspots**
> **Chan Chich Lodge, Río Bravo, Chiquibul NP**

SEABIRDS

*Only the male **magnificent frigatebird** has an inflatable throat pouch.*

***Brown boobies** are the most common booby species, and often feed and loaf near jetties.*

*The **red-billed tropicbird** is the only tropicbird in the region and unmistakable in flight.*

Pelagic wanderers and aerial pirates

Many bird families use the sea as a food resource, but a few feed exclusively at sea and return to land only to breed or molt. Among them are penguins, represented in Central America only by vagrants from South America, and the petrels, shearwaters and storm-petrels – 'true' seabirds that wander widely over the oceans. The true seabirds (known to aficionados as procellarids) are represented by only a dozen or so species, most of which are irregular visitors. Hardly spectacular, they nonetheless make serious birders drool – birdwatchers love a challenge and procellarids are notoriously difficult to identify at sea.

In complete contrast, members of a third (but only distantly related) seabird group are large, spectacular and immediately recognizable. The brown pelican is probably the most familiar (see opposite), but boobies, tropicbirds and frigatebirds are almost exclusively tropical in distribution and some are easily seen in Central America. All use various strategies to catch fish at sea or in coastal waters, and nest on uninhabited islands (such as the red-footed booby shown inset) where they are safe from predators such as people, pigs and rats. Boobies got their unflattering name because seafarers found them easy to catch at their nests. Closely related to gannets, they are adept at catching fish by plunge-diving and their comical appearance is totally lost once they take to the wing: Feeding boobies plunge from great heights into shoals of fish like airborne torpedoes. The all-white, graceful tropicbirds are represented in the region by a sole species, the red-billed tropicbird.

But none can boast the supreme aerial elegance of frigatebirds – often seen floating effortlessly on narrow wings above coastal waters. Also known as man o' war birds, frigatebirds harass flying birds, such as boobies, into dropping (or regurgitating!) their catch, which they then scoop up in midflight. Aerial piracy is commonly practised, but frigatebirds are also capable of catching their own fish and may, in fact, obtain most of their prey this way. Male frigatebirds have an inflatable pouch under their bill; nearly invisible normally, during courtship he sits atop a bush, cocks his wings in a 6.6ft (2m) span, and inflates his scarlet pouch like a balloon to attract a mate (see photo on p62). ∎

> **Hotspots**
> **Central Panama** Magnificent frigatebirds common along the coast and Panama Canal. **Half Moon Caye** Belize's only colony of red-footed boobies; magnificent frigatebirds also nest. **Swan Caye (Bocas del Toro)** Red-billed tropicbirds and brown boobies.

Frigatebirds gather in great numbers as they return to their roosts and nests at night.

BROWN PELICAN

The fine art of plunge-diving

Few people will need an introduction to pelicans and Central America's representative of this family, the brown pelican, is common and easily seen along most stretches of coast. The brown is the smallest and most abundant of the world's seven pelican species and the most successful in the face of human disturbance: Brown pelicans are a familiar sight loafing on jetties, beaches and foreshores all over the region. Nonetheless, pelicans are vulnerable on land; these large, heavy birds need space to take off when threatened, and because they typically nest on the ground, they breed only on islands that are free from land-based predators. The young are born naked, but soon develop white down (inset) and band together in crèches when their parents are away feeding.

In the air the brown pelican is a different bird altogether. Like frigatebirds, pelicans commonly soar on thermals, yet they also glide over water just inches above the surface and flocks typically travel in V-formations, with each bird flapping then gliding in turn. The brown is the only pelican that feeds regularly by plunge-diving and it has developed this into a fine art. Selecting a fish from as high as 50ft (15m), brown pelicans plunge headfirst with mouth open and wings folded, thrusting back the wings and feet just before impact to increase speed. Dives are always made facing away from the sun and the bird usually disappears entirely underwater, although tiny air sacs under the skin give the brown pelican extraordinary buoyancy and they soon bob up again – always facing into the wind. Research has also revealed that adults make higher and steeper dives than juveniles; it may be that the more experienced adults can compensate for refraction before striking. Young birds are also robbed of their catch more often than adults – by the opportunistic frigatebirds, but also by laughing gulls, which may sit on a pelican's head to snatch a morsel. The best place to see pelicans plunge- feeding is at sea, where dozens may congregate around shoals of fish. ∎

Recognition Huge with unmistakable pouched bill. Gray-brown upperparts, darker below; white head and neck, hind-neck becoming dark brown in breeding plumage. Legs and feet black. 6.5–7ft (2–2.2m) wingspan.

Habitat Coastal marine waters, coasts, estuaries and bays; usually avoids open sea.

Behavior The most marine pelican, rarely visiting freshwater. Doesn't usually fish cooperatively. Often associates with magnificent frigatebirds. Most populations resident, but breeding colonies may shift according to food availability.

Breeding Year-round; forms colonies on flat islands. Lays 2–3 eggs in bare depression on ground or on stick platform in tree. Nestlings fledge after 63–75 days. Sexual maturity reached after 2–5 years.

Feeding Mostly fish, especially sardines and anchovies; also shrimps, carrion and fishing scraps. Young may take nestlings of other birds.

Voice Adults normally silent but occasionally grunt.

> **Hotspots**
> **Panama City; Islas Bolaños** and **Guayabo** (Costa Rica); **Caye Caulker, Ambergris Caye** (Belize)

HERONS & ALLIES

The **boat-billed heron** roosts in groups by day, but is a solitary nocturnal predator of fish.

Graceful wetland predators

Even casual birders will recognize members of the cosmopolitan order that includes storks, herons and egrets, and the distinctive spoonbills and ibises. There are only two stork species in the region: The jabiru (see opposite) and the wood stork (inset) are both large and unmistakable. The 20 members of the heron family found in Central America range from the 12in (30cm) least bittern to the 52in (132cm) great blue heron, and variations in between include egrets, night-herons, tiger-herons and the unique boat-billed heron.

At least one species is usually present at any sizeable waterway, including mudflats, mangroves, ponds or swamps; most are easily recognized (although all-white egrets and immature tiger-herons can look similar) and several species feed side by side without competing directly. All are deadly hunters of fish, frogs and other small animals, harpooning prey with speed and accuracy. Herons and egrets generally pose stock-still for long periods before striking; night-herons and the boat-billed heron are nocturnal; bitterns are cryptically colored skulkers of reedbeds; and cattle egrets snap up insects disturbed by livestock – behavior that has been shown to be much more

effective than hunting alone. Usually silent, herons often make harsh territorial calls at the nest; most species nest communally and heronries can be noisy places. Many species also roost communally, flying sometimes great distances in V-shaped flocks at dusk.

Juvenile tiger-herons, such as this **bare-throated tiger-heron**, sport more stripes than adults.

Like storks, ibises and spoonbills (see photo on p177) differ from herons most dramatically in the shape of their sensitive bills (and fly with neck extended, not in an S-shape as herons typically do). The flattened, spoonlike bill of spoonbills is swept from side to side as they feed on microscopic water creatures, filtered through fine sieve-like lamellae. The ibis bill is not flattened and curves strongly downward – designed for probing in mud and soft soil for crustaceans, snails and tadpoles. Ibises and spoonbills are close relatives: Occasionally ibises sweep their bills from side to side and spoonbills poke in soft mud. The roseate spoonbill is commonly seen in shallow, slow-moving waterways in the company of other waterbirds. ∎

As its name suggests, the **yellow-crowned night-heron** is primarily a nocturnal hunter.

The **white ibis** the region's most spectacular, if common, member of this wide-ranging family.

Hotspots

PN Tortuguero Bare-throated tiger-herons conspicuous among 14 species. **Crooked Tree WS** Many species, including boat-billed herons. **RNVS Caño Negro** Yellow- and black-crowned night-herons, boat-billed herons and several egret species.

JABIRU

The original and genuine

The jabiru is one of only two stork species found in Central America (the wood stork is the other – see photo on opposite page) and with a wingspan of 8.5ft (2.6m) is among the largest of flying birds. Popular lore has it that 'jabiru' is the Aboriginal name for Australia's black-necked stork, but in fact the name is derived from 'xabiru', a South American Indian word meaning 'blown in the wind'. The 'real' jabiru is found only in the Neotropics and was known long before Australia's stork was named by explorers.

The stork body plan is superficially similar to that of herons, ie, long legs, toes and neck – although a stork's neck is generally thicker, and storks fly with neck outstretched, making identification in flight straightforward. But no stork has a neck like the jabiru's – the base is inflatable and swells like a balloon during courtship rituals so the scarlet patch on the throat contrasts with the bare black skin. Like herons, storks are carnivorous, although most species have a heavier bill; in the jabiru's case, the bill is massive and acts as a powerful pair of tweezers adept at snatching small animals from shallow water. Jabirus are usually solitary, although pairs sometimes feed together and groups may aggregate during the dry season. Jabirus also may be seen in association with flocks of other large waterbirds, such as wood storks and ibises. Feeding associations are not unusual among birds, and probably have mutual advantages. For example, a flock moving through the shallows would undoubtedly stir or startle prey into the waiting gape of a jabiru; and a jabiru's extra pair of eyes – and imposing size – could act as a deterrent to any potential predators (jabirus also sometimes intimidate other birds into dropping their catch, which a jabiru will readily steal). Whether alone or not, jabirus feed by walking through the shallows, dipping their bill in the water with each step and probably locating prey both by sight and touch.■

Recognition Huge, completely white stork with unfeathered head and neck. Head, neck, legs and massive bill black except for red patch on swollen lower neck.

Habitat Large lakes, swamps and ponds; also estuaries and savanna.

Behavior Flies strongly, often soaring high in thermals. Congregates with other birds outside breeding season. Carries large fish to shore and beats young caimans to death before swallowing; groups may herd fish into shallows. Often nests far from water.

Breeding Solitary nester; builds a huge platform of sticks in a tall tree (see photo above), adding material in successive years. 2–4 eggs laid during dry season. Young fledge after 90 days.

Feeding Hunts small animals in shallow water: Mainly eels, but also other fish, frogs, turtles, crabs and young caimans.

Voice Silent, but claps bill when agitated and at the nest.

> **Hotspots**
> Crooked Tree WS, RNVS Caño Negro, PN Palo Verde

WETLAND BIRDS

A bonanza for birds and birders

Water is a magnet for birds and birdwatchers alike: The former are attracted to abundant food resources, especially late in the dry season when prey becomes concentrated in dwindling pools; and the latter to a myriad of birds in various shapes, sizes and colors – sometimes in staggering numbers. As a bonus for birders, wetlands often offer easy visibility from a boat or shore, uninterrupted by vegetation – although exposed to the elements, it's a great relief from craning one's neck into the forest canopy.

Wetlands attract many species of bird, mammal and reptile (as well as smaller animals) in search of food and safety, and the sum is a panoply of wildlife interactions: Birds hunting small animals, caimans lurking for unwary birds (and jabirus stalking

The **sungrebe**, one of the finfoot family, frequents slow rivers with dense overhanging vegetation.

The **sunbittern's** defensive coloration is like no other bird – by spreading its wings it reveals the eyelike markings that probably look like a large face to any would-be predator. Although uncommon, sunbitterns are not usually shy and can be readily observed.

Central America's two jacanas are distinctive in adult plumage – this is a **wattled jacana**.

young caimans), busy nesting colonies on overhanging boughs, and opportunists patrolling overhead. However, several bird families rely totally on wetlands for sustenance, protection or the rearing of young, and are best sought in this habitat. Most, such as ducks, herons and cormorants, will be familiar to birders from around the world (although naturally many species will be new) but, this being the Neotropics, there are also some unique families to look for.

Different birds occupy various wetland niches and an understanding of how they utilize their habitat will help you get the most out of wetland birding. Anhingas, whistling-ducks, ibises, spoonbills and herons all feed in water, but typically loaf on overhanging branches, larger species occupying the larger limbs and smaller species generally closer to the water (check the lowest branches for pygmy kingfishers).

The range of **northern jacanas** overlaps that of wattled jacanas in western Panama.

Black-bellied whistling-ducks are sometimes seen in large flocks and regularly perch in trees.

Similarly, open water of different depths is utilized in different ways: Many ducks upend in the shallows to reach food on the bottom, while masked ducks dive in deeper water; and anhingas and cormorants hunt fish underwater. At the water's edge, crakes and rails skulk in reedbeds, and plovers pick insects off the ground as mud is exposed by drying pools. Even the water's surface is exploited: Jacanas feed, nest and raise their young on mats of floating vegetation, their elongated toes spreading their weight so they can even walk across floating lilypads. Female jacanas hold territories containing several males with whom they mate; the male does all the incubation and rearing of the downy young, which are precocial and follow him around shortly after hatching.

Two uniquely Neotropical wetland birds, the sunbittern and limpkin, are of ancient and uncertain evolutionary affinities and both are the sole species in their respective families. Limpkins are vaguely ibislike in appearance, but are structurally akin to cranes and in behavior are more like rails. Like jacanas, they habitually walk on floating vegetation, among which they search for the water snails that make up most of their diet. The name comes from their peculiar gait, but limpkins also stand out for their loud, trumpeting calls.

The beautifully patterned sunbittern is most often found singly or in pairs along forested streams, but may also be seen near slow waterways. Few nests of this little-known bird have been found, although adult birds can be quite approachable. ■

*Although vaguely ibislike, the **limpkin** is unique and placed in its own family.*

Gray-necked wood-rails are large for a rail, but like most of their family are rather retiring in habit.

The roseate spoonbill's plumage can vary in color from almost white to rosy pink.

*The **anhinga** is closely related to cormorants and, like them, often perches with wings outstretched to dry. However, anhingas have a pointed bill with which they spear fish and normally swim with only head and neck showing above water.*

Hotspots
PN Palo Verde Migratory waterfowl by the thousand. **RNVS Caño Negro** Conspicuous roseate spoonbills, three ibis species and huge anhinga population. **Crooked Tree WS** Guaranteed limpkins, gray-necked wood-rails, sungrebes and northern jacanas.

*Like all members of its genus, the **masked duck** dives in deep water for plants and small animals.*

Common black-hawks are nearly always seen near water and feed mainly on crabs.

The *gray hawk* hunts lizards and small mammals in forest edge and savanna woodland.

Black-collared hawks swoop on aquatic prey such as fish from a perch overlooking water.

Snail kites pluck snails from aquatic vegetation and take them to a perch to eat.

BIRDS OF PREY

Aerial acrobats

Raptors, or birds of prey, are among the most widespread of birds and some, such as eagles, have inspired mankind as symbols of power and freedom since prehistoric times. Nearly all raptors are exclusively carnivorous, with talons to grasp prey and a hooked beak for tearing flesh. Varying proportions of wing length to wing breadth determine aerial maneuverability, speed, and therefore prey: Rounded wings enable forest-dwelling hawks to twist and turn in canopy pursuits; vultures have long, broad wings for energy-efficient gliding at great heights in search of carrion; and the long, narrow wings of falcons scythe through the air at great speed, building to deadly dives known as stoops.

The **turkey vulture** *is the second most common species of New World vulture in Central America, although unlike the ubiquitous black vulture it is not a generalist, feeding mainly on carrion which it detects with its fine sense of smell.*

In Central America an abundance of prey means an abundance of raptors – both in numbers and species. Neotropical raptors fall into four families: The osprey (the sole member of its family); the large cosmopolitan family that includes eagles, hawks, harriers and kites – known collectively as accipitrids; the so-called New World vultures, which are distinct from their counterparts in Eurasia (also accipitrids) and probably evolved from a storklike ancestor; and the falcons, which in the Neotropics include several large, rangy species called caracaras.

The osprey is a distinctive, cosmopolitan raptor that feeds almost exclusively on fish, which it catches near the water's surface by plunge-diving while flying overhead.

The 40-plus Central American species of accipitrid include both resident and migratory species that arrive en masse from North America along well-defined flyways. In size they range from the 10in (25cm) tiny hawk that ambushes birds as small as hummingbirds, to the world's most powerful raptor, the harpy eagle (see p180). And feeding niches are almost as varied as size: Freshwater specialists include the snail kite, which feeds almost exclusively on large snails that are extracted from their shells with its hooked bill. The various black-hawks typically perch near water, but run around after prey on the ground; the mangrove black-hawk is now considered a full species. The crane hawk has articulated legs that can bend backward to extract prey from crevices and under bark; and double-toothed kites snatch large insects disturbed by monkey troops.

Although most of Central America's four vulture species are carrion feeders, one, the black vulture, scavenges so successfully from human refuse that it has become ubiquitous around settlements. Flying vultures hold their wings in distinctive dihedrals: Lesser yellow-headed vultures drift low over grasslands with wings held in a steep V to cope with turbulence near ground level, while high-flying king vultures hold their wings flat and the dihedral of the other two species, which forage at different heights, falls in-between.

'Typical' falcons are among the swiftest of birds and most feed primarily on other birds taken on the wing. Forest-falcons and caracaras (named after their noisy calls) are unique to the Neotropics; the former are rather secretive birds that hunt through the forest canopy and most caracaras are generalist hunters that even feed on carrion (although one, the red-throated caracara, raids wasps' and bees' nests for eggs and larvae). ■

Crested caracaras stalk over the ground, looking for small dead animals and attacking live ones.

The *yellow-headed caracara* often feeds among cattle, dashing after mice, lizards and insects.

A black 'mask' and its raucous call readily distinguish the **laughing falcon** from all other raptors.

The **ornate hawk-eagle** is a large predator of lowland rainforests, where it hunts under the forest canopy for small mammals, iguanas, large snakes and birds as large as cracids.

Hotspots

Crooked Tree WS Good for water-associated raptors, such as crane hawks, snail kites and ospreys. **PN Corcovado** Many species easily seen, including yellow-headed caracaras and black-hawks. **PN Santa Rosa** Excellent for woodland buteos. **PN Darién** Forest raptors, including crested eagles.

Bat falcons have a typical falcon 'look', and catch bats and birds in rapid pursuits.

HARPY EAGLE

Recognition Huge. Adults white below with broad black chest band and faint leg barring; gray upperparts with prominent crest (see above). Strong wing bands prominent in flight. 6.5ft (2m) wingspan. Piercing yellow eyes; powerful yellow legs and bill.
Habitat Uninterrupted lowland primary forest, usually below 2600ft (800m); may hunt at forest edge.
Behavior May perch conspicuously in early morning; waits for prey beside salt licks and waterholes. Adults breed every three years, fledged young stay near nest for up to 12 months.
Breeding Usually nests in emergent tree (eg, *coiba*). One young, fledging after 6 months.
Feeding Hunts beneath the canopy, mainly for mammals (eg, monkeys, sloths, opossums, porcupines, anteaters and coatis), but also large snakes, iguanas and birds, eg, macaws and curassows.
Voice Eerie hoarse screaming by females at the nest and between mates.

Hotspots
PN Darién (Punta Patiño) Probably the best chance anywhere.

The mother of all eagles

Central America's most striking raptor is considered by many to be the most powerful bird of prey in the world. Unfortunately, opportunities to watch its prowess are few because harpies are now rare over much of their range – and are hard to find where they are common. But those who have had the privilege of watching one on the hunt often tell amazing tales. For instance, a harpy seen with a large male howler monkey writhing in her grip shifted her talons and with a resounding 'pop' crushed the monkey's skull so she could carry it unhindered. With massive claws as big as a grizzly bear's and legs as thick as a man's wrist, this is surely the mother of all eagles. It certainly has no competition in the Neotropics and the harpy is the peak avian predator between Belize and Patagonia, although its range is fragmented north of Panama: Harpies are now rarely seen in Costa Rica and even in their Amazonian stronghold they remain notoriously elusive.

A female harpy can weigh up to 20lb (9kg) and such a large predator obviously has high energy requirements: Harpies hunt all but the largest forest mammals, as well as large birds and reptiles. As a peak predator (like the jaguar), the harpy probably never occurred in high densities, but deforestation has removed much of its prey base and its habit of perching for long spells, even when people approach, makes it vulnerable to (illegal) human hunters.

Harpies rarely soar above the treetops and usually hunt by rapidly attacking prey through the canopy: Monkeys, including adult howlers and white-faced capuchins, are plucked from the foliage, unwary tayras and kinkajous are taken from boughs, and agoutis and young brockets are swept off the forest floor. But sloths make up a sizeable proportion of the harpy's prey and once a suitable candidate is found (sloths are most vulnerable when they bask in the morning sun), a harpy will sit nearby – sometimes for days – until it is hungry then take the sloth at its leisure. ■

KING VULTURE

Head of the pecking order

Vultures are unmistakable the world over, at least when perched, but Neotropical vultures are not closely related to their counterparts in Africa and Asia. They are, in fact, more akin to storks and are a remarkable example of convergent evolution, the process where ecological pressures cause unrelated creatures to evolve a similar appearance. African and Asian vultures are true raptors, while New World vultures show affinities with the storks and share with them weak feet, and various skeletal and muscular features. Whatever their origins, both Old and New World vultures have evolved to feed primarily on carrion, with a hooked bill for ripping open carcasses, a bare neck and face so feathers don't get matted in gore, and long, broad wings that enable them to soar with a minimum of energy as they search for dead animals.

The king is the largest of Central America's four vulture species and arguably the most attractive of the family (although such claims are of course relative). They are usually seen soaring alone and high over forest, and appear to scavenge primarily from the forest floor. But whereas the ubiquitous black vulture locates most of its food by sight and turkey vultures detect carrion with a keen sense of smell, king vultures appear to do neither. In fact, the king watches other vultures homing in on a corpse – its striking black-and-white plumage probably acting as a visual cue for others as it descends to feed. King vultures dominate other species at a carcass, but it's not a free ride: With its great size and strength the king can rip open tough carcasses that smaller vultures otherwise wouldn't have access to. And they are usually well-mannered at the dinner table: Kings don't loiter, feeding quickly then leaving smaller vultures to squabble over the remains; and the bizarre facial wattles (inset) are probably a dominance cue that keep others in line (they are usually not aggressive to each other when feeding). ∎

Recognition Adults white with gray 'collar'; black rump, tail and flight feathers; 6.5ft (2m) wingspan. Naked, multicolored neck and head; face wattles visible at close range.

Habitat Primary and secondary forest, woodland, forest mosaics of lowlands and foothills.

Behavior The highest-flying Central American vulture, soaring effortlessly as high as 3000ft (900m) for long periods with wings held flat. Spends little time at carcasses, although takes precedence when other vultures are present. Usually solitary, but family parties may forage together. Perches high in canopy.

Breeding One egg laid in hollow tree or even on ground during dry season. Chick fledges after 90 days.

Feeding Exclusively on carrion, specializing in skin and tough tissues such as sinews and tendons.

Voice Guttural croaks.

🔭 Hotspots
Mountain Pine Ridge FR, PN Corcovado, PN Darién

Band-tailed pigeons are birds of montane forests that may gather in flocks of up to 30.

*Look for the **pale-vented pigeon** at forest edges and even in parks in Panama City.*

PIGEONS & DOVES

Secrets of success

Unlike the multicolored fruit-doves that are such a highlight of Southeast Asian rainforests, most Neotropical pigeons and doves are rather drab birds. However, their camouflage is probably one of the secrets of their success and on forest trails it is not uncommon to be startled by one breaking from almost under your feet with a clatter of wings. All pigeons and doves fly well and explosive takeoffs are one of the secrets of their survival, along with loose-fitting feathers, which often leave a would-be predator empty-handed. They also have a rapid reproductive turnover: Most species are prolific breeders, although their nests are usually just a formality – typically a loose, untidy platform of twigs. The young grow faster than just about any other birds, developing for the first few days of life on a highly nutritious solution ('pigeon's milk') of digested seeds from the crop of the parent – a trait pigeons and doves share with parrots. Some species, such as ruddy ground-doves, have adapted to urbanization and can be readily seen in city parks and gardens; and the elusive quail-doves are ground-feeding birds of dense forest. ∎

> **Hotspots**
> **PN Santa Rosa** Inca doves, common ground-doves, white-winged doves and many others. **EB La Selva** Gray-chested doves, short-billed pigeons and ruddy ground-doves all common.

OWLS & NIGHTJARS

Birds of the night

Owls are essentially nocturnal hawks, armed with grasping talons, hooked bill, and soft plumage for silent flight. All are carnivorous and a disklike arrangement of facial feathers funnels sounds to their hypersensitive ears, enabling them to locate prey in almost total darkness. Admirable though these adaptations are, a nocturnal lifestyle usually makes seeing owls considerably more difficult than hearing them. Most are best seen by spotlighting, although they can sometimes be located during the day by the mobbing behavior of smaller birds.

Nightjars, nighthawks, poorwills and pauraques share the owls' soft plumage and silent flight, but are aerial hunters that locate flying insects with their large eyes, and snap them up in flight with their wide gape. They are probably more closely related to swifts, and have weak feet and long, usually slender wings. Most roost and nest on the ground, a trait for which they are superbly camouflaged in intricate patterns of brown, buff and black. Watch for them hawking over clearings; identification is often most reliably made using their distinctive calls. ∎

*The boldly-marked **spectacled owl** is a forest species that often hunts during the day.*

*Superb camouflage is a hallmark of all nightjars, including the **common pauraque** shown here.*

> **Hotspots**
> **Río Bravo** Mottled owls, black-and-white owls, Yucatán poorwills and nightjars, northern pauraques. **PN Soberanía** Eight owls, common pauraques and oilbird (vagrant).

COMMON POTOO

Master of disguise

Potoos comprise a small family of exclusively nocturnal birds that perform one of the most amazing disappearing acts in the Neotropical bird world. Like most other nocturnal birds, potoos are colored in subdued, but complex, patterns of brown, gray and cream. But unlike owls and nightjars, potoos roost during the day in an exposed position on a post or branch, relying on their amazingly bark-like plumage for camouflage. The 'normal' pose is somewhat relaxed with eyes closed and bill held horizontally, but potoos have loose eyelids with 'peepholes' and, although ostensibly asleep, when an intruder approaches they subtly morph into a stiff posture with bill pointing up and feathers slicked down to resemble even further the smooth outline of a branch. This is how most people see potoos during the day – if they can find one. Luckily potoos habitually use the same roost and once a roost is located, the bird can usually be found there on the following day or days.

After dark the lids lift on huge, bulging eyes (inset) that enable the potoo to see in most directions without turning its head. This is when they are readily seen by spotlighting, because although common, potoos rarely stray far from trees; much of their hunting is done from an exposed perch such as a fencepost. Adopting an owl-like stance – a look reinforced as they turn their head from side to side, although owls lack the potoos' long tail – they sally after flying insects which are snapped up in midflight. Like owls and nightjars, potoos have silent flight, but their feet are weak and prey is scooped up in their enormous gape before they return to their perch (a feeding technique that resembles that of the Australasian frogmouths). The common potoo is widespread from Panama to eastern Costa Rica (birds from northern Central America and Belize are now usually regarded as a separate species – the northern potoo). Among the bewildering array of Central American night sounds its call is easily recognized and commonly heard shortly after dark, particularly on moonlit nights. ■

Recognition Barred, streaked and mottled in variable bark-like shades of gray, brown and white or cream. Large yellow eyes. Eyes reflect intense orange at night. Length 15in (38cm).
Habitat Rainforest edge, woodland, mangroves and parks up to 5000ft (1500m); also farmland with trees.
Behavior Sedentary and mainly crepuscular. Roosts on stumps or posts; usually feeds near trees and rarely lands on the ground. Male attends nest during day, female at night.
Breeding Single egg laid December to March in a depression on a bare branch or stump.
Feeding Sallies after large flying insects such as beetles, moths, bugs and katydids; beetle larvae and small birds also recorded as prey.
Voice Four to eight mournful notes descending in volume and pitch, best described as *poor-me-all-alone*.

Hotspots
RNVS Caño Negro, PN Darién, Chan Chich Lodge (northern potoos)

PARROTS & MACAWS

Flying colors

Even nonbirders know a parrot when they see one and there is no better place in the world to observe these colorful birds – including the giant macaws – than the Neotropics. Nearly half of the world's 332 parrot species live exclusively in the Neotropics, and ornithologists have long realized that aspects of their behavior and morphology make them distinct from parrots elsewhere. No fewer than 27 species haunt Central American forests, with the richest variety in Panama where 22 species occur, including five macaws. Parrots are nothing if not forest birds and virtually every aspect of their biology is related to life in the trees. Their strong feet and claws – arranged with two toes pointing back and two forward – are ideal for grasping food and clambering through foliage. That distinctive hooked bill crushes nuts and tears bark apart, and acts as a 'third leg' when climbing; food is manipulated with the strong, thick tongue while being held in the feet. Many are predominantly green with patches of red, yellow or blue – coloration that provides camouflage by disrupting their outline among greenery and blossom. And parrots usually nest in tree hollows where the eggs are safe from all but monkeys, and a few arboreal snakes and mammals.

White-crowned parrots are noisy, sociable birds that form flocks of up to 50.

Blue-and-yellow macaws typically fly in pairs, although fledged birds may fly with their parents.

Although their basic form varies little, parrots range greatly in size, from the spectacular macaws (see opposite) to the spectacled parrotlet, which measures only 5in (12.5cm) in length. Apart from their size, macaws can be recognized by their huge bills, bare facial patch and long, tapered tails. Most amazons are about 12–15in (30–38cm) in length, with short tails and distinctive, shallow wing beats (the red-lored parrot shown inset is a typical amazon). And the various swift-flying parakeets tend to be noisy and gregarious, but can be very difficult to spot among foliage.

Watch for parrots at dawn flying above the canopy in small flocks, often alighting on exposed perches to take in the early sun. Parrots feeding in a tree typically make a cacophony of unmusical screeching, but when a potential threat appears they fall silent only to explode from the foliage in a burst of color in all directions, behavior that is thought to confuse predators. ∎

Great green macaws are canopy birds of lowland rainforest that seek out fruiting Dipteryx trees.

> ### Hotspots
> **PN Carara** Yellow-naped, white-crowned, red-lored and mealy parrots, plus orange-chinned parakeets. **PN Tortuguero** Great green macaws, and crimson-fronted and olive-throated parakeets. **Río Bravo** Many species, including endangered yellow-crowned parrots. **PN Darién** (Cana) Four species of macaw.

SCARLET MACAW

The real macaw

Sightings of the large, gaudy macaws are a highlight of any trip to Central America. Macaws are the largest parrots in the world and the scarlet is one of the biggest of the region's five species. Most macaws are usually seen in pairs flying close together, their wingtips almost touching, or in small family groups, although several parties may join together outside the breeding season and up to 50 may roost together. Early morning or late afternoon are the best times to watch for macaws as they fly to and from roosts with deep wing beats and sometimes perch conspicuously to bask. Their great size and brilliant coloration make them difficult to miss in flight, but when perched silently among foliage – as they do when feeding – macaws blend in and seem to disappear.

Scarlet macaws were revered as an oracle of the sun by the Maya and are still understandably popular as pets. But trapping for the pet trade – and the all-too-familiar refrain of habitat destruction – have extirpated these magnificent birds from much of their former range. Although it is readily seen at certain sites, the scarlet macaw is now extinct over most of Central America, including Costa Rica's entire Caribbean coast. Healthy populations now survive only on Costa Rica's Península de Osa and in parts of Belize. In Panama it is common on Isla de Coiba and historically was found only there and in parts of the adjacent mainland, but its fragmented distribution on the isthmus was actually due to a different reason. The scarlet macaw is also found in South America, and once ranged across a now-vanished part of the land bridge to Península de Osa and further north. Isla de Coiba is one of the few parts of its former range that survived a rising sea level, leaving relict populations of scarlet macaws. ■

Recognition Huge (33in/ 83cm); scarlet with blue flight feathers, rump and undertail-coverts, and yellow wing-coverts. Ivory-colored upper bill, black lower; bare face patch white.

Habitat Undisturbed lowland deciduous or pine forest; often in gallery forest and near exposed riverbanks.

Behavior Wanders seasonally in response to food availability. Young birds accompany parents after fledging, but flocks rarely number more than three or four during breeding season. Rests and feeds high in tall trees.

Breeding Nests in tree hollows or abandoned woodpecker nests 25–130ft (7–40m) high. Lays 1–2 white eggs in the dry season. Young fledge after 14 weeks.

Feeding Seeds, fruits, flowers and nectar of forest trees and palms; also bark, leaves and sap. Feeds while silently perched in the canopy.

Voice A loud, deep and hoarse squawking in flight.

> **Hotspots**
> **Cockscomb Basin WS, PN Corcovado, PN Isla de Coiba**

HUMMINGBIRDS

Pugnacious jewels of forest and garden

Hummingbirds are a Neotropical phenomenon and the greatest exponents of iridescence in the bird world. Although several species migrate as far as North America to breed (and migration is just one of many extraordinary features of this huge family), the center of their distribution is the tropics. With common names such as fairy, brilliant, starthroat and woodnymph, hummingbirds perhaps more than any other bird group evoke pictures of tropical splendor. And in real life they don't disappoint – the males of most species sparkle and glitter in dazzling shades of green, red and gold that shimmer in the light. Their rapid wing beats do sound like humming – it's more like

The **black-crested coquette** *usually feeds high in the canopy, venturing lower in treefall gaps.*

Measuring 6in (15cm) in length, the **violet sabrewing** *is Central America's largest 'typical' hummer. This species readily visits feeders, but away from gardens it is more often found in the understory of montane forest.*

Green-breasted mangos are hummers of more open country, such as savanna and plantations.

the lazy sound of bees at flowers on a drowsy afternoon magnified several times. But although many are common, their speed and agility can make them hard to see clearly, and difficult to identify (especially females and immature males).

'Hummers' (as birders call them) are important pollinators in tropical forests, and are especially attracted to red, orange and yellow flowers. Watch carefully at a flowering bush or tree, because several species may be in attendance and many pugnaciously defend territories (and don't forget to look for clumps of flowering epiphytes – many hummers feed high in the canopy). Large hummers chase off all comers, male or female, but smaller, more agile species such as coquettes dart in and steal a feed while territorial disputes rage around them. Ornithologists classify hummers into two subfamilies – hermits and 'typical' hummingbirds. Hermits are specialists of the lower forest layers, where they exploit large, showy blooms such as passionflowers. Most are soberly colored, although many sport

Violet-headed hummingbirds feed at small flowers at forest edge and secondary growth.

Rufous-tailed hummingbirds are common forest birds, but also visit gardens and feeders.

white tail plumes, and one or two of the region's eight species are commonly seen on forest walks: Hermits are highly inquisitive and will closely approach an observer – especially one wearing red – before darting off again.

'Typical' hummers are represented in the region by some 56 species, although hummingbird taxonomy is complex and several forms are split into different species by some references. Their extraordinary iridescence – sometimes complemented with extravagant adornments – is thought to play a role in threat and courtship displays. Iridescence is caused by a modified feather structure that weakens the feather and consequently does not occur on flight feathers, although in hummingbirds it can cover virtually every other surface. Iridescence changes according to the angle of the viewer, so when the bird moves its radiant colors can change instantly to dull tones or even black: It is thought that when a dull-looking male hummer suddenly turns to face a rival the interloper is met with an intimidating burst of dazzling color.

Males of many species display for females at leks, some also performing courtship flights; the leks of hermits can be low in the forest understory. Hummingbird nests are typically cuplike structures of soft material, camouflaged with lichen and moss on the outside, although hermits attach the nest to the underside of large fronds for shelter. Not every species has been studied, but it appears that females rear the young alone, feeding them regurgitated nectar and insects. ■

The *rufous-tailed hummingbird's* compact cup nest decorated with lichen is typical for the family.

The *magnificent* (or *admirable*) *hummingbird* inhabits montane forest above 6600ft (2000m).

Male *snowcaps* pugnaciously defend their patch against other snowcaps, but at 2.5in (6.5cm) they are easily displaced by larger hummers. Snowcaps typically feed at small canopy flowers, such as epiphytes.

Long-tailed hermits are commonly seen along forest trails, where they will investigate anything red.

After breeding, male *crowned woodnymphs* defend territories around heliconias.

Hotspots

Monteverde Twenty-six species, seven guaranteed close-up at Hummingbird Gallery. **PN Tapantí** Many notables, including purple-crowned fairies, white-bellied mountain-gems and black-bellied hummingbirds. **PN Volcán Poás** Highland species. **PN Darién** (Cerro Pirre) Endemic Pirre hummingbird and greenish puffleg; Chocó species such as tooth-billed hummingbird.

TROGONS

Colorful sit-and-wait predators

*A female **black-throated trogon** is considerably duller than the male, who sports green upperparts.*

Trogon origins have long puzzled researchers, but despite some affinities with kingfishers most now regard them as distinctive enough to be placed in their own order. But if anything defines these colorful forest birds it is their arboreal nature. All are medium-sized with a strong, broad bill and wide gape, and broad, rounded wings that give them excellent maneuverability among canopy foliage. Trogons have strong feet ideally suited to clinging and are most commonly seen perched on a horizontal branch in the middle layer of the forest with tail hanging vertically (like the slaty-tailed trogon shown inset). But with short, weak legs they are apparently incapable of walking and cannot even turn around on a perch without a flap of the wings. Trogons excavate nests in by enlarging cavities in decaying trunks, arboreal termite mounds or wasps' nests. Males and females both contribute to rearing the young.

Trogons probably evolved in Africa, but they reach the peak of their diversity in the Neotropics and it is here that they evolved into their most spectacular form, the resplendent quetzal (see opposite page). Males and females of the region's 11 'typical'

Collared trogons take a high percentage of insects in their diet as well as fruit.

trogons sport yellow, orange or red underparts contrasting with iridescent green or slaty-blue upperparts; and all have fine black and white barring (vermiculations) on the wings and/or underside of the tail. The combinations of color and undertail pattern are important field identification features, but locating the birds is the trick: Trogons seem to blend perfect-

ly into forest vegetation and, to further frustrate birders, can turn their head through a 180-degree arc so they often perch with their back turned, making their distinguishing marks hard to see. In fact, trogons are usually first spotted when they sally forth after a flying insect then return to their perch – this is their standard feeding method and is even used to pick fruits, although trogons also commonly drop from a perch to snatch prey from the ground.

*The **orange-bellied trogon** (this is a female) is sometimes regarded as a race of the collared trogon.*

Many species look similar and it's worth studying a field guide before you go birding in the forest – you could easily see several species in a day and confuse their identification features if you don't take careful notes. Salient points include breast bands and bare skin around the eyes, as well as undertail pattern and breast color. ■

> **Hotspots**
> **PN Carara** Five species, including the Costa Rica-Panama endemic, Baird's trogon. **PN Soberanía** Up to five species could be seen along Pipeline Rd and at other sites. **PN Darién** (Cerro Pirre) Central America's only site for golden-headed quetzal.

*Pairs of **slaty-tailed trogons** typically dig a nest chamber in an arboreal termitary.*

RESPLENDENT QUETZAL

The Maya bird of paradise

If birders were asked to name one 'must-see' Central American bird, most would immediately nominate this sometimes elusive denizen of the cloud forest. And it's not just birdwatchers who appreciate this extravagantly attired member of the trogon family: The quetzal was revered by the Maya civilization and is the national bird of Guatemala – even giving its name to the Guatemalan currency (although the bird is now rare there). But like many 'must-see' birds, the resplendent quetzal can be hard to find and inhabits often remote areas within a strict habitat requirement. Even there it can be hard to pin down, for unlike many trogons it is not terribly confiding and the high altitude forests it favors are often shrouded in mist, which can drastically reduce visibility at virtually any time of year.

Quetzals are still reasonably common in Costa Rica and Panama in the right habitat; the best time to look is close to the breeding season, when males grow a spectacular train (inset) and several males can congregate in a small area if there's a female nearby. The train is not actually the tail – like all trogons quetzals have rather short tails; it is in fact an extraordinary growth of the upper-tail coverts that in a breeding male can be over 30in (75cm) long. But even in this nuptial finery quetzals can be frustratingly difficult to see: In good light they show a golden iridescence to that emerald and ruby plumage, but once perched they disappear among the epiphytes that grow profusely in their preferred habitat, and the wispy train drifts in the slightest breeze like a filament of beard moss. Like most iridescent birds, when not in direct sunlight the plumage looks dull and, as an added vexation, quetzals (like other trogons) often perch motionless for extended periods. So, if you come across a likely looking tree, such as a fruiting avocado, wait and watch awhile before moving on, because a quetzal could easily be lurking somewhere among the foliage.■

Recognition Emerald-green, short crest; 15in (37cm). Males have elongated wing coverts, scarlet breast and belly; females duller with less red on underparts.

Habitat Epiphyte-rich highland forests above 4000ft (1200m), especially at forest edges and canopy.

Behavior Usually solitary or in pairs; several may feed at the same tree. Breeding males hop backwards off perch to avoid damaging their train.

Breeding Lays 2 eggs March–June in tree cavity 15–90ft (4.5–27m) high.

Feeding Mainly fruit, especially small avocados and figs, picked while hovering; also insects, snails, small frogs and lizards.

Voice Sharp cackles and a low, burbling whistle *keeeoo-keeeoo*.

Hotspots
RBBN Monteverde, **PN Volcán Barú**, **PN Volcán Poás**

RUFOUS-TAILED JACAMAR

Recognition Iridescent green with white throat; rufous belly and undertail. 9in (23cm).
Habitat Shady forest edges.
Behavior Sedentary.
Breeding Lays 2–4 eggs.
Feeding Flying insects.
Voice Loud whistle.

Hotspots
PN Carara, Cockscomb Basin WS, PN Corcovado

The flying letter-opener

Although their origins are uncertain, jacamars occur only in the Neotropics, and the long, fine bill of many species is unique (prompting one ornithologist to comment that it was 'better suited to opening letters than to catching insects'). Furthermore, many jacamars sport iridescent plumage and typically perch with bill angled upwards – features more reminiscent of hummingbirds. Three species occur in Central America: Great, rufous-tailed and dusky-backed jacamars, of which the rufous-tailed is most widespread and common (the dusky-backed jacamar is one of the specialty birds of Panama's PN Darién). All jacamars typically perch alone or in pairs at the forest edge or in the canopy, the rufous-tailed especially near streams. Ever on the lookout for the flying insects that comprise nearly all of their prey, they hunt low or in the forest midlevel. Jacamars ignore potential prey that isn't flying and this dietary predilection is thought to be the reason for their bill shape, which enables the bird to manipulate long-winged insects, such as dragonflies and butterflies, and dangerous wasps. Jacamars beat their prey against a branch to remove wings and dangerous stings; watch for their aerobatic dashes in pursuit of flying insects and look for carpets of discarded butterfly wings under perches. ■

PUFFBIRDS

White-whiskered puffbirds sit and wait for prey in the understory of forests and secondary growth.

The *white-necked puffbird* typically perches on a high, exposed branch in lowland forest.

'Kingfishers' of New World forests

Puffbirds spend much time perched and are generally approachable by humans, a trait that has earned them a reputation for sluggishness. But they are sit-and-wait predators and punctuate long spells of vigilance with mad dashes after prey. Their habit of fluffing out their feathers to give them a ball-like appearance probably serves as camouflage on exposed perches – and certainly earned puffbirds their common name. Unique to the Neotropics, eight species are found in Central America, including one each of the so-called nunbirds and nunlets. Ornithologists now place puffbirds in the same order as the jacamars, but their feeding technique is decidedly kingfisher-like; in fact, the presence of puffbirds probably explains why kingfishers don't occupy forest niches in the New World. When prey is spotted, a puffbird flies rapidly and directly to snatch it from the ground, trunk or air and returns to its perch, where it is beaten before being swallowed. Typical prey includes large arthropods, but small lizards and snakes are also taken; many species of puffbird are attracted to ant swarms and bird feeding flocks, and nunbirds take prey flushed by monkey troops. ■

Hotspots
PN Darién Gray-cheeked nunlets. Cockscomb Basin WS White-necked and white-whiskered puffbirds.

BLUE-CROWNED MOTMOT

Inconspicuous early risers

One of the most common sounds of the Central American dawn chorus is the double-hooting of motmots – a sound that undoubtedly earned the birds their common name. Motmots comprise a small family of 10 species endemic to the Neotropics – the only bird family whose stronghold is Central America; the blue-crowned motmot is typical of the family and also the most widespread species. Their calls are obvious and motmots themselves are common (in the right habitat you could easily encounter one or two of Central America's six species), but their habit of perching motionless for long spells makes them easy to overlook. Birders will note the similarity between motmots and bee-eaters: Both are brightly colored and related to kingfishers, but bee-eaters are unknown in the New World and motmots in the Old.

Like bee-eaters, motmots are also sit-and-wait predators that sally from a perch to snatch flying insects, although motmots are almost exclusively forest birds that do most of their hunting under the canopy. Blue-crowned motmots also take prey from the ground and even probe the soil for food. Most prey consists of arthropods – mainly insects, although rufous motmots (inset) are known to take scorpions, crabs, small fish and even poison-dart frogs – but motmots also eat fruit and have a serrated bill that presumably helps them grip such slippery food items. Another unusual motmot feature is a racket-like tail, formed when the lower part of the tail feathers wear away to leave two disks at the end. This may be a signal between mates that reinforces their bond: Adults stay in vocal contact when foraging; and a perched motmot often swings its tail from side to side like a pendulum. Indeed, this eye-catching movement may be your first inkling that one is nearby. ∎

Recognition Blue 'eyebrow', black mask and red eye diagnostic; upperparts and tail green, belly and breast variable but green to tan.

Habitat Rainforest, woodland and plantations up to 7000ft (2150m), especially at lower to mid-canopy levels.

Behavior Usually solitary or in pairs; may nest in colonies when nest sites are in short supply. Courtship behavior includes mutual feeding and possibly plucking and holding leaves and twigs. Sometimes attends ant swarms. Sometimes nests in Maya ruins.

Breeding Lays 3–4 eggs March to May in unlined chamber at end of 10–16.5ft (3–5m) tunnel. Young fledge after about 30 days.

Feeding Mainly large arthropods, but also fruits, snails, and small frogs, lizards, snakes and nestlings.

Voice Soft, deep, double-hooting *hoo-hoo*; pairs duet.

> **Hotspots**
> **RBBN Monteverde, PN Guanacaste, Central Panama**

Emerald toucanets move through montane forest in loose but frenetic flocks of 5-10 birds.

*The **fiery-billed aracari** is endemic to Costa Rica and Panama, and inhabits lowland forest.*

*Small flocks of **collared aracaris** are common in forest; this is the most widespread of the aracaris.*

TOUCANS

A most remarkable bill

Toucans are arguably the most recognizable birds in the Neotropics, and among the best-known birds in the world by birder and nonbirder alike. All seven Central American species are medium to large, colorful forest birds: Two of the largest species, rainbow-billed and chestnut-mandibled toucans, are common and easily seen in the right habitat, and the closely related Chocó toucan was recently identified in PN Darién, Panama. Smaller toucans are known as toucanets and aracaris: The former are represented by the emerald and yellow-eared toucanets; the latter by the collared and fiery-billed aracaris.

A toucan's most outstanding feature is of course that spectacular bill – in some species looking too heavy for the bird, although it is in fact full of air cavities and quite lightweight. Colorful and comical it may be, but the toucan bill is a powerful tool – serrations on the upper mandible help grip slippery fruits that comprise the birds' main diet. If fruit isn't available, or when their young require extra nutrients, the great reach comes in handy when toucans raid the nests of other birds for eggs and chicks; the bill probably also intimidates the hapless birds whose nests are being raided. Large species take predation a

step further: Chestnut-mandibled toucans (inset) have been known to take young coatis and monkeys. However, although toucans nest in tree cavities, they cannot excavate their own nest, relying instead on natural hollows or holes created by woodpeckers. This behavior restricts the distribution of most toucan species to mature forest, where fallen limbs create hollows in standing trees and there is an abundance of fruit for food; in fact, toucans are so adapted to flying from tree to tree in unbroken forest that they lose height if they must fly for long periods over open spaces.

It's hard to tire of watching toucans – their antics enhance their appearance as they preen each other (because of that large bill they can't preen themselves) and leap about in the foliage selecting fruits, craning and contorting to reach the most succulent morsels. A large fruit may take over an hour to digest, so toucans sometimes perch for extended periods, allowing superb viewing. ∎

Hotspots

PN Rincón de la Vieja Chance at yellow-eared toucanets. **PN Corcovado** Chestnut-mandibled toucans and fiery-billed aracaris. **RBBN Monteverde** Emerald toucanets guaranteed. **PN Guanacaste** Yellow-eared toucanets and collared aracaris.

*The large **chestnut-mandibled toucan** is also known as the yellow-throated toucan.*

RAINBOW-BILLED TOUCAN

The toucan formerly known as ...

Some books refer to this species as the keel-billed toucan, but one look will show that 'rainbow-billed' is a far better descriptor, especially as no other large toucan shares its brilliant bill coloration. Like many toucans it often perches in the open and, if seen well, there should be no mistaking it; the rainbow-billed toucan spends a lot of time calling and once you can recognize its call, you'll find it common in places. Singing birds jerk their head and tail, flashing their red undertail coverts; toucans are unique in having the last three vertebrae fused and attached to the end of the spine by a ball-and-socket joint. Thus, they can snap their tail back to touch the neck and sleep with the tail over their head.

Groups of up to 20 may gather in the same tree (sometimes alongside chestnut-mandibled toucans) ostensibly taking the sun, but probably also staking their claim on nearby food resources. Toucans are the dominant avian frugivore in Neotropical forests and their showy presence is usually enough to chase off any would-be competitors. The rainbow-billed toucan is a pleasure to watch as it feeds – usually in mid-canopy – that spectacular bill is sensitive enough to dehusk fruit before swallowing and males feed tidbits to females during courtship. Less glamorously, it can also pick apart large insects held down with its feet. The predatory nature of toucans may come as a surprise, but the rainbow-billed tears apart birds' nests and extracts eggs that it flips into its maw as delicately as any fruit. In flight, all toucans can be recognized by their undulating, flap-and-glide flight; groups of rainbow-billed toucans fly between trees one at a time, and the first bird has usually reached its destination before the next takes off. ∎

Recognition Black upperparts with white rump; bright-yellow breast, chocolate-brown belly and crimson vent. Lime-green facial patch and huge, multicolored bill; sexes alike. 18in (45cm).
Habitat Lowland rainforest and adjoining old secondary growth and plantations up to about 2600ft (800m).
Behavior Normally in pairs or family groups, but larger groups also occur. Visits fruiting trees in pastures, occasionally attends ant swarms. Drinks from bromeliads, bathes in arboreal cavities. Pushing duels with bill thought to be pair-bonding behavior. Roosts in groups.
Breeding Lays 1–4 eggs January to July in natural tree cavity 10–90ft (3–27m) up. Young fledge after about 45 days. Breeds when small birds are nesting.
Feeding Typically fruits, as large as 1in (3cm), swallowed whole; also beetles, cicadas, katydids, spiders, lizards, snakes and birds' eggs.
Voice A monotonous, creaking *crik-crik-crik*.

Hotspots
PN Soberanía, PN Corcovado, PN Guanacaste

FOREST BIRDS

A never-ending challenge

Ecotourists and birders flock to Central America's famous rainforests to get a taste of toucans, parrots, tanager flocks and the legendary army ant swarms. For a first-timer it can all be a bit overwhelming – a mixture of the familiar and bizarre, colorful and drab, skulkers in the undergrowth, gleaners in gloomy vine tangles and tiny silhouettes high in the canopy. But rest assured: Neotropical forests offer more birding excitement, variety and challenges than just about any other habitat on the planet.

Rainforests are among the most complex of ecosystems (although there are also other major forest types in Central America) and hundreds of Neotropical bird species rely on them exclusively

The 'clown face' of an **acorn woodpecker** is distinctive, as is its predilection for acorns.

Red-headed barbets typically investigate rolled leaves in search of insects and spiders.

Pairs and small groups of the striking **masked tityra** move through the canopy plucking fruit.

Orange-billed sparrows hop along the rainforest floor and even nest on the ground.

Like many of the crow family, **brown jays** are opportunists. Noisy parties travel through forest edge and secondary growth, restlessly searching for insects and other small animals, fruit and nectar.

for their livelihood. As in every bird community, some are specialists and some are generalists; there are species rare and abundant, quiet and vocal, seasonal and sedentary, and so on.

The incredible biodiversity of the Neotropics ensures a vast array of feeding opportunities at all levels of the forest; the corollary of this of course is that birders must search every one to find sometimes elusive birds, although many species habitually use only one or two. Thus, fruiting trees are exploited by toucans, barbets, parrots, tanagers and trogons that feed above the ground; and by others, such as guans and curassows that also eat fallen fruit. Foliage-gleaners, leaftossers, treerunners, woodcreepers and the more familiar woodpeckers ensure that sooner or later every crevice is probed and every leaf is turned in the search for insects and other small animals. And the banquet of flying insects is exploited by a legion of flycatchers and warblers (both resident and migratory), plus Neotropical specialties such as jacamars, puffbirds and motmots that sally forth from perches. Further, highly evolved Neotropical families include the hummingbirds, antbirds and manakins, all of which have evolved extraordinary coloration, adornment, behavior or all three in tandem with the forest's evolution (see the relevant sections in this chapter).

One of the most anticipated phenomena in any forest is a bird feeding flock, which can be composed of many species working all levels of the forest. Canopy flocks are most commonly encountered, but understory flocks with a different species composition also occur; sometimes the two join up temporarily, and then you'll have your work cut out for you trying to keep up with the constant procession. Feeding flocks also occur in dry forest, although in general they contain fewer species than rainforest flocks.

Many rainforest visitors expect to have their senses overwhelmed by flocks of colorful birds. In reality, birding tropical forests can be hard work: Apart from the difficulties of identifying birds often only glimpsed, there are more mundane problems such as rain to contend with (carry a light umbrella so you can continue birding during showers). Successful forest birding means tuning the senses to differentiate between rustling leaves and a foliage-gleaner; watching for glimpses of a skulking antpitta behind vegetation; being able to pick out the colors of a toucan or parrot where they blend into foliage; and knowing that even the largest birds, such as guans, can appear very small indeed when perched high in the canopy. It takes patience and practice, but be warned: Rainforest birding is addictive! ∎

The **collared redstart** is a common warbler of mossy montane forest above 5250ft (1600m).

The **brown-billed scythebill** has an extreme example of the woodcreepers' strong, probing bill.

Slaty flowerpiercers are found near patches of flowering shrubs from 4000ft (1200m) to the páramo above treeline. Competing directly with hummingbirds for food, they pierce the base of flowers with their bill and extract nectar with a brush-tipped tongue.

Long-billed gnatwrens work dense vine tangles low in forest edge habitat for insects and spiders.

The **olivaceous woodcreeper** feeds alone or in pairs at all levels of the forest.

Hotspots

Central Panama PN Soberanía offers an excellent introduction to Neotropical forest birding. **PN Corcovado** Many species, including woodcreepers, leaftossers and scythebills. **PN Santa Rosa** Dry forest specialties, such as Hoffmann's woodpecker.

Slaty antwrens are small, active antbirds of the forest understory that associate with feeding flocks.

The scaled antpitta is a rarely seen understory bird of middle elevations in montane forest.

Barred antshrikes usually move in pairs through vine tangles and undergrowth as they feed.

ANTBIRDS

Professional camp-followers

The most abundant and voracious predators in the rainforest are less than an inch long, but live in vast mobile colonies that bivouac at night in seething clumps (inset) and fan out by day to scour the forest floor like an army on the move. Any animal too slow is overwhelmed and eaten, and everything else gets out their way pronto. They are, of course, army ants and their role in rainforest ecology is so important that the daily, and even seasonal, routine of many birds is tied intimately with ant raids. However, antbirds don't actually eat ants – they wait on the flanks or near the head of a column and snap up any prey that is too agile or alert for the ants to overcome. Ant armies operate in regular cycles tied to breeding, and several antbirds, including bicolored, spotted and ocellated antbirds (see photo on p38), are known as obligate or professional antbirds because they always feed alongside army ants. The strident calls of obligate antbirds announce an ant swarm on the move to other birds; learn to recognize these calls and they should lead you to one of the most amazing feeding spectacles in the natural world. Following ant swarms is not unique to antbirds (several species of thrush follow safari ants in Africa), but only in the

Neotropics has it evolved so dramatically and birds from many families do it regularly or opportunistically. Among the opportunistic ant-followers are birds as diverse as toucans and thrushes; and a 'killer' ant swarm can galvanize a host of birds to join the picnic, including sought-after species like rufous-vented ground-cuckoos.

The antbird family also includes many diverse members that normally ignore ants altogether, such as various antwrens, antvireos, antshrikes, ant-thrushes and antpittas. Antpittas and ant-thrushes are usually solitary, retiring and elusive birds that forage on the forest floor; antpittas resemble their Old World namesakes and ant-thrushes are crakelike birds that walk, rather than hop. Other antbirds are common and readily seen birds that utilize the tropical forest's myriad feeding niches. Thus, the rather shrike-like antshrikes work the vine tangles and take insects with their stout, hooked bills; and antwrens are active little birds that often accompany mixed feeding flocks. ■

The spotted antbird is an obligate antbird that nearly always feeds near army-ant swarms.

> **Hotspots**
> **Central Panama** PN Soberanía is great for obligate antbirds.
> **PN Darién** Killer ant swarms, plus a chance at chestnut-vented ground-cuckoos. **PN Carara** Five species of antbird are common, especially black-faced ant-thrushes.

CLOUD FOREST BIRDS

Life among the Gods

Central America's extraordinary birdlife is tied to the region's habitat diversity and, even though the overall landmass is small, the great height of several mountain ranges has enabled vegetation – and hence wildlife – to diversify in broad altitudinal bands. Thus, different bird communities are found in recognizable zones between sea level and páramo (alpine grassland that covers the highest peaks). Cloud forest is a term applied to the dense forest that grows on the upper slopes of high mountains, usually above 2300ft (700m) – a mysterious world of stunted trees thick with epiphytes that can disappear in swirling mist that deadens sound. High mountains can be, in effect, 'islands' of vegetation that isolate populations from similar species; thus, members of various families – including flycatchers, thrushes, finches and warblers – have become dis-

*Groups of up to 16 **prong-billed barbets** huddle together in hollows at night.*

tinct from closely related species at lower altitudes and on other mountain ranges. It is a zone to which birders gravitate because a large proportion of endemic birds is found only in this habitat. No bird family is unique to cloud forest (although the two species of silky flycatcher, long-tailed (inset) and black-and-yellow, are restricted to this habitat), but various

*Like many members of the thrush family, the **black-faced solitaire** has a beautiful song.*

sought-after specialties, such as the bare-necked umbrellabird, three-wattled bellbird (see p 199) and resplendent quetzal (see p189) are most easily seen here in the right season. Other groups, such as bush-tanagers and tapaculos, have several representatives in this habitat.

Living among the Gods presents its own set of survival problems, such as cold and almost constant rain or dampness, which in turn affect food availability. And some birds that breed in cloud forest disperse to lower altitudes to follow the availability of food, such as insects or fruit, which is also affected by seasonal change. These movements are still little understood for many species; for example, resplendent quetzals disperse widely after breeding and three-wattled bellbirds travel almost to sea level in the wet season. However, it is clear that to maintain the integrity of cloud forest communities, it is important to protect corridors of forest that cover both the breeding and dispersal range of these wanderers. ■

*Male **bare-necked umbrellabirds** display from March to May in 'exploded' leks in the canopy.*

Hotspots
RBBN Monteverde Many species, including three-wattled bellbirds. **PN Chirripó** Black-faced solitaires and mountain robins, as well as bellbirds and quetzals. **PN Volcán Barú** Several Costa Rica-Panama endemics, plus both silky-flycatchers.

*The **slaty-backed nightingale-thrush** is usually seen foraging on the ground or in the understory.*

MANAKINS

*The male **white-collared manakin** displays at a lek and puffs out his 'beard' during courtship.*

Golden-headed manakins are found from Panama east and south to Peru and Brazil.

Male Chiroxiphia *manakins, such as the **long-tailed manakin**, have an amazing lek display.*

*Female manakins are usually olive, but female **blue-crowned manakins** are green.*

Cartwheeling capers

The affinities of manakins are still in dispute; most are probably related to the cotingas, although some, such as the broad-billed sapayoa are apparently closer to tyrant flycatchers. Regardless of taxonomy, these small, chunky birds with large head and eyes, and short tail and bill, are forest-dwelling fruit-eaters unique to the Neotropics. A few are sedentary and none migrates; some, like the sapayoa, are solitary, rather plain birds of the lower forest levels. But males of several species are predominantly black with contrasting colors on the head, throat or back – typically in electric shades of blue, red or gold. Some carry things even further, with long tail plumes, and all these colorful species perform some of the most amazing displays in the Central American bird world.

Males display alone or in leks (a lek is an area used by several displaying males in competition for matings with females), and some manakins take these courtship performances to incredible lengths. For example, male long-tailed manakins perched about 1ft (30cm) apart leap straight up and down on the spot, the leaps getting lower as the dance intensifies. When a female arrives, they perform a 'cartwheel' routine, where each flies up and backwards to land at a spot that has just been vacated by the other

male. The point of all this of course is to copulate with the female, and if she likes what she sees, she will mate with this 'master of ceremonies' – the male with the most developed adult plumage.

Males of another genus, which includes the golden-collared and white-collared manakins, have 'beards' of feathers that are puffed out during courtship displays. Each male clears a court of leaves and forest detritus, in close proximity to others, and when displaying bounces rapidly between saplings, sidles up and down and makes a loud snapping sound with his wings (this sound can be replicated by striking the palm with two fingers – and may attract male manakins). Males of the genus *Pipra*, such as the red-capped manakin shown inset, also make 'wing-snapping' noises.

In complete contrast, females of these lekking species are invariably drably colored, but they need to be camouflaged because they incubate and feed the young alone. ■

Hotspots
PN Carara Good for long-tailed, blue-crowned and orange-collared manakins. **PN Corcovado** Red-capped, orange-collared, thrushlike and blue-crowned manakins. **Bocas del Toro** Distinct race of golden-collared manakin (possibly a distinct species).

THREE-WATTLED BELLBIRD

Beauty in the eye of the beholder

If any family epitomizes the extravagance of Central American birds, it is the cotingas – an exclusively Neotropical group that includes some of the most bizarre birds on earth. Most are eagerly sought by birders, including the umbrellabirds, fruitcrows and several known simply as cotingas. Cotingas are thought to be most closely related to manakins, although they resemble them primarily in behavior because many cotingas look like nothing else in the bird world. A quick flip through a field guide will reveal cotingas in livery ranging from pure white to turquoise (see p38); the black, purple-throated fruitcrow with a gorget like royal velvet; and the incredible, crow-sized umbrellabird adorned with an umbrella-like crest and pendulous throat-patch of naked, scarlet skin (see p197). And among the most bizarre is the three-wattled bellbird, the males of which sport three black, drooping, wormlike appendages from their bill.

Only male bellbirds make the call from which they get their common name, and only one species sounds like a bell (the white bellbird of South America). But if you can find a three-wattled bellbird in action it's a sight: He opens his mouth so the lower mandible is almost touching his breast (bellbirds are frugivores and that gape can cope with very large fruit indeed), then emits a far-carrying *honk* that may be heard hundreds of yards away. A soon as he has called, he jumps a short way off his perch, turns around and lands facing the opposite direction.

Males of many cotinga species attract females by performing in leks, but male bellbird are mainly canopy birds, where it is thought that greater visibility enables them to display solo in comparative safety. Bellbirds are one of the region's 'must-see' species, but despite their vocal prowess they can be almost invisible from the ground and are a source of much frustration to birders. ∎

Recognition Male (12in/ 30cm) rich chestnut with contrasting pure white head and breast, and three worm-like wattles attached to gape. Female (10.5 in/ 26cm) streaked yellow-olive all over and lacks wattles.

Habitat Mid to upper levels of montane forest to 7500ft (2300m) during breeding season; outside breeding season range higher (to 10,000ft/3000m) and descend to forested lowlands.

Behavior Males perch high in canopy when calling. Females cryptic and difficult to see, but visit male and exchange places with him at display perch. All nesting and parental care apparently performed by females. Males take several years to reach maturity.

Breeding Nest has never been found. Breeding season appears to be March to September.

Feeding Plucks fruits from forest canopy while perched, but sometimes in a sally.

Voice Loud *honk*, followed by various less far-carrying whistles.

Hotspots
EB La Selva, PN Chirripó, RBBN Monteverde

*The highly versatile **bananaquit** is a successful generalist and a common garden bird.*

*Like the house sparrow, the **rufous-collared sparrow** has adapted to life in cities.*

Roadside hawks perch above fields and verges and pounce on insects, reptiles and small mammals.

*Small flocks of **yellow-faced grassquits** search for seeds in pastures, verges and lawns.*

GARDEN & ROADSIDE BIRDS

Making sense of it all

Every first-time visitor to Central America will feel a bit over-whelmed by the diversity of birds on show – from virtually the minute you step off the plane you'll be craning your neck and rummaging through your bag for binoculars. Virtually every species and even many bird families will be new: To help you get a handle on it all, spend some time familiarizing yourself with common species in your hotel ground or in a nearby park. Members of many bird families are generalists and these are the species that usually adapt to disturbed environments such as

*The **scarlet rumped tanager**, a common garden visitor, was recently split into two species: Cherrie's and Passerini's tanagers. Males (above) hardly differ, but female Cherrie's tanagers are more richly-colored, and Passerini's tanagers are restricted to the Caribbean slope.*

towns and agriculture. Thus, while you would search for a sooty robin only on forested mountaintops, the closely related clay-colored robin can be easily seen feeding on suburban lawns like a North American robin or European song thrush. Likewise, various flycatchers, hummingbirds, raptors, tanagers and many others will be commonly encountered in urban spaces and along the road as you travel between national parks and other birding destinations. By learning to recognize these 'bench-mark' species, you'll be able to mentally compare them to new species as they are encountered. For example, by learning the 'jizz' (the general appearance of a bird in the field) of black vul-tures tilting and floating over rooftops, you'll be more alert to the differences when a similar species, such as a lesser yellow-headed vulture, drifts into view.

Spectacular flowering shrubs and trees grow in profusion in the Neotropics, both wild and tamed in suburban gardens. These in turn attract nectar-eaters such as hummingbirds and bananaquits. Many hotels and well-to-do homes also erect hummingbird feeders, which can attract several species right in the heart of large cities. The bananaquit in particular has made an apparently seemless transition from forest edge to urban gardens, where its eclectic diet makes it a common visitor to feeders. One or two species of pigeon and dove often do well in proximity to humans: Watch for ground-doves looking for fallen seeds on lawns, and pale-vented pigeons in palms and other trees. Several members of the finch family adapt well to the urban environment: The rufous-collared sparrow, a close relative of the cosmopolitan house sparrow, is common in Central American cities. Other urban finches include saltators, and several species of small specialists of grass seeds, including grassquits and seedeaters, which seem to thrive in rank grass that springs up along country roads.

Central America has yet to suffer the introduction of exotic pest species, such as starlings, that plague some other parts of the world. But one highly-adaptable species has prospered in disturbed environments in spectacular fashion. The great-tailed grackle, a relative of the orioles and blackbirds, has increased to massive numbers in some cities and towns, although its population remains at 'normal' levels away from settlements. Sometimes thousands gather at dusk to roost in city parks, and during the day great-tailed grackles can be seen boldly looking for scraps in virtually any urban niche. ∎

*The **great-tailed grackle** is an icterid that has adapted to urbanization with spectacular success.*

*Buff-throated saltators** usually travel in pairs in search of fruit, insects and nectar.*

*The untidy, nondescript **black vulture** can be seen at any (and every) human settlement, hunched on rooftops and power poles, picking over trash or soaring effortlessly overhead.*

*Fork-tailed flycatchers** commonly perch on roadside wires, from where they sally for insects.*

*The **clay-colored robin** is equally at home foraging in urban lawns or accompanying army-ant swarms.*

Hotspots

Panama City Parks near the Canal and along the foreshore support many birds; Juan Díaz mangroves excellent for grassland birds. **San José** Slim pickings in the city center, but try the university. **Belize City** Leafy Fort George district can be rewarding, otherwise head for the zoo for many species in the grounds.

FLYCATCHERS

Great kiskadees are large (9in/23cm), pugnacious flycatchers that take a variety of small animals.

*The very similar **boat-billed flycatcher** is best distinguished by its call and massive bill.*

Tropical kingbirds are so commonly seen at roadside perches that they're known as 'TKs'.

Variations on a theme

Insects are a rich food resource exploited by hundreds of Neotropical birds from many families. And none is as big as the so-called tyrant, or American, flycatchers, an exclusively New World family of nearly 400 species, which have evolved into a bewildering array of sizes to match the availability of different insect prey. Tyrant flycatchers range from the pugnacious great kiskadee, which hawks from exposed perches in clearings, to diminutive tody-flycatchers that work the forest understory. The most common flycatcher feeding technique – sallying after prey from a perch – is not practiced by many Neotropical species, which instead typically glean insects and other arthropods from foliage, some even switching to a diet of fruit when insects are scarce. Nesting strategies are also diverse, and include cup-shaped or suspended nests of woven vegetation, holes in trees and even theft: The fruit-eating piratic flycatcher pesters birds such as caciques and oropendolas into giving up their nest for its own use.

More than 100 species of tyrant flycatcher occur in Central America, including migrants from both North and South America escaping their respective winters; but to confuse matters, the distinction between some large tyrants, such as becards and tityras, and the cotingas remains controversial. Some tyrants are difficult to misidentify, such as the fork-tailed (see photo on p201) and scissor-tailed flycatchers, and the unique royal flycatcher (inset). And others exploit a specific feeding niche, such as the torrent tyrannulet of mountain streamsides. But many tyrants look unspectacular (names like bran-colored flycatcher and paltry tyrannulet speak volumes) or are confusingly similar, decked in gray or brown above, with yellow underparts and black-and-white head markings. Males and females rarely differ and some species are difficult to tell apart even in the hand, with only minor variations in plumage detail or bill size. Calls are a good way to identify flycatchers, but otherwise you'll need patience, research – and dedication, especially when there are so many colorful birds to look at. Stick with it: Tyrant speciation and diversity alone are fascinating, and new species are being described almost every year. ∎

*The **tufted flycatcher** is a small species, typical of montane forest edges and clearings.*

Hotspots

Central Panama Fork-tailed flycatchers at Juan Díaz mangroves. **Lamanai Outpost Lodge** Many species easily seen and good chance at royal flycatchers. **PN Tapanatí** Excellent for forest species, such as tufted and black-capped flycatchers.

ICTERIDS

Familiar residents and surprising migrants

Their collective name may be unfamiliar, but representatives of this widespread New World family include many common North American birds, such as meadowlarks, blackbirds, orioles and cowbirds. Indeed, many of these same species migrate to Central America to escape winter, and orioles in particular may be seen in feeding flocks alongside Neotropical specialties. There are also resident species of each group that never stray north and all resemble their migratory counterparts, even if the details differ. Highly migratory species such as bobolinks and meadowlarks may seem out of place in tropical grasslands, but icterids are foremost a Neotropical family, and migratory behavior is a strategy adopted by some to take advantage of the brief boreal summer of plenty, before they retreat to their tropical homeland (not the other way round, as we so often suppose). Icterids in fact reach their highest diversity in the Neotropics, and none are as spectacular as the oropendolas and caciques.

Male **black-cowled orioles** display the bright, two-tone patterning common in the genus Icterus.

Like most other icterids, both caciques and oropendolas have a pointed, conical bill, piercing pale eyes and powerful feet; and when you hear them call you'll understand where their names came from. But oropendolas stand out from the crowd for many reasons: They are among the largest of passerines, some reaching 20in (50cm) in length; many have rich coloration; and all are noisy, gregarious birds that build beautiful pendulous nests in colonies (most caciques also build hanging nests (inset) – sometimes in association with oropendolas).

The **yellow-rumped cacique** of Panama often associates with chestnut-headed oropendolas.

Caciques and oropendolas are opportunistic feeders, taking insects and other small animals, as well as nectar and fruit as the availability dictates. Feeding in groups, they often deplete the resources of a tree before moving on, and numbers of other canopy-feeding birds are noticeably depleted near colonies. But nobody gets a free ride in nature, and these busy, hanging colonies are often raided by toucans, which are big and bold enough to intimidate oropendolas, and take their eggs and chicks. Many cacique colonies have a resident pair of piratic flycatchers, which pester the caciques into giving up their nests for their own ends. ∎

The **Montezuma oropendola** is the largest and most colorful of Central American oropendolas.

Hotspots

PN Darién Yellow-billed caciques (Cana) and black oropendolas (Punta Patiño). **EB La Selva** Montezuma oropendolas common. **Río Bravo** 16 species, including resident yellow-billed caciques, giant cowbirds and Altamira orioles.

A **chestnut-headed oropendola**, showing the pointed, conical bill typical of most icterids.

Common bush-tanagers frequent cloud forests, where they probe epiphyte clumps for insect prey.

Red-legged honeycreepers forage in small flocks, typically in the canopy but also in gardens.

Uncharacteristically plain, the palm tanager is common in gardens, plantations and near palms.

The emerald tanager is nearly always seen with other tanagers or in mixed flocks.

TANAGERS

A colorful mix

Experienced birders know that rainforest birding generally alternates between quiet spells, with few birds moving, and periods of frenetic activity when you hit a bird wave: Suddenly all hell breaks loose in the scramble to see and identify a procession of birds including flycatchers, woodcreepers, warblers, furnariids and, especially, tanagers. Tanagers form a large family unique to the New World (several species also migrate to North America to breed), although their affinities with other groups are constantly debated by taxonomists. Most references now include honeycreepers, dacnises and the unique swallow tanager in the tanager family, but whatever their affinities, tanagers are among the most colorful and eagerly sought of Neotropical birds.

Green honeycreepers are usually seen in the canopy, feeding on fruits like typical tanagers or probing flowers for nectar. This adaptable species may be seen in pairs (this is a male), traveling with feeding flocks and even visiting bird feeders.

'Typical' tanagers are 5–6in (12.5–15cm) in length with stout bills, and most are predominantly fruit-eaters. Most are brilliantly colored, some with patches of iridescence, and as several species may travel together in a feeding flock, they promise a nonstop procession of color and movement. And in Central America color does not necessarily equate rarity: Several colorful tanagers and honeycreepers are commonly encountered in urban gardens and as visitors to feeding tables.

A typical tanager flock moves through the canopy and midlevels of the forest, each individual in a never-ending search for fruit and berries, which they reach at any angle with strong legs and feet, or by sallying on relatively long wings. Filling up quickly they move on, constantly on the alert for predators and covering great distances daily. Tanager flocks move through the forest every day of the year, shifting their movements according to the availability of food; flocking tanagers not only increase their own feeding efficiency, they distribute a vast number of forest seeds in their droppings.

Not all species move in tanager flocks: The mainly insect-eating white-throated shrike-tanagers act as sentinels in mixed flocks, snatching prey flushed by woodcreepers, furnariids and others in the group. Euphonias and chlorophonias have stubby bills and short tails, and specialize in eating mistletoe berries; chlorophonias are brightly colored (see photo opposite), but many euphonias are confusingly (at least for identification purposes) attired in blue-black and yellow, with varying degrees of yellow on the crown. Dacnises and honeycreepers have slender, decurved bills that enable them to probe flowers for nectar; some join flocks and some associate more often with their own kind. Not all tanagers are canopy or midlevel birds: The rosy thrush-tanager is partly a ground-dweller; and the ant-tanagers (some of which attend ant swarms, especially in areas where antbirds are not common) are understory birds. Nor are all brightly colored: The so-called bush-tanagers are primarily olive above with yellowish underparts and dark head markings; and males of several other species, such as white-lined and white-shouldered tanagers, are predominantly black.

North American birders should recognize the half-dozen migratory tanager species that mix with resident species in their Central American wintering grounds, among them the hepatic, summer and scarlet tanagers. Males attain splendid coloration before starting their northward migration. ■

Speckled tanagers move through the upper levels of forest in small flocks of three to six birds.

The golden-hooded tanager is a common bird of lowlands and foothills, and often visits gardens.

Golden-browed chlorophonias are 'stubby' tanagers that inhabit wet, misty montane forest above 3000ft (900m). Small flocks moving through the canopy feed primarily on the berries of mistletoe and epiphytes. Chlorophonias often nest among clumps of bromeliads.

Like many tanagers, bay-headed tanagers may search under leaves and branches for insects.

The blue-gray tanager is common in gardens, as well as forest, throughout Central America.

Hotspots
PN Darién Tanager flocks on Cerro Pirre include lemon-spectacled tanagers. **PN Soberanía** Good for getting acquainted with the tanager flock phenomenon. **PN Carara** More than 20 species commonly seen; four species of euphonia. **RBBN Monteverde** Mixed tanager flocks almost guaranteed.

AMERICAN CROCODILE

Recognition Usually olive-gray, less than 15ft (4.5m).
Habitat Beaches, lagoons, mangroves and cayes.
Behavior Often basks.
Breeding Lays 30–60 eggs, hatching May to June.
Feeding Fish, turtles and mammals. Hatchlings eat mainly insects.
Voice Hatchlings squeak.

Hotspots
PN Palo Verde, RB Carara, PN Santa Rosa, Turneffe Atoll

Misunderstood giant

Reaching lengths of 23ft (7m), the American crocodile is the largest reptile in Central America and sufficient reason to be cautious when swimming. Really big crocs are rare because it takes them decades to grow and widespread persecution has claimed most of the old-timers. Even so, a 20ft (6m) male killed a volunteer conservationist in 1997 near Costa Rica's PN Tortuguero. In reality, the chances of an attack are tiny: most arise when crocs are breeding (during the dry season, December to April) and defending their territories; people are bitten as intruders rather than as prey.

American crocodiles occur mainly along the coastal zone and can tolerate saltwater – Belize's largest population actually occurs on the Turneffe Atoll 18 miles (30km) offshore. However, crocs dehydrate in salty surroundings and have to drink brackish or fresh water. It's critical for hatchlings, so females locate nests upriver or in lagoons and estuaries where salinity is lower. Hatching usually coincides with the arrival of the rains, which dilute the salinity in the lagoons and create better nurseries. American crocs apparently don't defend the nest with any great zeal as some croc species do, but nesting females in Panama have been seen attacking (and eating) green iguanas competing for the same beach space. ■

MORELET'S CROCODILE

Recognition Usually dark brown to deep olive. Rarely more than 10ft (3m) long.
Habitat Freshwater marshes, ponds and lagoons.
Behavior Diurnal or nocturnal. Basks during the day.
Breeding Lays 20–40 eggs. Hatch August to October.
Feeding Mainly fish. Hatchlings take insects.
Voice Hatchlings squeak.

Hotspots
Chan Chich, Lamanai, Crooked Tree WS

Back from the brink

Found only in Belize, Guatemala and Mexico, the range of Morelet's crocodile overlaps that of the American croc, but the former is found mostly in freshwater habitats. The best places to look are inland lagoons: Oxbows on riverine floodplains are productive, especially in the dry season when crocs aggregate in the dwindling pools. The wet season presents more of a challenge, for croc-watchers and crocodiles alike: Rising water diffuses the croc congregations and may also flood their nests; crocodiles are air-breathers and embryos drown in submerged eggs. Even though nests are better located in isolated wetlands protected from flooding, the lagoons apparently act as 'rearing yards' for hatchlings and will usually contain youngsters. They migrate there shortly after emerging, probably because floating vegetation mats provide shelter and good hunting grounds.

Morelet's crocodiles furnish high quality leather and the skin trade almost wiped them out in the 1960s. Belize banned hunting in 1981 and they have been making a gradual comeback, enough that they have even returned to canals near Belize City and Orange Walk. They also persist in sugarcane country because wetlands are usually left intact, although their stronghold remains Belize's remote northern swamps. ■

SPECTACLED CAIMAN

The common croc

As the most abundant and widely distributed crocodilian in the New World, the spectacled caiman is the species most often seen by wildlifers. Their success is due, in part, to people. Caimans are unusual among crocodilians in having bony scutes lining their belly skin, making them less attractive to hunters than smooth-bellied American and Morelet's crocodiles. It meant that not only were they largely ignored by hunters until quite recently, but they also benefited from the removal of other croc species. As larger, ecologically dominant species like the American croc disappeared, the caimans moved in and can now be seen in areas where they may never have occurred naturally.

Aside from anthropogenic leg-ups, the spectacled caiman is a natural colonist, able to live in a wide variety of freshwater habitats and capable of reproducing while still quite small. This adaptability has helped consolidate their human-fostered prevalence, which is especially fortunate because they are no longer overlooked by the skin trade. By the 1950s, the numbers of species preferred by hunters were so low that they turned their attention to spectacled caimans. Even though only the smooth, scute-free skin of the flank is usable, over half a million caimans are legally harvested each year – most from South America where some nations farm them to reduce pressure on wild populations.

Known also as the brown or common caiman, this species nests at different times throughout its enormous range, but in Costa Rica it mostly happens early in the wet season. The hatchlings emerge between September and October, when water levels are high and provide abundant habitat; dry-season hatchlings would have far less water in which to hide from herons and storks. The downside to the strategy is that some nests will be flooded as the wet season progresses and, indeed, flooding is the main cause of mortality for developing embryos. Raccoons and coatis also excavate nests, but like many crocodilians, female caimans guard nests; more unusually, they also occasionally protect the hatchlings. Conditions permitting (a harsh dry season can force migration to permanent water) females may remain with their offspring for as long as 18 months. ■

Recognition Usually dark brown. Caimans have shorter, rounded snouts compared with other crocodile species in region. Maximum length 9ft (2.8m); average about 3–5ft (1–1.5m).
Habitat All low-altitude freshwater wetland habitats in region. Occasionally mangroves.
Behavior Diurnal or nocturnal, best seen by spotlighting at night. Often basks during the day. Mostly occupies permanent canals and lagoons in dry season, dispersing to open wet grasslands and swamps following rains.
Breeding Lays 20–40 eggs. Hatchlings emerge September to October. Nests usually located in riverine forest lining rivers and canals. Female and occasionally male open the nest to aid emerging hatchlings.
Feeding Mainly fish, amphibians and carrion. Occasionally birds and small mammals. Hatchlings take mainly insects and spiders.
Voice Adults growl when threatened. Hatchlings squeak to adults when emerging.

Hotspots
RNVS Caño Negro, PN Tortuguero, RNSF Barra del Colorado

SNAKES

*Growing as large as 2.5m, the venomous **fer-de-lance** is a species best given a wide berth.*

Eyelash vipers are named for the pointed scales above their eyes; their function is unknown.

*The **green parrot snake's** name is no indication of diet: It eats mostly frogs and lizards.*

*The **Central American coral snake** is the most common species of coral snake in the region.*

Beauty in the beast

Unless you're a herpetologist, snakes are probably rather low on your wildlife want-list. Rest assured, the chance of encountering snakes in Central America is actually rather slim, but should you see one, take a moment to enjoy it; snakes never go on the offensive without good reason. And no Central American snake views people as prey. In theory, the largest boa constrictors could eat a person, but they don't. If treated with respect, snakes can be a beautiful and exciting inclusion in a Neotropical safari.

Of the 140-odd species here, only about 17 are really dangerous, so most encounters are with harmless types such as chunk-headed snakes with their pencil-thin necks and blocklike heads, zopilotas (also called indigoes, because of their color), and arboreal, lizard-eating vine snakes. Also common, the large snake-eating musarana has venom which has little effect on people, but is lethal even to the most deadly snake species.

Of course, people are always more fascinated by venomous snakes, and Central America has a few which should be enjoyed strictly at a distance. Most poisonous snakes in the New World are vipers or pit vipers, so-called because they have heat-sensing cavities lining their upper jaw that help locate warm-blooded prey. The three largest species, the infamous fer-de-lance (usually called *terciopelo* in Central America and tommy-goff in Belize), the tropical rattler and the bushmaster have formidable reputations for unprovoked attack. Their notoriety is exaggerated, but they are fast-moving and readily bite if annoyed. Baby vipers also have a habit of hanging from trees like a vine, so be careful what you grab when hiking.

Highly venomous species that aren't part of the viper family include four species of brightly marked coral snakes (inset), as well as at least a dozen nonvenomous mimics that look more dangerous than they are. However, this ruse works only where coral snakes themselves are found: Predators eat the mimics outside coral snake range, but don't risk it where corals also live. The safest way to recognize the real thing is supposedly if the color pattern spells frog in Spanish ('rana': *rojo*/red, *amarillo*/yellow, *negro*/black, *amarillo*). But even within the same species color variations can be substantial; so to be sure – if it looks like a coral snake, treat it like one. ∎

> **Hotspots**
> **PN Rincón de la Vieja** Coral snakes and false coral snakes.
> **PN Corcovado** Eyelash vipers and many harmless species.

BOA CONSTRICTOR

A tight squeeze

The longest boa constrictor on record measured 18.4ft (5.6m) making this nonvenomous species the largest snake in Central America, although such giants are exceptional and a boa of 10ft (3m) is considered a very large one. As their name suggests, boas kill their prey by constricting, but they first have to catch it. Supreme ambush hunters, boas actively seek out the best places to spring a trap, such as rodent burrows, the forks of fruiting trees and cave openings. Once settled, they remain there, sometimes for days because well-chosen sites are usually rewarded: the burrow resident returns, birds visit the fruits, or bats exit the cave.

A lightning strike, with a mouth full of teeth like curved needles, makes the catch and the boa's enormously muscular coils usually seal its fate. Small prey is simply crushed to death, but larger animals like coatis actually die of cardiac failure rather than, as is often assumed, suffocation (the snake's enveloping embrace prevents circulation and the heart quickly fails, a considerably faster method than killing by asphyxiation. Boas can kill animals as large as young deer and there's at least one accurate record of an ocelot being consumed, but smaller prey is the norm, probably because large targets can fight back; one adult boa in Panama was killed by the tamandua it had grabbed. Even the largest boas aren't people killers, but they can inflict serious bites which easily become infected; boa mouths are rife with bacteria that are difficult to control once in a wound. Boas are placid if left alone; it's better for boas and people alike if they're not picked up.

Although sometimes killed for their skins and caught for the pet trade, boas occur in a very wide range of habitats and often thrive near people; enlightened communities value them as rodent and bat killers. There are five additional species of boas in Central America: the rainbow boa, three species of tree boas and the northern eyelash boa. All are smaller than the boa constrictor and are mainly arboreal and nocturnal; look for them in trees on night-walks. ■

Recognition Tan or gray colored with dark blotches. Young boas usually more brightly colored. Average length 6.5-10ft (2–3m). Top weight 100lb (45kg), usually less than 45lb (20kg).
Habitat Wide tolerance where not persecuted; most forest types, savanna, scrub and pastures. Rarely in highlands (above 3280ft/1000m).
Behavior Solitary and nocturnal/crepuscular. Terrestrial and arboreal; usually seen on the move on the ground, but often waits in trees for prey.
Breeding Bears 12–64 live young, usually between March to August. Newborn boas measure about 50cm (19.5 inches) and immediately disperse from the nest. There is no parental care.
Feeding Mostly small mammals, especially rodents and bats. Also lizards, birds and occasionally larger mammals (including at times, domestic cats and dogs).
Voice Hisses loudly when threatened; usually indicates a bite is imminent!

Hotspots
PN Palo Verde (especially Isla Pajaros), **PN Corcovado, Río Bravo**

LIZARDS

*Known as the old man lizard in Belize, the **helmeted iguana** is actually related to basilisks.*

3D hunters

After snakes, lizards are the most diverse group of reptiles in Central America and are far more common. In fact, in total numbers, lizards are the most abundant vertebrates in many Neotropical habitats. Their success lies in their diet: most lizards eat invertebrates, an extremely abundant resource which lizards exploit to the fullest by foraging in three dimensions. Most lizards are as comfortable above ground as on it, so aerial insects and tree-dwellers make as good a lizard-meal as burrowing bugs and worms. Lizards tend to be either active hunters or patient ambushers. Anoles and skinks are mostly the former, using their excellent vision to locate prey and then securing it with lightning dashes. Anoles cling to tree trunks and adopt a characteristic head-down posture, probably to search for the rich insect life of the leaf litter. Other very active hunters of the leaf litter, whiptails search more vigorously, scratching and nosing through it for prey. In contrast to this constantly mobile strategy, other species adopt sit-and-wait tactics, usually feeding less often, but concentrating on larger prey. Many geckos and spiny lizards use such a method and are very easily seen laying in wait for insects near porch lights.

*The **green spiny lizard** is one of the few Central American lizard species found above 2000m.*

Oddly, the largest Central American lizards start out as bug-hunters, but convert to vegetarianism. Green iguanas and ctenosaurs feed on insects while young, but turn mainly to leaves, flowers and fruits as they age, perhaps because large bodies are very difficult to fuel with small, invertebrate meals. The extraordinary basilisk (inset) or Jesus Christ lizard (there are actually three species in Central America) overcomes the same challenge by eating virtually everything, including other lizards, snakes, fish, small mammals, fruits and flowers. Hatchlings of their larger relatives, the iguanas and ctenosaurs, are apparently much favored basilisk prey when they emerge in May. Named for its ability to run on water (youngsters are much better at it than adults), the diurnally active basilisk sleeps in trees overhanging water so it can make a speedy escape if discovered by nocturnal predators.

Green iguanas (female pictured) are very common and confiding where they are protected.

A number of lizard species are seasonally territorial, especially when males defend a patch in the hope of attracting females. Head-bobbing, dewlap-extending displays of anoles, and head-wagging and chasing of ctenosaurs, are among the more visible manifestations on show. ■

*A member of the iguana family, the **ctenosaur** is also known as the black spiny-tailed iguana.*

Hotspots
PN Manuel Antonio Ctenosaurs, green iguanas. **PN Santa Rosa** Guanacaste endemics. **PN Chirripó** Green spiny lizards.

TURTLES

Aquatic sliders and snappers

With about 23 species throughout the region, turtles are not the most diverse group of reptiles, but some species are conspicuous and well worth looking for. Water-dependent species are usually called terrapins or turtles, but just to confuse things, pond turtles feed mostly on land and are often called 'land turtles'. Among them, the brown land turtle, the red turtle and Belize's furrowed wood turtle are usually found in moist vegetation near rivers and swamps, but are sometimes spotted up to 1km (0.6mi) from water. Pond turtles are very active after rain and easily found on wet trails and paths. The black river turtle is an aquatic herbivore, but often leaves the water to feed at night on riverbank vegetation.

*The **red turtle's** coloration is especially vivid in youngsters and may mimic deadly coral snakes.*

Largely aquatic except when they trek overland in search of water during dry season, all other inland species are primarily carnivorous. Mud and musk turtles concentrate on aquatic snails, although land invertebrates are also taken; and one of the largest aquatic species, the snapping turtle, also takes birds, reptiles and small mammals. ∎

PN Tortuguero Tropical sliders, brown and black wood turtles. **Crooked Tree WS** Good for Central American river turtles. **PN Palo Verde** Red-cheeked mud turtles, snapping turtles.

*The **common slider** is the only freshwater turtle with orange throat stripes in the region.*

OLIVE RIDLEY

Beach battalions

Probably the most abundant of the world's seven sea turtle species, the olive ridley is also the smallest, rarely exceeding one-tenth the weight of the massive leatherback. Individually, they're less than spectacular, but collectively they provide one of the most extraordinary turtle-viewing events on the planet. Usually solitary nesters, females occasionally synchronize their laying in mass nesting events called arribadas (Spanish for 'arrivals'). Arribadas average around 40,000 to 50,000 females, but they can be much larger: In 1996, approximately 500,000 turtles laid en masse at Ostional Beach in Costa Rica. Mass nesting may result in 'predator swamping' – providing so many eggs that there are just too many for predators to eat – but the extreme competition for nesting space probably defeats the advantage. Females nesting in arribadas risk losing their eggs to later females that, inadvertently, dig them up to deposit their own clutch. In fact, it's estimated that at least 95% of arribada nests fail because of disturbance by other females.

Recognition Olive-green, smooth carapace, up to 28in (70cm) in length; and 50kg.
Habitat Tropical Pacific, Atlantic and Indian Oceans.
Behaviour Solitary; entirely marine except for nesting. Nests throughout its range, but arribadas only occur in Mexico, Central America and India.
Breeding Laying peaks in September–October. Average of 110 eggs.
Feeding Small crustaceans, jellyfish, marine vegetation.
Voice None.

Ridley arribadas last only about three to ten days and predicting them is chancy; they're more frequent around the first and the last quarter of the moon and during the wet season (peak: September-October). Ridleys nest all over the region's Pacific coast, but there are only three arribada beaches (see Hotspots). ∎

Hotspots
PN Santa Rosa, RNFS Ostional, Isla de Cañas

FROGS & TOADS

Weighing more than 3lb, the **marine toad** *is Central America's largest amphibian.*

Fleischmann's glass frog has a translucent belly that allows the internal organs to be seen.

Name aside, **green-and-black poison-dart frogs** *can be blue, yellow or green with black spots.*

Deadly jewels and lumpy landlubbers

The profusion of wet, humid environments in Central America makes ideal habitat for amphibians and, collectively, frogs and toads are the region's most prolific herps (reptiles and amphibians, from the Greek *herpeton* – a creeping animal). Of the 150-odd species, around 20 are toads and the rest are frogs. What's the difference? In fact, toads are just a type of frog with some important but mostly obscure anatomical differences. More significantly, a clear ecological difference makes most of them easy to tell apart: frogs are tied to water whereas toads are not. So, toads have dry, lumpy skin that prevents water loss, whereas frogs are usually smooth and moist. Even so, all Central American toads return to water to breed and there are froglike toads and toadlike frogs. The smooth-skinned splendid harlequin frog (inset) is actually a toad, while the litter toad looks like a tree frog (though it lives in leaf litter). Unmistakably a toad, the large marine or cane toad is more common near towns than in many natural habitats because of its ability to eat anything its own size or smaller. Marine toads have large parotoid glands (lumps just behind the eyes) which secrete defensive poisons that can be highly irritating if absorbed through cuts.

For truly breathtaking toxins, a family of frogs, not toads, tops the scale. Wearing flamboyant colors to advertise their toxicity, poison-dart frogs are used famously by Colombian Chocó Indians to coat their blowdart-tips. Subsisting on small, diurnal prey like ants and termites, it's thought the frogs' defenses arose because they spend so much time foraging in the open. Poison-dart frogs are mostly easy to recognize; look for vivid, almost 'unnatural' reds, blues and greens, often combined with glossy black. Completely harmless, but also strikingly colored, tree frogs like red-eyed tree frogs and splendid leaf frogs can be distinguished by their catlike, slit pupils. Given that the poison from a single blue poison-arrow frog is enough to kill 100 people, it's wise not to touch any brightly colored species unless you're with an expert.

Frogs and toads are found by carefully exploring wet habitats; streams, ponds, moist leaf litter, rock crevices and under logs. Most frogs are nocturnal so go on night-walks and shine upwards; alongside tree frogs, arboreal groups include translucent-skinned glass frogs and rain frogs. ■

The most common poison-dart frog, **strawberry poison-dart frogs** *are also called blue-jeans frogs.*

> **Hotspots**
> **PN Corcovado** Endemic poison-dart frogs, giant smoky jungle frogs. **PN Tortuguero** Tree frogs, abundant marine toads.

GOLDEN TOAD

Absent amphibians

The story of the golden toad is an extraordinary one. Unknown to science until 1964, the excitement over its discovery turned to alarm when it became apparent that the entire species was restricted to a four square mile patch of elfin forest in Costa Rica's Tilarán mountains. In 1972, the creation of the Monteverde Cloud Forest Preserve secured their tiny range, a triumph which should have been enough to protect the species – although remarkably local in distribution, the toad was abundant. Then, in 1988, a lone toad was the only arrival at the most important breeding pools where the year before 1500 toads had appeared. A year later, Monteverde's total count of toads didn't make double figures and they haven't been seen since.

What happened? Nobody knows for certain, but disaster didn't befall the golden toad alone. Since 1987, 20 species of frog and toad have disappeared from Monteverde along with two endemic highland anoles, and many remaining species are vastly reduced. Theories abound, but the most compelling blames a combination of global warming and deforestation far from Monteverde's borders. As climate change heats up ocean temperatures, Monteverde's dry season has become drier and the number of misty days has decreased. Amplifying the effect, felling forests in the lowlands results in less moisture making it to the mountains; evaporation from forests yields many times the moisture than does pasture, meaning cleared lands don't give rise to clouds. How warmer, drier days kill toads is still a mystery; but they may increase their vulnerability to skin infections by fungi, or the toads may simply be unable to cope with higher temperatures.

A few scientists hold hope that golden toads are simply waiting underground until better conditions return. Even when they were abundant, they mostly stayed hidden in moist underground burrows and were rarely sighted outside of the breeding season. Given that they haven't been seen for 13 years, it seems unlikely. And even if there are survivors, assuming the climate theories are correct, conditions may never improve enough for them to re-emerge. ■

Recognition Males are brilliant orange, females are black with red-orange spots. Juveniles look like a pale female. 1-2in long.
Habitat Elfin forest; only recorded from Monteverde.
Behaviour Elusive and rarely seen outside breeding season, but not shy when observed; poisonous parotid glands on the neck protect it against most predators. Diurnal when breeding.
Breeding Breeds March-June with the onset of heavy rains. Large numbers congregate at breeding pools and compete fiercely for access to mates. Eggs are deposited in shallow puddles.
Feeding Unrecorded, but probably small insects among leaf litter.
Voice Fairly quiet; a low trill and a soft 'tap' sound.

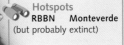

Hotspots
RBBN   Monteverde
(but probably extinct)

BUTTERFLIES

After mating, the **postman** deposits a repellent chemical on the female to deter other males.

Red-moon satyrs have an unusual diet of sugar-rich rotting fruit and decomposing fungi.

The **tiger mimic-queen's** diet of bird droppings furnishes nitrogen, critical for egg production.

Pollinators and predators

Of the world's 20,000-odd butterfly species, Central America has more than 10%, which means it's possible to see over 2000 species here. However, most of them require expert help to identify and some have not even been properly described by science. In fact, Neotropical butterflies somewhat blur the species boundary – over a quarter of species in some well-known families crossbreed with each other, producing fertile hybrids. Interspecies sex aside, the better guides can point out the more common and striking species such as the famously iridescent blue morpho (there are actually about 80 morpho species), but names are not especially required to enjoy butterflies. If you wanting to dig deeper, see the Resource Guide.

Caterpillars, the larvae of butterflies and moths, can sport impressive defences. Coccoons (right) are known as **chrysalids**; shiny ones are thought to mimic water drops or toxic beetles.

No matter which terrestrial habitat you're exploring, butterflies will be present. Indeed, some migratory species have even been spotted far out to sea, but the richest places are, not surprisingly, those with lots of flowers. Most butterflies feed on nectar, so environments with a constant supply have the greatest diversity and numbers; evergreen forests are among the best. In drier habitats, butterflies can be less abundant, but the onset of the rainy season brings a flush of migrants and breeding activity; indeed, this is the best time for butterfly viewing throughout the region, especially June to July.

As nectar-feeders, butterflies are very important pollinators, however, their offspring are far less useful to plants. In fact, nearly all butterfly caterpillars are herbivores, consuming leaves after hatching, occasionally enough to entirely defoliate a tree. Neotropical butterflies are well known for having specific 'host'

Glasswing butterflies feed on bird droppings and dead insects.

Cramer's 88 butterfly is one of two butterfly species that, inexplicably, have '88' markings.

Zebra butterflies often roost in groups of as many as 30 adults. Males patrol for females every morning and wait on female chrysalids – and mate with the female as she emerges.

plant preferences, in which many species lay their eggs only on a particular plant or group of plants. Toxic compounds deter some feeding, but caterpillars have a suite of methods for thwarting a plant's defences: they eat young leaves with fewer toxins, snip the transport veins so the compounds don't reach their destination and even recycle them for their own use. Some of the most colorful butterflies get away with their flamboyance because, as larvae, they are able to repackage the plant's poisons into their own distasteful defenses.

While butterflies don't see color as we do , many have a preference for yellow, purple or red flowers. Sit near one for a butterfly procession, especially in the morning: most species have activity peaks between 8am and 2pm. Allowing for wind direction, you could also station yourself near carrion, rotting fruit or dung – a few unusual butterfly species shun nectar for these more pungent dietary options. ■

The blue morpho is perhaps the world's most collected butterfly. Only buy them from breeders.

The chrysalids of the scarce bamboo page resemble bird droppings, and are always found on poison vines. Adults usually live high in the canopy.

Hotspots
RBBN Monteverde (el Jardin de Mariposas) Dozens of species in live displays. **PN Rincón de la Vieja** Four morphos.

The common blue morpho feeds on fallen fruit as well as carrion and mud.

OTHER INVERTEBRATES

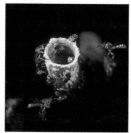

Helicopter damselflies rely on water-filled tree-holes or bromeliads for laying their eggs.

The sometimes elaborate nests of **wasps** are fashioned from mud or saliva-glued woodchip.

The **leaf-footed bug's** vivid coloring warns predators of its distasteful toxins.

The **herbivorous hordes**

In its myriad forms, the rainforest's profuse greenery represents an inexhaustibly rich resource for the creatures that can exploit it. However, leaves laced with cellulose and tannins are tough to stomach, which is partly the reason why there aren't huge herds of mega-herbivores crowding the forest. The rainforest equivalent has six legs. In more forms than we have yet been able to catalog, insects are the great consumers of plants here. If you were able to amplify the sounds of the forest only a little beyond the range of human hearing, you would hear the unceasing hiss of millions upon millions of tiny mandibles harvesting a massive salad.

The insect equivalent of farmers, **leafcutter ants** may even use pesticides: They culture an antibiotic-producing bacteria that kills parasites attempting to invade their nests.

Having said that, many insects need help with their diet and find it in the most ingenious forms. Leafcutter ants alone have been estimated to utilize as much green stuff as the combined browsing of all vertebrate herbivores in the forest – but they don't eat it. They transport it to their nest and mulch it for a type of fungus which occurs nowhere else. The fungus feeds on the leaves and the ants eat the fungus. Indeed, neither can survive without the other – an example of an intricate relationship called obligate mutualism. Termites are similarly mutualistic with microscopic gut-living protozoans; termites alone can't digest wood but that's the protozoans' specialty. Whatever the method, the insect herbivores of the forest are crucial for converting locked away nutrients into protein. As such, they inevitably become food for a multitude of predators, most of which are also invertebrates.

Tarantulas in Central America can deliver an irritating bite, but are otherwise harmless to us.

As well as disguise from predators, this **mantid's** camouflage is for ambushing prey.

The extraordinary camouflage of **katydids** even includes patches of false caterpillar herbivory. Their leaf mimicry is designed to deceive predators.

Hunters of the forest floor

Perhaps the most notorious are army ants. They have a reputation for unstoppable voracity, but other insects make up the bulk of their prey. Nomadic and constantly mobile, columns of army ants capture anything that can be subdued (the largest catches are skink-sized) and form temporary nests that are shifted as often as prey availability dictates. If you encounter army ants on the move, the worst you'll get is bitten toes – simply step to one side to really enjoy them and their various camp followers: Army ant marches attract antbirds that mop up fleeing bugs and they, in turn, are attended by 'army ant butterflies', which extract minerals from the birds' droppings.

Potentially far more dangerous hunters are not insects but arachnids (eight legs rather than six). Scorpions, tarantulas and wolf spiders are all mainly nocturnal and, like the ants, they're unlikely to do any real harm unless you bother them. ■

About 13 specialized species of Central American **weevil** feed exclusively on bromeliad leaves.

Jewel scarabs are prized by insect collectors and fetch as much as $500 per beetle. So long as their cloud forest habitat is protected, collecting by enthusiasts is probably not affecting populations.

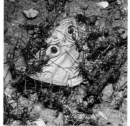

Army ants are not as formidable as their reputation suggests – except to other insects.

Hotspots

Lamanai Four tarantula species. **Monteverde** Dozens of jewel scarabs. **PN Carara** Huge leafcutter nests, termites and acacia ants.

RESOURCE GUIDE

The following information isn't intended to be comprehensive so if you don't find it here, it doesn't mean it isn't worth checking out. But we've included some key references and contacts which we know are reliable starting points to help you find what you're looking for.

RECOMMENDED READING

Field guides

Mammals Easily the best guide for the region is F Reid's *Field Guide to the Mammals of Central America & Southeast Mexico*, with superb colour plates and excellent field information – marine mammals are also included. *Neotropical Rainforest Mammals: A Field Guide* by L Emmons covers rainforest species from Central and South America, most with distribution maps and colour plates. *Costa Rica Mammals* by E Carillo, G Wong & J Saenz is an excellent introductory title which has just been revised; the second edition is widely available in Costa Rica.

Cetaceans *Whales, Dolphins & Porpoises* by M Carwardine is light-weight, covers all known species with superb illustrations and includes practical watching tips. The Sierra Club *Handbook of Whales & Dolphins* by S Leatherwood & R Reeves is pocket-sized and comprehensive. It's a little bulky for a field guide, but a superb up-to-date reference, get is *Sea Mammals of the World, A Complete Guide to Whales, Dolphins, Seals, Sea Lions and Sea Cows* by R Reeves and co-authors.

Birds *A Guide to the Birds of Mexico & Northern Central America* by S Howell & S Webb, has extremely comprehensive coverage as far south as central Nicaragua and is the guide of choice for Belize. The definitive guide for Costa Rica is *A Guide to the Birds of Costa Rica* by FG Stiles & A Skutch. For Panama, take R Ridgely & J Gwynne's classic *A Guide to the Birds of Panama with Costa Rica, Nicaragua & Honduras;* make sure you get the extensively revised second (1989) edition.

Reptiles and amphibians A trio of recently published guides all come highly recommended. T Leenders' *A Guide to Reptiles and Amphibians of Costa Rica* is excellent and is small enough to fit in a jacket pocket; it also covers most of the species seen in Panama. For Belize, take your pick from two equally worthwhile titles: *A Guide to the Reptiles of Belize* by P Stafford & J Meyer, or the slightly more comprehensive (and heavier) *A Field Guide to the Amphibians and Reptiles of the Maya World: The Lowlands of Mexico, Northern Guatemala, and Belize* by J Lee.

Invertebrates Field guides for the smaller denizens of the bush are a little patchy but Inbio (see the following Bookshops section for contact details) publishes very nice introductory titles on *scorpions, beetles, butterflies* and *Diptera* (flies, fruit flies and mosquitoes) as well as online guides to many others (in Spanish). *An Introduction to Costa Rican Butterflies* by M Goode covers behaviour, mimicry and practical advice on finding butterflies. The weighty, two-volume *Butterflies of Costa Rica & their Natural History* by P DeVries is for the more technically minded.

Marine life The *Collins Pocket Guide to the Coral Reef Fishes of the Indo-Pacific & Caribbean* by E Lieske & R Myers is an invaluable identification tool for divers, with illustrations of over 2100 species. E Kaplan's *Peterson Field Guide to Coral Reefs of the Caribbean & Florida* is also excellent and covers sponges, mollusks and corals as well as fish. Lonely Planet's *Diving & Snorkeling Belize* outlines all the top dive sites and the *Pisces Guide to Caribbean Reef Ecology* helps you to identify common species and explains how they interact.

Background reading and references
Eminently readable, J Kricher's *A Neotropical Companion – An Introduction to the Animals, Plants & Ecosystems of the New World Tropics* is the classic read-before-you-go text covering everything from evolution to conservation in Central and South America. *Tropical Nature* by A Forsyth & K Miyata covers similar ground, but concentrates on the most intriguing species and relationships in a very entertaining collection of essays. For a readable account of Central America's role as a bridge for wildlife exchange between North and South America, get a copy of *The Monkey's Bridge* by D Wallace. D Janzen's encyclopedic *Costa Rican Natural History* was published 20 years ago and while some of it is out of date, it is still the most comprehensive technical reference for the region. Also technical but more condensed and accessible, *Central America: A Natural and Cultural History* by A G Coates covers everything from plate tectonics to Paseo Pantera.

Ornithologists will find *Trogons, Laughing Falcons, and Other Neotropical Birds* by the legendary A Skutch a fascinating mixture of field stories and observations collected over 70 years. For frog-lovers, M Crump's *In Search of the Golden Frog* tells the adventures of a field biologist in Costa Rica and throughout Latin America. A Rabinowitz's *Jaguar* is a compelling read about the struggle to establish the world's first jaguar reserve in Belize; written by the 'Indiana Jones of conservation' it reveals a few hard-learned realities about field work in the tropics.

For some background on the conservation history of Central America, both D Wallace's *The Quetzal and the Macaw; The Story of Costa Rica's National Parks* and *The Green Republic; A Conservation History of Costa Rica* by S Evans are worthwhile. *Green Phoenix* by W Allen covers the restoration of Guanacaste's tropical dry forests.

Bookshops
Most of the titles we've recommended can be ordered from the following mail-order natural history bookshops; several have a web catalogue and online ordering service. As well as recent books, most of them can help with out-of-print titles but if not, try www. book finder.com

- **American Birding Association** (USA & Canada ☎ 800-634 7736, fax 590 2473; International ☎ 719-578 0607, fax 9705; **w** www.americanbirding.org/abasales), PO Box 6599, Colorado Springs, Colorado 80934, USA.
- **Andrew Isles Natural History Books** (☎ 03-9510 5750, fax 9529 1256, **e** books@AndrewIsles.com, **w** www.AndrewIsles.com), 115 Greville St, Prahran, Victoria 3181, Australia.
- **Buteo Books** (☎ 800-722 2460 (orders – USA and Canada), 434-263 8671, fax 263 4842, **e** allen@buteobooks.com, **w** www.bu teobooks.com), 3130 Laurel Rd, Shipman, VA 22971, USA.

- **Inbio** (244 0690, ext. 802, Fax 244 2816, **e** editorial@ inbio.ac.cr **w** www.inbio.ac.cr/editorial), P.O. Box Apdo. 22-3100, Santo Domingo de Heredia, Costa Rica. (Costa Rica's National Institute of Biodiversity, it produces many publications on Costa Rican natural history.)
- **Natural History Book Service** (☎ 1803-865 913, fax 280, **e** nhbs@nhbs.co.uk, **w** www.nhbs.com), 2–3 Wills Rd, Totnes, Devon TQ9 5XN, England.
- **Subbuteo** (☎ 870-0109 700, fax 699, **e** info@wildlifebooks.com, **w** www.wildlifebooks.com), The Rea, Upton Magna, Shrewsbury SY4 4UR, England.
- **ZooBookSales** (☎ 507-467 8733, fax 467 8735, **e** zoobooks@acegroup.cc) 403 Parkway Avenue N., PO Box 405, Lanesboro, MN 55949, USA.

TOUR OPERATORS

Tour operators abound throughout Central America; the best ones are accredited and licensed by relevant tourist boards (contact details below). Even then, not all tours are informative or environmentally sound. The following operators we feel know their stuff and will offer safe, informative and interesting wildlife-watching experiences.

International
International wildlife conservation organizations such as the World Wildlife Fund (**w** www.worldwildlife.org/travel) run natural history tours to Central America. It's also worthwhile checking listings of international wildlife tour operators in well-regarded wildlife magazines (like *BBC Wildlife*). Several specialist wildlife, nature and bird tour companies that use only professional guides schedule regular trips to Central America.

EcoVentures (☎ 804-296 1582, fax 296 0487, **e** KenKlotz@ ecoventures-travel.com **w** www.ecoventures-travel.com), PO Box 3881, Charlottesville, VA 22903-0881, USA.
Field Guides Inc (☎ 512-327 4953, fax 9231, **e** fgileader@aol.com, **w** www.fieldguides.com), PO Box 160723, Austin, Texas 78716-0723, USA.
Naturetrek (☎ 1962-733 051, fax 736 426, **e** inquiries@nature trek.demon.co.uk), Chautara, Bighton nr. Alresford, Hampshire SO24 9RB, England.
Sunbird (☎ 1767-682 969, fax 692 481, **e** sunbird@sunbird .demon.co.uk, **w** www.sunbird.demon.co.uk), PO Box 76, Sandy, Bedfordshire SG19 1DF, England.
Victor Emanuel Nature Tours (☎ 512-328 5221, fax 2919, **e** infro@ventbird.com, **w** www.ventbird.com), PO Box 33008, Austin, Texas 78764, USA.
WCS (Wildlife Conservation Society) (☎ 212-439 6507, **e** travel@wcs.org, **w** www.wcs.org), Adventure Travel, 830 Fifth Avenue, New York, New York 10021, USA.
Wings (☎ 520-320 9868, fax 9373, **e** wings@wingbirds.com, **w** www.widdl.com/wings), 1643 N. Alvernon Way, Suite 105, Tucson, Arizona 85712, USA.

Belize

Ecotourism & Adventure Specialists (☎ 337 0009, fax 337 009, **e** info@ecotourism-adventure.com, **w** www.ecotourism-aadven ture.com), 4 avenida 7-95 Zona 14 2nd level, Guatemala City 01014, Guatemala.

International Zoological Expeditions (☎ 5-22119, fax 5-23152; USA 508-655 1461, toll free 800-548 5843, fax 508-655 4445, **w** www.ize2belize.com), 210 Washington St, Sherborn, Massachusetts 01770, USA.

Lamanai Outpost Lodge (☎ USA toll-free 1-888-733 7864, **e** reefs ruins@aol.com, **w** www.lamanai.com); arranges excellent itineraries for the whole of Belize.

Costa Rica

Canopy Tour (☎ 257 5149, fax 256 7626, **e** canopy@canopy tour.com, **w** www.canopytour.com), Interlink 227, PO Box 25635, Miami, Florida 33102, USA.

Costa Rica Expeditions (☎ 257 0766, 222 0333, fax 257 1665, **e** ecotur@expeditions.co.cr, **w** www.costaricaexpeditions.com), Calle Central, Avenida 3, San José; Dept 235, PO Box 025216, Miami, Florida 33102-5216.

Costa Rica Sun Tours (☎ 296 7757, fax 4307, **e** info@crsun tours.com, **w** www.crsuntours.com), Calle 36, Avenida 4, San José; PO Box 025216-1660, Miami, Florida 33102-5216, USA.

Costa Rica Trekking Expeditions (☎ 771 4582, fax 771 8841, **e** trekking@racsa.co.cr, **w** www.chirripo.com) Apdo. 352-8000, San Isidro de el General. In **USA**: Selva Mar, 1641 NW 79th Avenue, Miami, FL 33126-1105, USA.

Green Tropical Tours (☎ 229 4192, fax 292 5003, 380 1536 cellular, **e** information@greentropical.com, **w** www.greentropical.com). PO Box 675-2200, Coronado, San José; forwarding address: Dept 252, PO Box 025219, Miami, Florida 33102, USA.

Horizontes (☎ 222 2022, fax 255 4513, **e** info@horizontes.com, **w** www.horizontes.com), Calle 28, Avenidas 1 & 3, San José; postal address: Apdo. 1780-1002, San José, Costa Rica.

Los Caminos de la Selva (Jungle Trails; ☎ 255 3486, fax 2782), Calle 38, Avenidas 5 & 7, San José, Costa Rica.

Tikal Tours (☎ 223-2811, 257-1494, fax 223-1916), Avenida 2, Calles 7 & 9, San José, Costa Rica.

Panama

Ancon Expeditions of Panama (☎ 269 9415, fax 264 3713, **e** info@anconexpeditions.com, **w** www.anconexpeditions.com), Box 0832-1509 (WTC), Panamá, República de Panamá. Canopy Tower (☎ 264 5720, **e** stay@canopytower.com, **w** www.canopy tower.com)

Iguana Tours (☎ 226-8738, fax 226-4736, **e** iguana@sinfo.net, **w** www.nvmundo.com/iguanatours), PO Box 6655, Panamá 5, República de Panamá.

Preferred Adventures Ltd (☎ 651-222 8131, 800-840 8687, fax 651-222 4221, **e** travel@preferredadventures.com, **w** www.pre ferredadventures.com), One West Water St, Suite 300, St Paul, Minnesota 55107, USA.

Wildland Adventures (☎ 206-365 0686, 800-345 4453, fax 206-363 6615, **e** info@wildland.com, **w** www.wildland.com), 3516 NE 155th St, Seattle, Washington 98155, USA.

TOURISM BOARDS

Belize Belize Tourism Board, Level 2, Central Bank Building, PO Box 325, Belize City, Belize (☎ 501-2-31913/31910, fax 501-2-31943 **w** www.travelbelize.org).
Costa Rica Institute Costarricense de Turismo (ICT) Plaze de la Cultura, Avenidas Cenrtral & Calle 5, San José (☎ 222 1090, **e** info@tourism-costarica.com, **w** www.tourism-costarica.com).
Panama Instituto Panameño de Turismo (IPAT), Apartado 4421, Centro de Convenciones ATLAPA, Vía Israel, Panamá 5, Republic of Panamá (☎ 226 7000 or ☎ 226 4614/3164, fax 226 5046, **e** infotur@ns.ipat.gob.pa, **w** www.ipat.gob.pa).

PARKS & CONSERVATION AUTHORITIES

Belize Ministry of Natural Resources, the Environment and Industry (contact Permanent Secretary, Belmopan ☎ 822 2630, fax 822-2333).
Costa Rica SINAC (Sistema Nacional de Areas de Conservation) Ministry of Natural Resources and Mines, Calle 25, Avenidas 8/10, San José; postal: Apdo. 10094, San José 1000 (☎ 283 8004 or information line ☎ 192, fax 283 7343, **w** www.sinac.go.cr).
Panama Instituto Nacional de Recursos Naturales Renovables (INRENARE); ☎ 232 5886/6667, fax 232 6717, **e** inrenare@ns.in renare.stri.si.edu, **w** www2.usma.ac.pa/⌐eco1 Apartado 2016 Paraíso - Ancón, Panamá City, Republic of Panamá.

CONSERVATION ASSOCIATIONS

The following local and international organizations run projects and activities in Central America. Most of them have opportunities for volunteer work or to join research and conservation expeditions.

ANAI (National Association of Indigenous Affairs) San José, Costa Rica ☎ 224-6090/3570, fax 253 7524, **e** anaicr@sol.racsa.co.cr.
ANCON (Asociacion Nacional para la Conservacion de la Naturaleza), Apartado 1387, Panama 1, Republic of Panama (☎ 314 0060, fax 314-0061, **e** ancon@ancon.com, **w** www.ancon.org).
Belize Audubon Society P.O. Box 1001,12 Fort Street, Belize City, Belize (☎ 223 5004, fax 223 4985, **e** base@btl.net, **w** www.belize audubon.org).
BirdLife International Wellbrook Court, Girton Rd, Cambridge CB3 0NA, England.
Canadian Organization for Tropical Education and Rainforest Conservation (COTERC) Box 335, Pickering, Ontario L1V 2R6, Canada (☎ 905-831 8809, Fax: 905-831 4203, **e** info@coterc.org, **w** www.coterc.org).
Caribbean Conservation Centre US (☎ 800-678 7853, **w** www.ccc turtle.org; Costa Rica ☎ fax 506-224 9215, 710 0547).
Monteverde Conservation League (☎ 645 5003, fax 645 5104, **e** acmmcl@sol.racsa.co.cr **w** www.monteverdeinfo.com/mon teverde_conservation_league.htm).
Panama Audubon Society (☎ 224 9371, fax 224 4740, **e** audupan@pananet.com, **w** www.orbi.net/audubon/).

Programme for Belize Eyre Street, P.O. Box 749, Belize City, Belize (☎ 227 5616, fax 227 5635, **e** pfbel@btl.net, **w** www.pfbelize.org).
The Nature Conservancy 4245 North Fairfax Drive, Suite 100, Arlington, VA 22203-1606 (☎ 800-628 6860, **e** comment@tnc.org, **w** www.nature.org/wherewework/centralamerica/).
Wildlife Conservation Society 2300 Southern Blvd, Bronx, NY 10460, USA (☎ 718-220 5111, fax 364 4275, **e** feedback@wcs.org, **w** www.wcs.org).
Worldwide Fund for Nature UK (☎ 1483-426 444), Panda House, Weyside Park, Godalming, Surrey GU7 1XR, UK. **USA** World Wildlife Fund 1250 24th St, NW, Washington DC 20037-1175, USA (☎ 202-293 4800, fax 293 9211, **w** www.worldwildlife.org).

WEB SITES

The following web sites offer useful background information on wildlife, wildlife-watching and wildlife research in Central America.

www.agroecoturismo.net Costa Rican organization which runs various community-based ecotourism operations.
www.belizeecotourism.org Belize Eco-tourism Association's site. 'Current Issues' link posts up-to-date notices on conservation challenges in Belize.
www.camacdonald.com/birding/birdcentral.htm Resources for birdwatching in Central America.
www.cccturtle.org Homepage of the Caribbean Conservation Corporation with details of volunteer opportunities at Tortuguero.
www.communityconservation.org Robert Howich's grassroots conservation group was instrumental in establishing Belize's Community Baboon Sanctuary and other projects.
www.crbirdingclub.tripod.com Home page of the Birding Club of Costa Rica.
www.dmoz.org/Recreation/Outdoors/Scuba_Diving/Regional/Central_America/ Directory of dive operators in Central America.
www.earthwatch.org/region/camerica.html Describes research projects coordinated by Earthwatch in which paying participants can contribute.
www.fundelfin-costa-rica.org Nonprofit foundation dedicated to conserving the cetaceans of Costa Rica's Drake Bay.
www.naturephotogallery.com/places/costa_rica Biologist and photographer Greg Basco's site which has useful tips on wildlife photography in the tropics.
www.ots.ac.cr The detailed pages of the Organization for Tropical Studies including information on visiting their research stations in Costa Rica.
www.pactbelize.org A non-profit trust fund dedicated to the promotion, conservation, and sustainable development of Belize's protected areas.
www.savethejaguar.com Wildlife Conservation Society's jaguar conservation program.
www.trekforce.org.uk Trekforce is a UK-based charity which organizes conservation, community and scientific expeditions in Central America.
www.worldtwitch.virtualave.net/belize_bird_reports.htm Birdwatching in Belize.

GLOSSARY

adaptation – physical or behavioral trait that helps an organism survive or exploit an environmental factor.

aestivate – to enter a state of dormancy in seasonal hot, dry weather, when food is scarce.

algae – primitive water plants.

alpha male or **female** – dominant animal in a hierarchy, eg, primate troop.

altricial – helpless at birth, requiring prolonged parental care, eg, primates (*compare with* precocial).

amphibian – animal that lives part of its life cycle in water and part on land, eg, frog.

aquatic – living in water or a behavior that takes place in water (*compare with* marine).

arachnid – eight legged invertebrates, includes spiders and scorpions.

arboreal – tree-dwelling.

arribada – mass nesting aggregations of marine turtles (especially olive ridleys).

arthropod – invertebrate characterized by a segmented body and jointed legs, eg, insects, spiders, crustaceans.

avian – characteristic of birds, eg, avian behavior.

binocular vision – vision with overlapping field of view to give heightened perception of depth; in mammals, best developed in primates and carnivores.

biodiversity – faunal and floral richness of an area.

biomass – total weight of living organisms in an ecosystem.

bipedal – standing or walking on two legs, eg, humans.

birder – a birdwatcher.

blind – *see* hide.

bluff – behavior to convince a predator or rival that the bluffer is stronger.

bromeliad – a type of epiphyte (*see* entry).

brood – group of young animals produced in one litter or clutch.

browse – to eat leaves and other parts of shrubs and trees (*hence* browser).

cache – (*noun*) a hidden store of food; (*verb*) to hide food for future use.

camouflage – coloration or patterning that helps an animal blend into its surroundings.

canid – any member of the dog family (Canidae), eg fox, coyote.

canine – doglike; also relating to or belonging to the dog family.

canines – the four large front teeth at the front of the mouth in mammals; well developed for killing in carnivores.

canopy – uppermost layer of forest foliage, often well-defined as a distinct 'roof'.

carapace – upper 'shell,' usually applied to marine turtles and crustaceans.

carnassials – shearing teeth near the back of carnivores' jaw.

carnivore – a meat-eating animal; (*adj.*) carnivorous.

carrion – dead or decaying flesh.

cetacean – collective term for whales and dolphins.

class – a major division of animal classification, eg, mammals, birds, reptiles etc.

climax forest – mature forest.

cohort – subgroup within a species having a common demographic, eg female adults, male juveniles etc.

colony – aggregation of animals (eg, birds, bats) that live, roost or breed together (*hence* colonial).

commensalism – relationship between two unrelated animal species in which one species benefits from the interaction and the other is unaffected.

convergent evolution – evolution whereby unrelated species develop similar characteristics, usually seen among geographically separate species occupying similar niches, eg, sloths and koalas (*also called* convergence).

courtship – behavior (often ritualized) to attract a mate.

crèche – gathering of young birds or mammals for safety or play.

crepuscular – active at dawn and dusk.

crustacean – arthropod with gills, which can breathe underwater or survive in damp condiions on land.

cryptic – behavior, appearance or lifestyle that helps conceal an organism from predators.

deciduous – characteristic in plants of shedding leaves, usually in response to seasonal shortages in nutrients or water.

decurved – downward-curving, eg in beaks or claws.

digit – finger or toe.

dimorphism – having two forms of color or size, eg, spotted and black jaguars (*see* sexual dimorphism, polymorphism).

dispersal – movement of non-adult animals (fish 'fry', immature birds, subadult mammals etc) or plants (seeds) away from their natal home range; generally assumed to be a mechanism ensuring individuals don't breed with their parents (*compare with* migration).

display – behavior transmitting information from the sender to another, often associated with threat, defense of territory, courtship etc.

diurnal – active during daylight hours (*opposite of* nocturnal).

dorsal – pertaining to upper (top) surface, ie the back, on most animals (*opposite of* ventral).

down – loose, fluffy feathers that cover young birds and insulate plumage of adults.

drey – squirrel nest.

dung – animal excrement (feces).

echolocation – method by which bats and cetaceans determine their surroundings by reflected high frequency sounds; often used to locate prey.

ecology – scientific study of relationships between organisms, their environment and each other.

ecosystem – community of living organisms and their physical environment.

ecotone – transition zone between two habitats, eg savanna and forest – hence edge species (*also called* edge).

emergent tree – tallest trees in the forest which 'emerge' above the canopy level.

endangered – in danger of imminent extinction if trends causing its demise continue.

endemic – native and restricted to a certain area, eg, ocellated turkey is endemic to Yucatán.

epiphyte – plant which gathers nutrients and water from the air, usually growing on another plant for support, eg, orchids on a tree. Sometimes called air plant.

equatorial – on or near the equator.

erectile – can be erected, eg, hair or feathers erected in defense or courtship displays.

estrus – *see* oestrus.

eutherian – a mammal with a placenta that gives birth to fully-formed young; also called placental (*compare* marsupial).

family – scientific grouping of related genera, eg, Felidae (the cat family).

feces – excrement.

feline – catlike; also related to or belonging to the Felidae (cat family).

feral – running wild, especially escaped domestic stock or introduced species.

fledgling – young bird able to leave the nest, ie, to fledge.

flight distance – distance at which an animal will flee from a perceived threat.

flight feathers – large wing feathers (*also called* primary feathers).

foliage – leafy vegetation, eg, on trees.

folivore – a leaf-eating animal; *adj.* folivorous.

fossorial – burrowing or digging lifestyle or adaptations, eg armadillo.

frugivore – a fruit-eating animal; *adj.* frugivorous.

gallery forest – forest growing along watercourses, may extend into adjoining well-watered habitat (*also called* riverine forest).

gap – human-made or natural opening in the canopy admitting light which reaches the forest floor.

genera – plural of genus.

genus – taxonomic grouping of closely-related species.

geophagy – eating rock or soil, usually to acquire minerals.

gestation – period that young mammals develop in the womb before birth.

gland – *see* scent gland, and inguinal, interdigital and preorbital glands.

granivore – a grain-eating animal; adj. granivorous.

gravid – pregnant (also applies to reptiles or birds carrying eggs).

graze – to eat grass (*hence* grazer).

gregarious – forming or moving in groups, eg, herds or flocks.

guano – phosphate-rich excrement deposited by seabirds or bats, usually accumulated over generations.

hackles – long, loose feathers or hairs on nape or throat, often erectile.

harem – group of females that mate with one male; the male defends his harem against other males.

hawk – to fly actively in search of prey such as insects, usually caught in the open mouth.

helper – animal, usually from a previous brood, which helps parents raise subsequent offspring.

herbivore – plant-eating animal; adj. herbivorous.

herd – social group of mammals; usually applied to herbivores.

herp – enthusiast's term for any reptile or amphibian.

herpetologist – zoologist who studies reptiles or amphibians.

hide – artificial construction, usually of wood, for the observation of animals while keeping the observer hidden (*also called* blind).

hierarchy – order of dominance among social animals, usually with a dominant individual or caste and one or more tiers of status or function, eg, termites, primates.

hive – home of bees or wasps.

holt – otters' den.

home range – the area over which an individual or group ranges over time (*compare with* territory).

host – organism on (or in) which a parasite lives; bird that raises young of parasitic species.

hybrid – offspring, usually infertile, resulting from a mating between two different species; rare among vertebrates.

immature – stage in a young bird's development between juvenile and adult.

incisor – front (ie, cutting) teeth.

inguinal gland – scent gland in groin area.

insectivore – an insect-eating animal; adj. insectivorous.

interdigital gland – scent gland between toes or hooves, eg, on dogs.

invertebrate – an animal without a spinal column or backbone, eg, insects, worms.

iridescence – metallic sheen on many insects and birds, eg, hummingbirds.

juvenile – animal at the stage between infancy and adulthood (mammals) or with first feathers after natal down (bird).

lamellae – comb-like plates in the bill of some birds (eg, spoonbill) that filter food particles from water.

latrine – site where mammals habitually deposit dung or urine (*compare with* midden).

lek – communal arena for courtship displays and mating, mainly in birds; also verb.

liana – vine which begins as a terrestrial shrub and grows upwards throughout the canopy.

loaf – to laze about, especially used in describing bird behavior.

localized – restricted to a small or distinct area.

mammal – a warm-blooded, usually furred or hairy animal (except cetaceans) that gives birth to and suckles live young.

mandible – lower part of beak or jaw in vertebrates or the main mouthparts in invertebrates, eg 'pincers' in biting ants.

marine – living in the sea.

marsupial – a mammal that lacks a placenta and give birth to 'premature' offspring which complete their development in a pouch (*compare* eutherian).

matriarchal – female dominated.

matrilineal – relating to kinship or descent among related females.

melanism – naturally occurring excess of dark brown pigment that produces black forms of some animals, eg, jaguars, variegated squirrels.

midden – accumulation of dung as a territory marker, often accompanied by scent-marking (*see* latrine).

migration – regular movement, often en masse, from one location to another usually in response to fluctuating levels of a critical resource, such as food, eg, shorebirds (*hence* migrant, migratory).

milpa – Belizean term for slash and burn agriculture in which plots are abandoned after a season or so.

mixed flock – a feeding party of birds, especially in forest, containing various species (also called bird wave or bird party).

mob – to harass a predatory animal (eg, small birds mobbing an owl); often in response to a distress call.

monogamous – having one reproductive partner for life or breeding season.

montane – living or situated on mountains.

molt – to shed and replace all or certain feathers, skin or fur, usually prompted by seasonal or behavioral factors, eg, courtship, onset of summer etc.

mortality – (*as used here*) an environmental factor causing death.

mutualism – an interaction between two species where both benefit.

natal – pertaining to birth.

nectarivore – animal feeding primarily on nectar eg many butterflies, hummingbirds and bats; adj. nectarivorous.

Neotropics – the tropical regions of the New World, ie most of Latin America (*see* tropical).

nestling – young bird until it leaves the nest (*compare with* fledgling).

nest parasitism – laying eggs in the nest of another bird species and taking no further part in rearing the offspring (*also called* brood parasitism), eg cuckoos.

nictitating membrane – semi-transparent membrane that draws across eyes of most birds and some mammals and reptiles.

nocturnal – active at night.

nomadic – wandering in search of resources, eg, food or water, with no fixed home range or territory.

oestrus – period when female mammal is ovulating and therefore sexually receptive; *adj.* estrus (referring to behavior).

omnivore – an animal that eats both plant and animal matter; adj. omnivorous.

order – grouping of one or more related animal families, eg, cats and dogs belong to order Carnivora (carnivores).

pair bond – social ties that keep mated pair together, reinforced with grooming, calls etc.

parasite – plant or animal that obtains nourishment during all or part of its life from another life form, usually to the detriment of the host.

pelagic – living at sea, ie, in or above open water.

photosynthesis – the process whereby plants convert sunlight, water and carbon dioxide into organic compounds.

pioneer – the first animal or plant species to colonize an area; most often applied to rapidly growing tree species which appear first after clearing.

piscivore – fish-eating animal; adj. piscivorous.

placental – *see* eutherian

plumage – birds' feathers, often used to describe total appearance, eg, drab plumage.

polyandry – female having access to more than one reproductive male.

polygamy – having access to more than one reproductive mate.

polygyny – male having access to more than one reproductive female.

polymorphism – having more than one adult form, size or color.

precocial – well-developed at birth or hatching; usually highly mobile and/or independent (*compare* altricial).

prehensile – flexible and grasping, eg, tail, fingers.

preorbital gland – scent gland in front of the eyes, used to mark territory.

primary feathers – *see* flight feathers.

primary forest – undisturbed, old growth forest (*see* secondary forest)

primate – a monkey, prosimian or ape.

primitive – resembling or representing an early stage in the evolution of a particular group of animals.

pouch-young – juvenile marsupials while still in the pouch.

pug – footprint or other imprint left on the ground by an animal; usually applied to carnivores.

quadruped – four-legged animal.

quarter – to systematically range over an area in search of prey, eg, coyotes, birds of prey.

race – *see* subspecies.

raptor – bird of prey, eg, hawk, falcon, vulture.

recurved – upward-curving, eg, bill of avocet.

regurgitate – to bring up partly digested food from crop or stomach, particularly when feeding young.

relict – remnant of formerly widespread species, community or habitat.

resident – an animal remaining in a particular area for the reproductive stage of its life cycle, usually associated with territorial behavior. Also, as applied to birds, remaining in a region or country for its entire life (*compare with* migration).

riparian – *see* riverine.

riverine – living in or always associated with rivers or streams (*also called* riparian).

rodent – any of the many species of rat, mouse, squirrel etc.

roost – area where mammals (eg, bats) or birds gather to sleep, sometimes in large numbers (*also verb*).

ruminant – ungulate with four-chambered stomach (rumen) that chews the cud (*hence* ruminate).

rump – upper backside of mammal or bird, often distinctively marked for signaling, eg, deer.

rut – the deer mating season; (*verb*) courtship behavior of male deer during this period.

saddle – mid to lower back area on mammals and birds.

sanguivore – a blood-eating animal, eg vampire bat; *adj.* sanguivorous.

scavenger – animal that feeds on carrion or scraps left by others.

scent gland – concentration of special skin cells that secrete chemicals conveying information about the owner's status, identity, reproductive state etc.

scrape – shallow digging in soil used by some mammals (especially carnivores) as a territorial marker; often with feces or urine.

secondary forest – forest which has been felled and is regenerating.

selection – process by which environmental or behavioral pressures weed out traits that are detrimental to an organism's reproductive success or favor traits which aid that success.

sexual dimorphism – differences in color, size or form between males and females of the same species, eg, many spectacular examples in birds, antlers in male deer.

sibling – related offspring with the same parents (*hence* foster sibling in brood parasites).

signal – behavior or display that conveys information from one animal to another, eg of danger.

slough – to shed skin when growing, eg reptiles.

spawn – eggs of fish and amphibians, usually laid in water (*also verb*).

speciation – process whereby species develop from a common ancestor.

species – organisms capable of breeding with each other to produce fertile offspring; distinct and usually recognizable from other species.

spoor – the track or tracks of an animal.

spraint – otter feces, used as territorial marking.

spy-hop – behavior in marine species (whales and sharks) of peering above water's surface apparently to check bearings, threats, etc.

stage – level in development of an organism.

stoop – powerful predatory dive of a bird of prey.

streamer – long decorative feather, eg of male quetzal.

subadult – last stage of juvenile development, usually characterized by near-adult coloration, size or plumage; distinct from adult in generally being non-reproducing.

subordinate – an animal that is ranked beneath another in a social hierarchy, eg in monkey troops.

subspecies – population of a species isolated from other populations (eg by landforms) that has developed distinct genetic, physical or behavioral traits over many generations (*also called* race); can interbreed successfully with other subspecies of the same species but usually does not owing to discrete distributions.

symbiosis – *see* mutualism.

taxonomy – scientific classification of organisms according to their evolutionary relationships (*also called* systematics).

tectonic – pertaining to changes in the earth's crust caused by movement of molten rock below its surface.

termitarium – earthen mound constructed by a termite colony (*also called* termitary).

terrestrial – living on the ground.

territory – area inhabited by an individual, defended against others of the same species (and usually the same sex) to provide exclusive access to resources such as food, mates, den sites, etc (*compare with* home range).

thermal – rising column of warm air, used by birds especially raptors to gain height; (*also verb*).

troop – group of monkeys.

tropical – found within the tropics, ie, between Tropics of Cancer and Capricorn.

understory – layer of vegetation growing beneath the canopy.

ungulate – a hoofed mammal.

vent – the urogential opening of cetaceans, birds, reptiles and fish (occasionally applied to female land-mammals).

ventral – pertaining to lower (under) side of an animal (*opposite of* dorsal).

vertebrate – an animal having a backbone, ie, bony fish, amphibians, reptiles, birds and mammals.

vocalization – sound made orally by an animal usually with a specific communicative meaning.

volplane – steep, controlled dive on outstretched wings, eg by vultures to a kill.

waders – shorebirds and related families, eg plovers.

warm-blooded – maintaining a constant body temperature by internal regulation, eg most birds and mammals (*correctly known as* homeothermic).

waterfowl – general term for swans, geese and ducks.

wattle – fleshy, sometimes brightly colored growth on head or neck, usually prominent in courtship, eg on birds.

yearling – a mammal in its second year of growth.

PHOTO CREDITS

Gavin Anderson 42 top David Andrew 25, 33, 35, 39, 50, 51 bottom ARDEA 62 , 137, 176 column 4, 177 column 3, 179 column 4, 188 column 1, 195 column 3, 195 column 4, 196 column 4, 201 column 2, 203 column 1, 204 column 4, 205 column 3 ARDEA/D Avon 202 column 1 ARDEA/David Dixon 204 column 1 ARDEA/JS Dunning 200 column 4 ARDEA/MD England 194 column 2, 196 column 3, 198 column 2, 198 column 3, 202 column 2 ARDEA/Kenneth W Fink 178 column 4, 179 column 2 ARDEA/Francois Gohier 173 bottom, 178 inset, 179 column 3, 211 column 3 ARDEA/A Greensmith 201 column 3 ARDEA/M Watson 59 ARDEA/Wardene Weisser 203 column 4 Michael Aw 42 bottom Greg Basco 5 column 1, 5 column 2, 5 column 4, 15, 27, 46 bottom, 47, 52 top, 53, 54, 64, 67, 148 bottom, 150 top, 155 top, 186 column 4, 187 column 2, 193 bottom, 197 inset, 208 column 2, 208 column 3, 210 column 1, 212 column 2, 214 inset (main), 214 inset (small), 216 inset (small), 217 inset Jim Beveridge 211 column 2, 150 bottom, 152 column 2, 158 bottom, 166 bottom, 167 bottom, 169 top, 174 column 4, 177 column 2, 179 inset, 182 column 3, 184 column 2, 187 column 1, 192 column 3, 201 column 1, 206 top, 209 top Tom Boyden 6 column 4, 16, 43, 45 top & bottom, 55 top, 61 top, 63 bottom, 83, 88, 90, 96, 100, 110, 114, 120, 121, 122, 124 right, 142, 153 top, 156 bottom, 157 top, 158 top, 159 bottom, 162 bottom, 163 bottom, 165 top, 165 bottom, 168 bottom, 169 bottom, 170 column 3, 172 column 3, 174 inset, 175 top, 177 column 1, 178 column 3, 179 column 1, 180 bottom, 181 bottom, 184 column 4 & inset, 188 column 2, 188 column 4, 188 inset, 189 top, 190 column 1, 191 top, 194 column 1, 200 column 2, 200 column 3, 200 inset, 201 column 4, 203 column 2, 203 inset, 204 column 2, 205 column 4, 206 bottom, 207 top, 210 column 2, 210 inset, 212 column 3, 212 column 4, 214 column 2, 214 column 4, 215 inset, 215 right middle, 215 top left, 216 column 3, 216 column 4, 216 inset (main), 217 right bottom, 217 top left, 217 top right Cheryl Conlon 157 bottom Scott Doggett 126, 134 Wade Eakle 201 inset Jason Edwards 161 bottom John Elk III 59, 65 top Michael & Patricia Fogden 6 column 1, 18, 30, 56, 58, 105, 144 column 1, 144 column 2, 144 column 3, 145 top, 145 bottom, 146 top, 146 bottom, 152 column 1, 152 column 3, 152 inset, 153 bottom, 154 column 1, 154 column 3, 160 top, 160 bottom, 167 top, 168 top, 170 column 1, 170 column 2, 170 column 4, 174 column 1, 176 column 1, 176 column 2, 176 column 3, 176 inset, 181 top, 182 column 1, 182 column 2, 182 column 4, 183 bottom, 183 top, 184 column 1, 186 column 1, 186 column 2, 186 column 3, 186 inset, 187 column 3, 187 column 4, 187 inset, 188 column 3, 189 bottom, 190 column 2, 191 bottom, 192 column 1, 194 column 3, 194 column 4, 194 inset, 195 column 2, 195 inset , 196 column 1, 196 column 2, 196 inset, 197 column 1, 197 column 2, 197 column 3, 197 column 4, 198 column 1, 198 column 4, 199 top, 199 bottom, 200 column 1, 202 column 3, 204 inset, 205 column 2, 205 inset, 207 bottom, 208 column 1, 208 column 4, 208 inset, 209 bottom, 211 column 1, 212 inset, 213 top, 213 bottom, 216 column 1 Roberto Soncin Gerometta 215 right bottom Ralph Hopkins 5 column 7, 6 column 2, 6 column 3, 32, 36, 44 top, 44 bottom, 51, 53 bottom, 74, 94, 102, 133, 141, 148 top, 149 bottom, 151 bottom, 156 top, 163 top, 171 top, 172 column 1, 172 column 2, 172 column 4, 172 inset, 173 top, 184 column 3, 185 top,

185 bottom, **195** column 1, **204** column 3 Luke Hunter **46** top, **54** bottom, **55** bottom, **57** top, **57** bottom, **60**, **61** bottom, **70**, **72**, **79**, **82** left, **92**, **98**, **106**, **109**, **116**, **119** bottom, **125** right, **154** column 2, **159** top, **161** top, **162** top, **163** top, **164** top, **164** bottom, **166** top, **171** bottom, **174** column 3, **177** inset, **178** column 1, **210** column 3, **210** column 4, **214** column 1, **216** column 2 Greg Johnston **28**, **63** top, **68**, **76** Casey Mahaney & Astrid Witte **149** top Alfredo Maiquez **1**, **5** column 3, **5** column 6, **20**, **24**, **49**, **84**, **123**, **124** left, **130**, **139**, **147** top, **151** top, **178** column 2, **180** top, **192** column 4, **193** top Andrew Marshall & Leanne Walker **41**, **82** right Debra Miller **65** top Carolyn Miller Carlstroem **29** Nature PL **147** bottom, **175** bottom, **177** column 4, **198** inset John Neubauer **34** Mark Newman **5** column 5, **37**, **125** left, **155** bottom, **192** inset, **212** column 1, **214** column 3, **215** top right Louisa Preston **40** bottom Stephen Saks **119** top, **174** column 2 VIREO **192** column 2 VIREO/R & N Bowers **38** bottom VIREO/John Cancalosi **205** column 1 VIREO/J Dunning **190** column 3 VIREO/Steven Hold **38** top VIREO/Doug Wechsler **202** inset, **203** column 3 David Watson **135**, **202** column 4, **217** right middle Mark Webster **40** top

INDEX

LONELY PLANET

You already know that Lonely Planet produces more than this one guidebook, but you might not be aware of the products we have on this region or our other Watching Wildlife guides. Here is a selection of titles that you may want to check out as well:

Watching Wildlife East Africa
ISBN 1 86450 033 6
US$19.99 • UK£12.99

Watching Wildlife Southern Africa
ISBN 1 86450 035 2
US$19.99 • UK£12.99

Watching Wildlife Australia
ISBN 1 86450 032 8
US$19.99 • UK£12.99

Travel Photography
ISBN 1 86450 207 X
US$16.99 • UK£9.99

Costa Rica Spanish phrasebook
ISBN 1 86450 105 7
US$7.99 • UK£4.50

Latin American Spanish phrasebook
ISBN 0 86442 558 9
US$6.95 • UK£4.50

Diving & Snorkeling Belize
ISBN 1 74059 047 3
US$16.99 • UK£10.99

Read This First: Central & South America
ISBN 1 86450 067 0
US$14.99 • UK£8.99

Healthy Travel Central & South America
ISBN 1 86450 053 0
US$5.95 • UK£3.99

Costa Rica
ISBN 1 74059 118 6
US$19.99 • UK£12.99

Belize
ISBN 1 74059 276 X
US$14.99 • UK£9.99

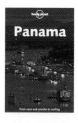

Panama
ISBN 1 86450 307 6
US$16.99 • UK£10.99

Available wherever books are sold

RESEARCH

The authors visited as many of the national parks and other reserves as possible during the research for this book. In cases where access was not possible, material was drawn from sources such as scientific papers and authoritative publications, and corroborated by experts.

In their research the authors have drawn on their experience, their contacts and their personal observations. They have not necessarily been able to see everything in the parks they visited, and they have not gone on every available tour. Instead, they have used their expertise to judge what to bring together in as accurate a picture of a place as possible.

Common names for many wide-ranging Central American mammals and birds vary across the region; and no two references agree completely on names (scientific or common). Bird names in this book follow Stiles, Skutch & Gardner (Costa Rica), Ridgely & Gwynne (Panama) and Howell & Webb (Belize); see Resource Guide for full titles. Mammal names follow Reid.

We welcome feedback to help us improve new editions. All information is passed on to the authors for verification on the road. The best snippets are rewarded with a Lonely Planet guidebook.

Send all correspondence to the Lonely Planet office closest to you:

Australia Locked Bag 1, Footscray, Victoria 3011
USA 150 Linden St, Oakland, CA 94607
UK 10A Spring Place, London NW5 3BH
France 1 rue du Dahomey, 75011 Paris

Map Legend

HYDROGRAPHY

	Reef
	Coastline
	River, Creek
	Lake
	Intermittent Lake
	Beach
	Spring/Waterhole
	Waterfalls
	Swamp

ROUTES & TRANSPORT

	Freeway
	Highway
	Major Road
	Minor Road
	Vehicle Track
	Walking Track
	Fence
	Ferry Route
	Train Route & Station
A10	Route Number

BOUNDARIES

	International
	Provincial
	Marine Park

MAP SYMBOLS

♋	CAPITAL	National Capital
◉	CAPITAL	Regional Capital
●	CITY	City
●	Town	Town
●	Village	Village
●		Point of Interest
●		Geographic Feature
●		Hydrographic Feature
●		Reserve/Wildlife Park
✈		Airport
⊞		Airfield
▲		Camp Site
⌂		Cave
		Cliff or Escarpment
⊞		Forest
⋈		Gate
■		Hotel
⊡		Lodge or Hut
⊡		Lookout/View Platform
▲		Mountain or Hill
⊕		Picnic Site
⚑		Ruins
❶		Tourist Information
▲		Volcano
⊡		Zoo

AREA FEATURES

	Land
	Park
	Prohibited Area
	Savannah

ABBREVIATIONS

BR	Botanical Reserve
CA	Conservation Area
CP	Conservation Park
CR	Conservation Reserve
FR	Forest Reserve
GR	Game Reserve
MP	Marine Park
MNP	Marine National Park
MNR	Marine National Reserve
NP	National Park
NR	National Reserve
NrP	Nature Park
PN	Parque Nacional
RR	Regional Reserve
SF	State Forest
SR	State Reserve
WP	Wetland Park
WR	Wildlife Reserve

Note: not all symbols displayed above appear in this book

ABOUT LONELY PLANET GUIDEBOOKS

Lonely Planet published its first book in 1973 in response to the numerous 'How did you do it?' questions Maureen and Tony Wheeler were asked after driving, busing, hitching, sailing and railing their way from England to Australia.

Written at a kitchen table and hand collated, trimmed and stapled, *Across Asia on the Cheap* became an instant local bestseller, inspiring thoughts of another book.

Eighteen months in South-East Asia resulted in their second guide, South-East Asia on a shoestring, which they put together in a backstreet Chinese hotel in Singapore in 1975. The 'yellow bible', as it quickly became known to backpackers around the world, soon became the guide to the region. It has sold well over half a million copies and is now in its 10th edition.

Today an international company with offices in Melbourne (Australia), Oakland (USA), London (UK) and Paris (France), Lonely Planet has an ever-growing list of books and other products, including: travel guides, walking guides, city maps, travel atlases, phrasebooks, diving guides, cycling guides, healthy travel guides, restaurant guides, world food guides, first time travel guides, condensed guides, travel literature, pictorial books and, of course, wildlife guides. Many of these are also published in French and various other languages.

In addition to the books, there are also videos and Lonely Planet's award winning Web site.

Some things haven't changed. The main aim is still to help make it possible for adventurous travellers to get out there – to explore and better understand the world.

At Lonely Planet we believe travellers can make a positive contribution to the countries they visit – if they respect their host communities and spend their money wisely. Since 1986 a percentage of the income from each book has been donated to aid projects and human rights campaigns.

> Lonely Planet gathers information for everyone who's curious about the planet – and especially for those who explore it first-hand. Through guidebooks, phrasebooks, activity guides, maps, literature, newsletters, image library, TV series and Web site we act as an information exchange for a worldwide community of travellers.

LONELY PLANET OFFICES

Australia
Locked Bag 1, Footscray, Victoria 3011
☏ 03 8379 8000 fax 03 8379 8111
e talk2us@lonelyplanet.com.au

USA
150 Linden St, Oakland, CA 94607
☏ 510 893 8555 or ☏ 800 275 8555 (toll free)
fax 510 893 8572
e info@lonelyplanet.com

UK
10a Spring Place, London NW5 3BH
☏ 020 7428 4800 fax 020 7428 4828
e go@lonelyplanet.co.uk

France
1 rue du Dahomey, 75011 Paris
☏ 01 55 25 33 00 fax 01 55 25 33 01
e bip@lonelyplanet.fr
w www.lonelyplanet.fr

World Wide Web: w www.lonelyplanet.com *or* AOL keyword: lp
Lonely Planet Images: w www.lonelyplanetimages.com